The Life of Things

Therapy and the soul of the world

Bernie Neville

PCCS Books
Ross-on-Wye

First published in 2012
Reprinted 2013

PCCS BOOKS Ltd
2 Cropper Row
Alton Road
Ross-on-Wye
Herefordshire
HR9 5LA
UK
Tel +44 (0)1989 763900
www.pccs-books.co.uk

The Life of Things: Therapy and the soul of the world

A CIP catalogue record for this book is available from the British Library

ISBN 978 1 906254 46 9

Cover image by Hazel M Pickering BWS
Cover design by Old Dog Graphics
Printed by 4edge Ltd, Hockley, Essex, UK

Contents

Foreword *Godfrey Barrett-Lennard*   i

Introduction   iii

1   Imagining therapy   1

2   Healing the planet   23

3   The client-centred ecopsychologist   43

4   Rogers, Whitehead and the evolving universe   60

5   Counselling the five-minded animal   86

6   Self-realization and the ecological self   119

7   Entwined and entangled   144

Afterword   172

References   181

Index   191

For Max and Emily

FOREWORD

This book is alive, as a wonderfully rich, well-informed and searching conversational journey of inquiry and wisdom. It pulsates with ideas joined in a continually extending landscape of meaning. On one main level, the author situates client/person-centred therapy and theory in the context of other major understandings, historical and contemporary, of the human condition, living world and beyond. Sources include classical literature, modern philosophy, human and natural sciences and ecology. The result is a work of exceptional scholarship that is highly engaging to the thoughtful reader with or without a primary interest in therapy. Even the reference list is a goldmine.

On a broader level, this book is about humans discovering or recovering their sense not only of connection with the living world but of being an inherent part and expression of this world. The whole planetary world is likened to an organism, one in which humanity is a component organ necessarily dependent on the larger body and having its special significance and function within it – and through it in the inclusive larger cosmos. Our advanced consciousness is not just possessed uniquely by humans, in this perspective, but is one wave front and expression of the whole living world, of evolution and of what Rogers called the formative tendency in all of nature and, indeed, the universe.

To help to take care of or heal this world is also to heal ourselves. Thus Chapter 2, titled 'Healing the planet', is about the integral connection between planetary well-being and human health in its widest sense. It sets the stage and introduces themes further developed in the rest of the volume. Neville is careful throughout to emphasize that he is talking about ways of seeing or imaginatively understanding the world, not about final truths. As in his other works, he draws on highly evocative stories and figures in classical mythology, especially the diverse Greek and Roman gods, to illuminate varied perspectives on human nature, potential and approaches to helping. Diversity among the gods parallels diversity in ways of envisioning the person (and culture) and of desirable or healthy ways of being. The idea of Gaia, or Earth mother in Greek mythology, is soon introduced, since her 'sons' include Prometheus (hero and control freak) and Hermes (the versatile but also tricky messenger). She is an entry point also to a panoply of other distinctive god relatives that can each throw light on the human condition. The envisioning of Gaia and view of an animate world in which humans are one interwoven expression is creatively developed and refined through much of the book.

The whole perspective contrasts with any clockwork image of the world or deterministic understanding of persons in which specific causes produce singular effects. There is no absence of connection, influence or examination of vital ingredient features – for example in a therapeutic process – in the world as portrayed. Its reality, however, is always envisioned as complex, multi-faceted, interactive and often emergent with new properties as components combine: into a therapy dyad, larger grouping or community, or into still larger wholes. The idea that connection and process are the primary stuff of existence and that distinctive parts (including persons) flow from this, stands side by side with the complementary idea that new wholes emerge from prior components – within a fabric of growing complexity.

Though this book is a consummation of a life of study, action experience and reflection, Neville does not tell the reader how to do therapy or how anything must be understood. His search through a richly multi-sided world of connected meaning invites and opens the way to an enlargement of the reader's own perspective and knowing. Much more could be said about content information and subthemes, beyond this suggestive sketch, but the volume itself speaks so well from start to finish that further encouragement to harvest its potential riches seems superfluous. Once embarked on this 'harvesting' I found myself wholly engaged and could not put the book down.

Godfrey Barrett-Lennard, author of *Relationship at the Centre: Healing in a troubled world*. London and Philadelphia: Whurr.

INTRODUCTION

I intend in this book to engage with the question: What happens to counselling when we abandon the egocentric and anthropocentric assumptions on which it is conventionally based? In doing so I will be looking at therapy as understood by Carl Rogers and the many person-centred counsellors whose practice has been shaped by his ideas.

If I want to follow the ecopsychologists in shifting the discussion from personal pathology and healing to the pathology and healing of the planet I need to clarify a few of things. First, I need to state my understanding that the planet is not a lump of largely lifeless matter which we happen to inhabit, but a complex system of which we are (currently at least) an essential part. One element in this dynamic system is consciousness, and human beings, to the best of our limited knowledge, represent this in a unique way. We tend to see ourselves as subjects and address the planet as object. This is an attitude which has, in many respects, brought us to the present planetary emergency and the threat of global warming, environmental degradation and nuclear devastation.

Second, I also need to state my understanding that pathology is not an aberration, in contrast to some supposed perfectly healthy normality, but is part of the human condition. I have no supposition that there can be perfect health in the planet, any more than there can be perfect health in the individual – or perfect beauty or perfect goodness, for that matter. What we call pathology is omnipresent and is merely an aspect of the way we are. Moreover, when we talk about the pathology of the planet it is our own pathology that we are talking about.

Third, I want to declare that when I write in this way I do so on the premise that I am not stating facts about the planet or pathology, but rather presenting ways of imagining them. This is not to say that it is impossible to state truths about the planet, or to deny that we can accumulate credible evidence pointing to these truths. It is rather to assert that every examination of truth is made from a particular direction, a particular perspective, and that no single perspective presents truth in all its complexity. It is also to suggest that in our attempts to find meaning in our experience of the world, we find imagining easier and more natural than thinking, and we often confuse the two.

Person-centred theory and therapy are conventionally based on a number of premises: that client and therapist are essentially distinct entities, with their separate personal boundaries; that it is the client's subjective experience of the world which shapes the client's behaviour; that the success of therapy hinges on the therapist's ability to form a relationship with the client through which he or she can enter and articulate the client's experience of the world. Both client and therapist are assumed to act in and on a world which is essentially 'other'. The focus of therapy is the quality of the individual's functioning and experience of life. In ideology and method, person-centred therapy privileges subjectivity and personal autonomy.

Ecopsychology, which has its roots in deep ecology – a perspective first developed by the Norwegian ecophilosopher Arne Naess – challenges the anthropocentric assumptions on which most therapies, including person-centred therapy, are based. It abandons any essentialist notion of a boundary between self and the world. It does not perceive the world as 'other'. In such a perspective, human beings do not live within 'the environment'. They *are* the environment. Adequate human functioning is living 'naturally' with no conflict between the demands of self and the demands of nature. It demands an expansion of the notions of 'self' and 'self-realization' not only to the species but to the whole of non-human reality. If subjective, individualised experience is acknowledged and valued, it is acknowledged and valued as a manifestation of the 'mind of the world'. From this perspective the focus of therapy shifts from the individual to the planet. In its most radical expressions, it proclaims that the uniqueness of the individual is illusory, or at most irrelevant.

Naess' distinction between 'shallow' and 'deep' ecology is similar to distinctions made between 'technocentric' and 'ecocentric' environmentalism (O'Riordan, 1999), 'environmentalism' and 'social ecology' (Bookchin, 1980), 'homocentric' and 'transpersonal' ecology

(Fox, 1990), 'reformist' and 'radical' approaches to environment (Devall & Sessions, 1985). Deep ecologists argue that the non-human world should be conserved, preserved and valued for its own sake rather than because of its use value to humans. They dispute the dualism which places 'the environment' outside of humans to be either exploited or conserved for our benefit, and base their theorizing in an intuitive sense of the unity of all life. The European philosophical foundations of deep ecology are to be found in Martin Heidegger, Baruch Spinoza and Alfred North Whitehead. It is not surprising that many of the most influential figures in the deep ecology movement are Buddhists.

Client-centred therapy, on the other hand, has deep roots in the Enlightenment conviction that there is something very special about human beings. We are reasonable, decision-making individuals, capable of works of great rigour and beauty. We are on the earth but are essentially separate from it. We identify with the contents of our minds. We are not condemned to accept a particular view of the world forced upon us by religious or secular authorities, but can observe the world critically and act to change it. What defines us as human is not our objective existence as part of the planet, but our subjective experience of being separate individuals. I believe there is a point in forcing a meeting between these two perspectives.

The ideas I bring to this discussion, apart from those of Rogers and his intellectual heirs, come largely from four sources: archetypal psychology, ecopsychology, process philosophy and cultural psychology. For all their difference, there is one very strong thread which connects these perspectives. They all advise us to look outside the psychology of the individual when seeking understanding and engaging in action. Ecopsychology, drawing on the ecophilosophy of Arne Naess, calls our attention to the planet and suggests that we should see our individual selves not as centres of value and meaning in themselves, but as cells of a greater organism. Archetypal psychology, following Carl Jung and James Hillman, argues that, for all our sense of personal uniqueness, our lives are embedded in ancient patterns which are collective and cultural. Whitehead's process philosophy argues that the cosmos of which we are a part is not a machine but a living organism. Jean Gebser's cultural psychology reminds us that we are five-minded animals and are seriously mistaken if we identify ourselves only with our recently acquired rational consciousness. The contribution of person-centred theory to this line of thinking is the notion that the self-actualization of the individual is part of a larger process, and that the basic therapeutic conditions of empathy, acceptance and congruence apply not only to our relations with the individual client but to our relations with the species and the planet.

One of the great attractions of Rogers' thinking, as far as I'm concerned, is his deep belief in the radical ordinariness of the person-centred approach. The attitude and skills he first discovered to be at the heart of effective counselling he later recognized to be at the heart of all creative relationships. Indeed he found them to be at the heart of the good life. What began as a radical technique for professionals assisting people in mental distress eventually became for Rogers a radical 'way of being'. He believed that:

> the philosophy of interpersonal relationships which I have helped to formulate ... is applicable to all situations involving persons. I believe it is applicable to therapy, to marriage, to parent and child, to teacher and student, to persons with high status and those with low status, to persons of one race relating to persons of another. I am even brash enough to believe that it could be effective in situations now dominated by the exercise of raw power – in politics, for example, especially in our dealings with other nations ... I go along with Martin Buber and the ancient Oriental sages: 'He who imposes himself has the small, manifest might: he who does not impose himself has the great, secret might.' (Rogers, 1980: 45)

In *A Way of Being* (1980) Rogers makes it clear that his objection to 'imposing' does not only apply to our relations with other human beings. Like Buber, Mahatma Gandhi, Naess and 'ancient oriental sages' he believes that this respectful, compassionate, non-oppressive stance must extend beyond humankind to the whole of creation.

In the final pages of this, his final, book, Rogers expands on his 'person-centred scenario for the future'. The 'person of tomorrow', he suggests, will 'feel a closeness to, and a caring for, elemental nature'. People will be 'ecologically minded' and get their pleasure from an 'alliance with the forces of nature, rather than in the conquest of nature' (Rogers, 1980: 351). Rogers was convinced that humankind was experiencing a paradigm shift, citing with approval the statement of Nobel prizewinning chemist Ilya Prigogine that 'we are at the dawn of a new period, with all the excitement, the hopes and also the risks which are inherent in a new start' (Rogers, 1980: 348). In the present global emergency, when we have no guarantee of any future at all, we can only hope that he was right. Business as usual can only lead to disaster.

Rogers began his thinking about human beings and their place in the world with a focus on the one-to-one relationship between a counsellor and a client, testing the theory and practice first of 'non-directive', then of 'client-centred', therapy. What he discovered was something deeply significant about humanity, relationship and the good life – a way of being which came to be called 'the person-centred approach'. I have attempted in the following pages to say something of interest both to those who have a professional interest in the one-to-one therapeutic relationship, whether they call themselves counsellors, therapists or psychotherapists – labels I use interchangeably – and those who have a more general, non-professional curiosity about Rogers' ideas.

My own thinking about these matters owes a lot to Jung, Gebser, Whitehead and Naess. I find little acknowledgement of Jungian ideas in the person-centred literature, and even less mention of Rogers by Jungians. The counselling literature knows nothing of Gebser. Jung himself never refers to Gebser's work, though they were well known to each other, and though Gebser devotes some space to a commentary on Jung's contribution to an emerging integral psychology. Gebser mentions Whitehead but seems to know little about his philosophy. Whitehead's process philosophy stands apart, though it seems to have had an indirect influence on Rogers. Naess' language of deep ecology came too late to have an influence on any of the others. Ecopsychologists occasionally call on Jungian ideas, but Rogers barely rates a mention in their discussion.

Academic and professional literatures tend to exist in isolated silos, ignorant of each other's contents. Nevertheless, all five philosophers have been significant in the way my own approach to counselling – and life – has developed over the past decades. What I have attempted to do here is to take the postmodern turn, stand on the windswept plain between the five silos, and attempt, like William Wordsworth, to 'see into the life of things'.

The philosophy which underpins this book is sometimes labelled by the awkward words 'organicist' or 'organismic', contrasting it with the mechanistic worldview which has dominated science since the Enlightenment. While this way of thinking leads me to make plenty of assertions in the course of this book, I am reminded by Whitehead to beware of what he calls 'the fallacy of dogmatic finality':

> *There remains the final reflection, how shallow, puny, and imperfect are efforts to sound the depths in the nature of things. In philosophical discussion, the merest hint of dogmatic certainty as to finality of statement is an exhibition of folly. (Whitehead, 1929/1978: xiv)*

Some of the following chapters have been adapted from earlier publications. Chapter 1 appeared in *Perspectiven Psychotherapie,* Chapter 2 began as an article in *Psychotherapy in Australia,* Chapter 3 appeared in *The Person-Centered Journal* and Chapter 4 has been adapted from papers in *ACP: Pratique et Recherche* and *The Person-Centered and Experiential Psychotherapies.* Chapters 5–7 have not been previously published. At this point I wish to acknowledge and thank the numerous friends and colleagues in the Rogerian, Jungian, Whiteheadian and Gebserian communities who have shaped my thinking through their conversations over the years. No doubt they will recognize their ideas when they come across them in the following pages.

1

IMAGINING THERAPY

Alfred North Whitehead argued that: 'Every philosophy is tinged with the colouring of some secret imaginative background, which never emerges explicitly into its train of reasoning' (Whitehead, 1927: 7). We can say much the same about counselling theory and practice. Though the theory may be set out in persuasively rational terms, it is the imaginative background which gives it its resonance. We can see the image of the machine behind cognitive behavioural therapy and the hydraulics of psychoanalysis. We can detect the Hero's journey in narrative therapy and the scientific experimentation with life in personal construct therapy. We find Carl Jung caught between an academically credible, mechanistic image of energy exchange and his unfashionable sense of an ensouled universe. In Reichian and many other body therapies we find not a machine-like individual in a machine-like universe, but an organism subsisting on the life-energy of the universe.

In the following discussion of Carl Rogers and client-centred therapy, my interest is in a particular kind of complexity I find in his ideas. I do not find in Rogers a single 'secret imaginative background' shaping a rationally coherent theory. There are paradoxes and contradictions inherent in the person-centred approach, paradoxes and contradictions that I believe should be acknowledged rather than explained away.

Jung's notion of archetype provides a framework for my reflections. The notion of archetype is central to Jung's psychology, and archetypal psychology has become a useful tool for cultural analysis as well as an approach to individual therapy. Jung was intrigued by the recurring patterns he found in his clients' behaviour and imaginings, patterns which could not readily be understood in terms of learning. He found collective behaviour to be patterned in similar ways. Those

1

of us who take Jung seriously would argue that the concept of archetype is one of the most important ideas to have emerged in the twentieth century, an idea with enormous implications for the way we think about ourselves.

In his writing, Jung swings through a number of variations on the notion of archetype. He sometimes wrote as though archetypes are pre-existent, as though they are eternally there, outside of our time and space, existing independently of our consciousness, manifesting themselves in various ways in individual behaviour and human history. At times he was careful to point out the distinction between the archetypes as such and the archetypal images through which we become aware of them. At times he seemed most interested in their physical manifestation, in instinct or pathology. At times he described them as our archaic heritage – a 'living system of reactions and aptitudes that determine the individual's life in invisible ways' (Jung, 1979, CW 8, para. 339). He argued that 'they can only be explained by assuming them to be deposits of the constantly repeated experiences of humanity' (Jung, 1979, CW 7, para. 109). At other times he emphasized that they were not inherited habits, or even inherited ideas, but inherited *possibilities* of ideas and behaviour. All our ways of perceiving, thinking, feeling, valuing and behaving are shaped by particular possibilities. Our ancestors saw these patterns as representing primal energies, which they personified as gods.

More recently, archetypal psychologists like Michael Conforti have argued that it makes most sense to think of archetypes as fields which predate the existence of matter, and out of which matter and form emerge. Others, like Anthony Stevens and John Haule, suggest that the archetypal patterns in human behaviour are the result of evolutionary adaptation, noting that Jung himself had moments of Darwinian insight:

> *This whole psychic organism ... preserves elements that connect it with the invertebrates and ultimately with the protozoa. Theoretically, it should be possible to 'peel' the collective unconscious, layer by layer, until we come to the psychology of the worm, and even of the amoeba. (Jung, 1979, CW 8, para. 322)*

If we see these two ideas as contradictory it may say less about the nature of archetype than it does about the nature of our thinking.

What is important here is the notion that the universe we live in is patterned in specific ways, and that these patterns can be detected even in apparently trivial aspects of human experience.

James Hillman, the central contemporary figure in the school of thought known as archetypal psychology, does not make Jung's distinction between the archetype per se and the archetypal image, nor his distinction between the personal and collective aspects of the unconscious, so that for him every image is an archetypal image, and these archetypal images structure all our experience and behaviour. For Hillman, the proper work of psychology is *seeing through* our personal and collective experience to the archetypal images which shape them.

Hillman's argument takes him inevitably into a multi-perspectivist understanding of reality. As a framework for his multi-perspectivism he takes the gods of the Greco-Roman pantheon. Each of the gods personifies a 'mode of apprehension' (Jung's term), which gives distinct and observable shape to our encounter with the world. This is distinct but not discrete, for the archetypal patterns interpenetrate in ways which are represented by the relationships (familial and erotic) between the gods. The Greek pantheon is chosen because its images are embedded in European culture – even in the culture of positivist science. Hillman (1975) suggests that if we want to understand ourselves we should *see through* our behaviour all the way to the god image and the god-story in which it is embedded. And we need to experience these god stories the way our ancestors did, not just as interesting stories which we hear and remember and tell to our children, but as grand narratives within which we live our lives.

Jean Gebser argued that we will find five distinct 'structures of consciousness' manifested in culture. First, there is the basic 'archaic' structure which experiences the world with little or no awareness. Second, there is the 'magic consciousness' which emerged with the first humans and experiences a world of 'vegetative entwinement' in which everything is connected. Third, there is the 'mythical structure' through which we live our lives embedded in particular tribal narratives which give them meaning. Fourth, we have a 'mental' consciousness which enables us to think, objectively and rationally, as individuals. Finally, the 'integral' structure of consciousness – a structure which integrates all the others – enables us to experience the universe transparently. Archetypes shape our experience through all of these structures: in our body; through health and disease; in our instincts; in our behaviour; in our emotions; in our values; in our ideas.

If we accept the notion that all human behaviour is archetypally constellated, we might expect to be able to *see through* any philosophical system or political ideology to the images that give it its form. This should apply no less to the theories and methodologies of psychotherapy than to the grand narratives of our culture. Each therapy will be a manifestation of a mode of apprehension, a value system, a form of energy, a notion of truth and a vision of the good life which can be personified in a god – or in more than one god. In a world where truth has been increasingly relativized, counselling theory and technique is less likely than before to be constrained to a single perspective on what it means to be human, and may hold various perspectives and values in creative tension.

Jung brought us the notion of 'inflation', a condition in which the individual is taken over by a complex, or a nation or culture is taken over by a particular archetypal energy. We may find inflations of all kinds in our professions, and in the personalities of those who profess them. Taking the lead from Hillman, we can attempt to *see through* the theory and practice of therapy, and find the energy and perspectives of the Greco-Roman deities. When we look at therapists and the professional sub-culture within which they exercise their skills we may find both the wisdom which comes with embracing the perspective of a particular god, and the pathology which comes with excessive worship – when the therapist is inflated by the energy of one god at the expense of all the others.

The Greek pantheon provides us with a language for talking about a wide range of distinct philosophies, value systems, energies, feeling states, habits of behaviour and communication styles as they can be observed in the counselling profession and the counsellor–client interaction. It is a language which is not dominated by a single philosophy or theory but welcomes contradictory perspectives. The gods are many, and if we follow the advice of the ancient Greeks we will be careful not to neglect any of them – and not to get too carried away in worshipping any single one of them.

MANY GODS, MANY THERAPIES

The first of the Greek gods is Zeus. Zeus is the father of the gods, the patriarchy personified, generally benevolent but ready to punish if annoyed. He is sometimes grouped with the older, pre-Olympian gods – Uranus, Kronos, Saturn – as the Senex, the old man, the image both of autocratic power and of ancient and unchanging wisdom. He is the image of transcendent divinity which we have inherited from the three great religious traditions of the ancient Middle East.

When the Senex is supreme in a society, therapy as we understand it has no place. Political or religious authority tells people how to live and that is the end of it. Where patriarchal power is breaking down, the Senex counsellor may take the client, as Freud did, from a state of hysterical desperation to the state of 'ordinary unhappiness' that comes with adjustment to the strictures of society. It has been argued that, regardless of the intentions or ideology of the therapist, the political function of therapy is to soften dissent and to divert challenge to an oppressive political system. There are plenty of Senex counsellors still around, even in a society where patriarchal power is no longer assumed to rule by absolute right. They have unambiguous notions of right and wrong, and their mode of counselling is to advise their clients how they should live. There are many clients who seek only this from their counsellors.

Zeus–Senex is not actually the first and oldest of the gods who inhabited the Greek peninsula. When the Hellenic tribes (known to us as the Greeks) first arrived there in the second millennium BCE they found that the indigenous inhabitants worshipped the Earth as the Great Mother who gave them life (without the assistance of any male gods) and took them back into herself when their time was up. She had a lot of different, local names, as though there were multiple mother-goddesses. The Greeks incorporated her into their religious system in a number of ways. The identified all the local goddesses with Zeus' consort and Queen Hera (a name which simply means 'lady'). They invented stories about Zeus seducing or marrying the local goddesses and having children by them. They made Gaia (the Earth) the grandmother of Zeus and his five siblings. Gaia holds a place in the classical Greek religious system rather as an impersonal force than as a superhuman being with a personality of her own like the Olympian gods. She is, however, personified in her different aspects in the different female gods of the pantheon. Demeter, Athena, Aphrodite, Artemis and Hera are different, and limited, manifestations of the Great Mother, as are various nymphs, Titans and mythical mortals.

Hera, queen of the Olympian gods, is the archetypal image of marriage, family, social bonds and social roles. Her authority supports that of Zeus. A therapy grounded in such values will be socially conservative, based on notions of social rights, obligations and duties, and the maintenance of proper roles. Hera has no problem with giving advice, and her advice is likely to focus on the need to adjust to society's demands. Systems approaches to therapy come out of a Hera perspective, and it is no coincidence that they provide family therapy with its orthodoxy.

Demeter is the mother. A therapy which functions by providing the kind of support and nourishment which encourages growth in the client belongs to Demeter. So does the therapy which controls by giving and withdrawing affection, and the therapy which develops emotional dependence.

Apollo is the god of clarity, reason and understanding. He has been powerfully present in some therapies, notably psychoanalysis, logotherapy and cognitive therapy, which are shaped in different ways by the notion that human beings have a basic urge to understand, to find meaning, and that change in behaviour tends to follow more or less inevitably on the insights gained through therapy. It should be noted that Apollo is notoriously inept in his relationships.

Artemis is the goddess of the moon, sisterhood, and untouched nature. She is most obviously present in radical feminist therapies, for she has no interest in giving men power or pleasure. She cares for the new-born and fragile, and sees the good life as one lived in harmony with nature and its rhythms. Like Demeter she is a manifestation of the original Great Mother, Gaia. She is the personification of wild nature, in contrast to Demeter, who personifies the nurturing earth.

By contrast, Athena is the goddess who accommodates the feminine to the patriarchal world. She is the warrior goddess, the goddess of common sense, the goddess of expertise and professionalism, of civilization, of normality. She is, significantly, goddess of democracy. We find her in therapies based on the sharing of power between therapist and client, and in therapies whose aim is the sharing of understandings and the solving of problems rather than the sharing of feelings and the building of relationships. Feelings and relationships are not of much interest to her.

Ares, god of war, might not seem to have much of a contribution to make to therapy, but we can find him present in confrontative therapies and in the confrontational style of therapists from many persuasions. We find him wherever the counsellor challenges the client to fight. We find him in a somewhat domesticated form in assertiveness training. Ares is not terribly smart, and prefers the simplistic solution, but he is passionate and certainly knows how to stimulate action.

Hephaistos, the craftsman, forms the perspective of the counsellor who sees counselling essentially as a craft. In Greek myth, Hephaistos is the only god who does any work. He is the god who convinces us that the creation of something beautiful is worth long hours of hard and intensely focused work, slaving over the forge. He is wedded to Beauty (Aphrodite) but in spite of his obsession with her, and the toil and pain of his crafting, he never manages to please her.

Aphrodite has many aspects. She is most commonly worshipped under the aspect of sexual attractiveness, but she is also the goddess of spiritual beauty. In any case, under one aspect or another, she is the driving force behind much of what we do in counselling as anywhere else. Leaving aside the psychoanalytic notions of transference and projection, and leaving aside the all too frequent cases of sexual exploitation, it is arguable that therapy often works by way of seduction, so that the attractiveness of a therapist's personality or the attractiveness of a therapist's view of life makes a powerful contribution to the client's healing. For the Aphrodite-driven therapist, counselling is an aesthetic activity – an art rather than a science or a craft.

The son of Aphrodite is Eros, the god of relationship, who is central to most humanistic conceptions of therapy. Eros has his own truth, that healing occurs through the coming together of therapist and client in a relationship which is truly mutual and truly caring. For Eros, the key ingredient of successful therapy is love.

Dionysos is the god of 'the flow', of fertility, growth, impulse, and spontaneity, of spiritual ecstasy and emotional freedom. Dionysos is fervently worshipped by psychodramatists, and by different species of expressive therapists. As the divine child, the god of death and resurrection, he is worshipped also by rebirthers and holotropic therapists. Our society, no less than that of Greece, has a tendency to regard his activities as subversive of good order and morality. No less than the Greeks we pay a heavy price when we ignore him.

Hestia is the quiet goddess, the goddess of the hearth, of the home, of focus and 'centring'. Therapies which work through meditative introspection, such as psychosynthesis and experiential focusing, carry her power. She is responsible for the healing which comes simply through being still. She is the sense of safe containment in a therapeutic encounter.

Classical psychoanalysis and classical behaviourism, grounded as they are in the mechanistic and positivistic assumptions of nineteenth century science, point to the myth of Prometheus, the ancient hero who stole fire from heaven and taught men how to use it to gain control of the world and free themselves from the power of the gods. The Promethean fantasy of ego-driven emancipation through technology also shapes such diverse therapies as neurolinguistic programming, biofeedback and biomedical psychiatry.

And so on. Each archetype is manifested in its particular perspective on the world, its peculiar system of values, its own pathology, its own vision, its own methodology, and the particular energy which drives it. Each god has their own truth and their own morality. Reality is not single and simple, but multiple and complex.

Yet even this statement about the nature of reality is archetypally constellated. When we look at the world and see not the one truth but relative and local truths, when we see not facts but images, when we acknowledge the paradoxical and the irrational, we are taking a particular archetypal perspective – the perspective of Hermes. I suggest that Hermes is the god of a postmodern consciousness and provides the energy and the vision of both Jungian and Rogerian therapy. The Greeks worshipped him as the god of travellers, the god of exchange, the god of information, the god of flexibility, the god of transformation. He is the god who insists that all the gods must be worshipped.

PERSON-CENTRED PLURALISM

When I first encountered the work of Rogers in the late sixties, what most impressed me was his focus on relationship. As a teacher I suspected that my ability to teach my students effectively was somehow related to the quality of my relationships with them. The Beatles were still singing 'All You Need Is Love'. Hippies in San Francisco were apparently wearing flowers in their hair. Dialogue and encounter were entering the vocabulary of many teachers. Rogers gave me a language to talk about this in a legitimately psychological manner, and to share my excitement with colleagues who were making the same discoveries.

Another notion which made a big impression on me was the notion of process. Reading *On Becoming a Person* (1961) confirmed me in my sense that what really mattered in teaching was the immediacy of what was happening. I accepted the obvious truth of Rogers' assertion that the information that children pick up in their schooling is far less important than the processes by which they pick it up, that what matters is that they learn to adapt creatively to the future, rather than learn to repeat the past.

I was also impressed by his insistence that power be shifted from teacher to student, his confidence that students are perfectly able to decide what was good for them, and his conviction that their teachers should respect this ability and desist from telling them what to learn and what to do. I enthusiastically embraced the notion of 'facilitation'. It became obvious to me that my prime function as a teacher was to develop and maintain an emotional and intellectual climate which was both nurturing and challenging, in which my students would be encouraged to initiate and take responsibility for their own learning. As a young teacher with countercultural tendencies, I saw education in terms of growth, freedom, dialogue, sharing, discovery, relationship, nurturance and creativity.

When I now try to look at all of this archetypally I find the language of relationship clearly pointing to the god Eros, the god of love and of the creativity which springs from relatedness. The language of growth, freedom and new beginnings points to Dionysos, the god of fertility, of impulse and spontaneity. The language of nurturance points to Demeter, the mother. The language of process, dialogue and discovery points to Hermes, while the language of power-sharing, co-operation and problem-solving points to Athena.

When I left the classroom in 1970 to do my PhD, I found that there were other gods involved in client-centred therapy and student-centred teaching. I read what Rogers had to say about the organization of personality in *Client-Centered Therapy* (1951) and in his 1959 paper 'A Theory of Therapy, Personality and Interpersonal Relationships'. I noted his respectful acknowledgement of the perceptual theory of

Snygg and Combs, and read *Individual Behavior* (1959) with great excitement. I came to understand behaviour as the rational response of the organism to the world as perceived. I became persuaded that the essence of therapy and education (from the client's and student's point of view) is the search for clarity; the unending endeavour to construct a meaningful world out of one's experience. This is the work that the therapeutic conditions make possible. When my colleagues tried to trivialize the client-centred approach by locating it in a fantasy of touchy-feely countercultural cosiness and put scorn on the notion that empathic understanding is an essential component of effective teaching, I argued that empathy is essentially a cognitive operation, that it involves entering another's world in order to know how the other perceives and understands – not in order to share the other's feelings. I took both therapy and education to be concerned with an expansion of consciousness which enables greater freedom of action. This perspective on the person-centred approach was clearly that of Apollo, the sun god, the god of clarity and rationality, the god of understanding.

Working on my PhD at a graduate school which was at the time avowedly empirical in orientation, I was attempting to 'operationalize' Rogerian therapeutic conditions, in order to develop testable hypotheses related to educational outcomes. When I came across Robert Carkhuff's *Helping and Human Relations,* which had been published in 1969, it was just what I needed. I was soon immersed in a self-consciously tough-minded fantasy of levels of functioning, personal effectiveness, the development of human resources and, above all, of training and skilling. It is apparent to me now that Carkhuff's vision of highly effective people training less effective people in the skills of effective living belonged, as did his operationalism, his evangelical fervour and his focus on human resources, to the fantasy of Prometheus, the heroic liberator, the technologist.

The work of Carkhuff, Charles Truax and their associates was taken up by Gerard Egan, and still has an enormous impact in the field of counsellor training. However, I believe there has been a shift from Carkhuff's Promethean vision of interpersonal skilling as a way of emancipation to a notion of interpersonal skills as marketable commodities. This is, in part, a criticism of 'Eganism', but the phenomenon is much more broadly based than that. I find that there are many people and organizations willing and able to pay me to teach them (or at least their employees) 'interpersonal skills' and 'negotiation skills', and I find empathy, positive regard and congruence being bought and sold by people whose language comes from Rogers but whose commitment to a person-centred philosophy is doubtful.

The charm of Hermes

This brings me back to Hermes, who I mentioned earlier as the god of exchange and, accordingly, of dialogue and process. He is, above all, the god of the marketplace. Hermes, the entrepreneur, has been peculiarly powerful in the last decades of the twentieth century, and it is not surprising that his presence should be felt in the person-centred approach. I believe that Rogers' own thinking about counselling was increasingly dominated by a postmodern, Hermetic consciousness, and that this consciousness is manifested in the person-centred approach.

The very existence of the profession of counselling is an illustration of the postmodern condition as Jean-Francois Lyotard describes it. Human interactions which used to be tied to the structures of society, to tribe, church, family and friendship, have entered the marketplace. Advice on how to live is bought and sold, as is emotional support, attention, listening, understanding, healing, even love. The increasing commercialization of therapy, no less than the commercialisation of knowledge and the commercialization of the arts, points to the contemporary Hermes inflation.

We know that Rogers had an enormous influence on establishing and legitimizing the profession of counselling. We know that he did not go along with the popular psychoanalytic notion that the exchange of money is an enormously significant part of the therapeutic interaction. We know that he preferred to counsel without receiving money from his clients, and was able to avoid doing so. We know, further, that he succeeded in laicizing and democratizing both the theory and the profession. It is largely through his influence that counselling is no longer restricted to the medical profession, nor even to psychologists, and that it is possible now to argue that the qualities which make counselling effective are qualities which are reflected in every positive relationship. We should note that when he substituted the language of 'client' for the language of 'patient' he was, consciously or unconsciously, placing counselling in the marketplace. However, we should remember that Hermes is not only the god of the marketplace. He is the god of every crossroad and every boundary, every point where one person's pathway or territory meets another's, and that he dwells in these ordinary places rather than in a temple like the other gods.

Hermes is the facilitator, the god who makes things smooth and easy. I used to be enchanted with the word, when the notion of facilitation was an exciting and refreshing alternative to the dogmatism and oppression of the Senex. It has lost some of its enchantment, as I see the word and the notion embraced and abused by a postmodern culture of management and manipulation. I am also a little more sensitive to my own Hermes pathology than I used to be.

The person-centred counsellor does not set out to intervene in people's lives in order to change them. The initiation and direction of change come from the person who wants to change, not from the helper, who simply devotes his or her skills and attention to facilitating the exploration and insight which lead to change. There is, however, plenty of scope for self-deception in this. Hermes is, after all, the god of illusion and disguise. In my own teaching and counselling I am aware how easy it is for me to cross the gap between facilitating people's discovery of insights of their own and guiding them towards the discovery of insights which I have consciously or unconsciously prepared for them.

The person-centred ideal of a mode of counselling or teaching that withholds advice or instruction – in the conviction that client and student are themselves the experts in deciding on what is best for them – remains revolutionary after 50 years of practice. It attracts a Hermes energy which can transform people's lives, yet it is always threatened by a 'Hermes pathology'. Hermes, the facile, the one who makes things easy, the smooth talker, the persuader, is equally present in facilitation at its best, and manipulation at its worst.

When Rogers pointed out that the task of the therapist is not the expansion of the client's consciousness, but companionship on the client's journey, he was placing the approach within the image of Hermes. Hermes is the companion and protector of travellers. In the image of Hermes, the person-centred therapist accompanies the client on the client's sometimes frightening journey to the underworld.

> *This can only be done by people who are secure enough in themselves that*
> *they know they will not get lost in the sometimes bizarre world of the other,*
> *and that they can comfortably return to their own world if they wish.*
> *(Rogers, 1951: 483)*

We should note that companionship is different from facilitation. There are many therapists who will happily facilitate a client's journey to his or her personal underworld, and there are many techniques available to assist in this. However, many of these therapists, like travel agents, facilitate this journey for the client without going there themselves. It seems to me that the essence of Rogers' approach is that the therapist must go all the way into the client's underworld at the client's side and must be prepared, like the client, to be permanently changed by the experience.

Hermes as messenger of the gods and guide to the underworld is present in a very obvious way in the psychology of Jung, for whom it is apparent that the gods dwell in our personal and collective unconscious. While client-centred therapy seems conventionally to ignore the notion of the unconscious, Rogers acknowledges the significance of unconscious processes in the therapeutic interaction, though he shuns anything approaching psychoanalytic language. Even in the phenomenological model proposed in his 19 propositions in *Client-Centered Therapy* (1951), he acknowledges that when he talks about experience he is not limiting his discussion to conscious experience. In his discussion of empathy in *A Way of Being* (1980) Rogers acknowledges that our experiencing moves ahead of our awareness, and sees the counsellor's task as tuning in to what is present but unconscious in the experiencing of the client, so as to assist the client to articulate it. 'Empathy', he says:

> *involves being sensitive, moment by moment, to the changing felt*
> *meanings which flow in this person, to the fear or rage or tenderness or*
> *confusion or whatever it is that he or she is experiencing ... it means*
> *sensing meanings of which he or she is scarcely aware, but not trying to*
> *uncover totally unconscious feelings, since this would be too threatening.*
> *(Rogers, 1980: 143)*

It is not only in the client that felt meaning moves ahead of symbolization. When the therapist tunes into the client's experiencing, it is her own organismic sensing of the interior state of the client which is the point from which the articulation of the client's meanings begin to emerge. It is Hermes, not Apollo, who provides the perspective which enables Rogers to claim that at his best his counselling was based on intuitively sensing the felt meanings of the client and even to note that this was sometimes associated with a trance-like state.

Another image in Hermes mythology is that of untying knots. It seems to me a fitting image of process in client-centred therapy. The client begins the process stuck, tied up, knotted and, in thoroughly experiencing and examining the knots, finds a way to untie them, so as to continue on his or her way without this encumbrance. Hermes, who negotiates the release of Persephone from the underworld and of Odysseus from Calypso's island, shares the title of 'loosener' with Dionysos, another god of transformation. But the patient work of the client-centred therapist is in contrast with the Dionysian fantasy of liberation through catharsis and ecstasy.

Hermes is obviously present in a therapy which focuses on dialogue rather than on training or emotional ventilation. Rogers comes back again and again to the notion that the essence of counselling is listening. The therapist has no interest in conveying her own message. Instead, she attempts to state the client's message even more accurately and completely than the client. Hermes is the information-carrier, not the information-giver, and has no message of his own.

In Lyotard's (1983) analysis of the postmodern condition he points to the replacement of the 'grand narratives' by 'local narratives'. The gradual abandonment of the great missionary and universalizing dogmatic systems is echoed in a postmodern science by the disappearance of an absolute material object about which one can make 'truthful' statements. The Apollonine myth of an absolute reality which can be made manifest to the human intellect if we think hard enough is fading, and is being replaced by a much more flexible, subjective, relativistic and ambiguous approach to reality – an approach which is in the image of Hermes rather than Apollo. Rogers' thinking is in tune with this shift in consciousness.

> *I think that men and women, individually and collectively, are inwardly and organismically rejecting the view of one single and culture-approved reality. I believe that they are moving inevitably towards the acceptance*

of millions of separate, challenging, exciting, informative, individual perceptions of reality. (Rogers, 1980: 106)

This statement comes from *A Way of Being* (1980), in Rogers' eighth decade, but this thinking is implicit in the person-centred approach from the beginning. The approach operates on the understanding that, as far as the client's behaviour is concerned, the only truth which is functional is the subjective truth of the client. The therapist must abandon any illusion that he or she knows more about the truth of the client's world than the client does, and must take the client's truth seriously, whether that truth comes from Zeus, Hera, Aphrodite or Dionysos, and whether it represents health or pathology. Hermes acknowledges all the gods and supports their worship. Empathy and unconditional regard are both necessary here. For Rogers it remained 'a basic fact of all human life that we live in separate realities' (Rogers, 1980: 107). Without getting into a postmodern circularity with regard to the relativity of even this 'basic fact', we can assert that even client-centred therapists live in separate realities, and we should not be surprised that any push to establish an orthodoxy of belief and practice in the person-centred approach is likely to have trouble dealing with the inevitable paradox.

Indeed it appears to me that some, at least, of the strength of the person-centred approach comes from its multidimensionality and its ability to contain logical contradictions without splitting apart. In the language of archetypal psychology, the approach is polytheistic rather than monotheistic.

A POLYTHEISTIC THERAPY

On the one hand, the Hermes archetype gives the person-centred approach its energy and defines its vision of the good life. As Rogers expresses it:

For the client, this optimal therapy would mean an exploration of increasingly strange and unknown and dangerous feelings in himself...

The good life is a process, not a state of being.

It is a direction, not a destination.

If a person could be fully open to his experience, however, every stimulus ... would be freely relayed through the nervous system without being distorted by any defence mechanism.

The individual is becoming more able to listen to himself, to experience what is going on within himself.

Such living in the moment means an absence of rigidity, of tight organization, of the imposition of structure on experience. It means instead a maximum of adaptability, of structure in experience, a flowing, changing organization of self and personality.

Yet the deeply exciting thing about human beings is that when the individual is inwardly free, he chooses as the good life this process of becoming. (Rogers, 1961: 183–196 passim)

On the other hand the other gods are fully acknowledged. The gods quarrel constantly, but Hermes remains on friendly terms with them all.

Many therapies are monotheistic. They acknowledge only one truth, one value system, one version of reality, and frame both their successes and their failures in terms of this reality. Client-centred therapy is not like this, although we sometimes try to make it so by defining too single-mindedly what we take to be the truth. Neither is it mindlessly eclectic or shapelessly flexible. It has a distinctive truth and a distinctive form, but both its truth and its form are comfortable with paradox.

To expand on this notion I will continue to use the metaphors of archetypal psychology and speak of the presence of the gods, though clearly the notion could be developed in quite other ways.

Rogers first developed his radical ideas within the framework of scientific psychology, but they first became widely known in the context of a counterculture dominated by the archetypes of Eros and Dionysos. This gave his ideas plenty of exposure, but it also distorted them with the pathology of Eros and Dionysos. For in the minds of many (apologists as well as critics), a person-centred approach seems to involve mindlessly indiscriminate intimacy, an absolute priority of feeling over thought, narcissistic self-indulgence, total absence of social awareness, general permissiveness and romantic soft-headedness.

This is not the person-centred approach and it is not the positive manifestation of Eros and Dionysos.

In our thinking and behaviour, the young gods seem to stick together, so it is not surprising to find Eros and Dionysos associated with Hermes in the person-centred approach. We can, if we like, make a case that client-centred therapy is essentially an Eros therapy, that the understanding and practice of genuine loving is the core of its theory and method. We can theorize that what confused or suffering clients need more than anything else in the world is the experience of a relationship in which another person genuinely cares for them and desires what is good for them, and we can theorize (and experience) that this in itself is healing. Or we can make a case that client-centred therapy is a Dionysos-charged therapy, that its essential theoretical notion is the existence of the actualizing tendency, the drive towards growth, towards emergence of the true, vital, free, spontaneous self from the sterility of introjected values and incongruent behaviour, and that its essential practice is the provision of the conditions which will best support this growth.

On the other hand, we might argue that client-centred therapy is essentially an Athena therapy, that its key assumption is the existence of the client's practical wisdom, his or her innate (though often repressed) ability to decide what is best, and that its key practice is the genuine sharing of power between therapist and client in a purposeful and co-operative exploration and resolution of a problem. Athena is goddess of democracy, and it may be argued that client-centred therapy is as much an artefact of Rogers' political convictions as of his psychological ones.

We might argue, again, that client-centred therapy is essentially the work of Hephaistos, that it has taken the commonplace elements of human relating and shown us how to craft them, to make them beautiful and powerful. We can demonstrate that, for both client and therapist, therapy is focused, dedicated and patient work. The client-centred therapist often resembles Hephaistos, who works away at the forge below the mountain, aware (perhaps resentfully) that other gods are attracting a lot of attention by doing brilliant and exciting things, but determined to stick at his unglamorous craft, for this is where beauty is created.

Or we might follow Carkhuff in proclaiming the truth of Prometheus, and see the therapeutic conditions as the skills of highly effective people, engaged in liberating and empowering their clients or students, who will thus, in their turn, become effective, productive, resourceful people and make an impact on the world. We might simply reiterate that client-centred therapy is not a way of life but a technique, that we should not be distracted by vague, soft-headed talk about person-centredness, but concentrate on perfecting our technique, for it is a powerful instrument for setting people free.

The truth of Hestia is very different. From the perspective of Hestia, client-centred therapy is inner work, a turning away from frantic or desperate action to find the still point within, where thinking and feeling are one and confusion dissolves. The centre of Hestia's worship in the classical world was the hearth (*focus*, in Latin), around which the family constantly rediscovers and reaffirms its unity. The person-centred counsellor's provision of a safe container for the therapeutic process and her attention to the immediacy and mutuality of the present moment points to Hestia, as does the centrality of focus in the language of experiential therapy.

We might argue, on the other hand, that this is the work of Aphrodite, that it is based on a confidence in the essential beauty of human beings, that it works through the practice of transparency and authenticity, of the beauty of what is simply and concretely and congruently there, in both therapist and client. We can certainly argue that, where many therapies operate within a fantasy that the liking of client for therapist or therapist for client is irrelevant, this is not the case in client-centred counselling or healing, or in student-centred education. The seductive presence of Aphrodite is central to the process, and for most people working in a person-centred framework it is inconceivable that it could be otherwise.

We can even claim a major place for Ares, for client-centred therapy is essentially about confrontation, about facing oneself and one's world as they are without pretence or avoidance. One distorted perception of the person-centred approach is that it is cosy and unchallenging. Any therapist who uses the approach with skill and commitment, and any client who has the good fortune to interact with such a therapist, knows that this is not true. The client-centred process demands courage and energy, a readiness to confront the frightening, to wrestle with demons and dragons if need be, to assert oneself, to be heroic. And this can be just as true for the therapist as it is for the client. We can argue that this perspective is absolutely central to the person-centred approach, that the truth of client-centred therapy is the truth of Ares, or of his protégé, the hero Herakles. We can argue that the process of client-centred therapy is the struggle of a 'self' trying to emerge from a tangle of introjected values and borrowed identifications and behaviours, and that this struggle deserves to be called heroic.

On the other hand, we can as legitimately argue that the truth of client-centred therapy is the very different truth of Demeter, the Great Mother, and that its effectiveness comes through the therapist's ability to offer support and nourishment. Very often what the client needs most is the security, the unconditional love, the emotional sustenance, the protection, which belong to the mother archetype, and which some therapeutic approaches actually deny. Client-centred counselling has the means to provide the mother's warm embrace to the client whose immediate need to be is childlike and dependent, and has the means also to assist that client to grow towards independence and self-reliance.

Then again, we might argue just as legitimately that client-centred therapy is the province of Artemis, the nature goddess who does not give birth herself but presides over childbirth and protects the fragile infant. The metaphor of Artemis, the midwife, is one which Rogers himself uses. It carries a lot of meaning for a therapist who sits beside someone in whom a new life is struggling to be born. So does the metaphor of Artemis the nature goddess, who cherishes and protects and affirms what is natural and what is feminine, and upholds the values of the natural and the feminine against a pathological patriarchy which would exploit or destroy them.

There is a great deal in Rogers' later writing which reflects the perspective of Artemis. His early writings, on the other hand, are dominated by the perspective of Artemis' brother, Apollo. Apollo is manifested in a perceptual theory which asserts that human behaviour is a rational response to the world as it is perceived, and in the value placed on scientific research as a means of reaching understanding of the process and impact of therapy. The Apollonine perspective has endured in the person-centred approach, both in a research tradition and in the Apollonine truth that it is the task of the therapist to assist the client to understand, to clarify, to symbolize, to find meaning in his or her world. We might argue that client-centred therapy is essentially an Apollo therapy, in that it acknowledges that we are driven to construct or discover a meaning for our lives; that our behaviour is consistent with the meaning we construct or discover, and that the therapist's task is to assist the client's attempt to understand, symbolize and articulate such meanings.

The person-centred approach is sometimes attacked for its perceived focus on the individual and its neglect of the social dimensions of life. Rogerian thinking, and humanistic psychology in general, is accused of being a manifestation of a culture of narcissism. Nevertheless, we can argue that Hera, queen of the gods, the goddess who attends to the stability of the family and other social structures, is very much a part of it. She certainly appears to have been powerful in Rogers' own personality. She appears in his assertion that the actualizing tendency takes us towards greater interdependence with others, that as the client in therapy becomes more congruent and self-affirming, he or she becomes more accepting of others, more socially aware, and more socialised. She appears in client-centred therapy in the modelling of a role-defined relationship driven by the therapist's conviction that people matter, and in the therapist's loyalty and commitment to his or her clients. Hera appears also in client-centred therapy's acknowledgement of every client's essential dignity, an acknowledgement which not every form of therapy is prepared to make.

Where does the old man, Zeus, come into all of this. Non-directive therapy, Rogers' early formulation of the approach, was by name and nature an attack on the assumptions of the patriarchy, and the person-centred approach has preserved this stance. I think that Rogers had a blind spot with regard to Zeus. He saw authority as essentially abusive. When he wrote about education he used 'traditional' as a pejorative term. In the Rogers–Buber dialogue he appeared unable to acknowledge what to Buber was obvious – that there is a genuine power differential between therapist and client. It seems to me that, to use Jung's language, issues of power and authority are strongly constellated in the 'shadow' of the person-centred approach. One manifestation of this shadow might be our ability, individually and collectively, to deny any interest in power while unconsciously behaving in ways which enable us to dominate clients or colleagues. I believe another manifestation is the tendency (which I am demonstrating here) to turn Rogers into the wise old man and his writings into sacred texts. I suggest that the Senex will not be denied, even in a philosophical position dedicated to overthrowing him.

And what of Gaia? We can, of course, see her in the shadows behind the Olympian goddesses, including the image of the 'safe container' provided by Hestia, as we sit and contemplate our glowing coals in the therapeutic relationship. Furthermore, we can point to Rogers' inclination to imagine the world organically rather than mechanistically, especially in his writing about the 'formative tendency', where he depicts human beings as cells of a greater organism and each person's therapeutic growth as the manifestation of an actualization process which involves the whole universe (Rogers, 1980: 124). It is an aspect of Rogers' worldview which has been little understood or appreciated until fairly recently.

It seems a very commonplace observation that we can use a range of such metaphors to give a sense of the person-centred approach, that we can find a number of very different 'truths' about the nature of therapy, all of which seem central to the person–centred approach. However, it ceases to be a commonplace observation when we try to apply the same approach to other therapies. For many of them it simply cannot be done. They operate on the basis of a single truth and are blind to all other perspectives. Try to find all the gods debating within cognitive behavioural therapy, primal therapy, rational-emotive therapy, psychoanalysis, neurolinguistic programming, hypnosis, existential therapy and electro-convulsive therapy. You will be lucky to hear more than one voice. They are monotheistic therapies, existing in a fantasy of a single way of knowing. I suggest that the ambiguity and paradox that the person-centred counsellor learns to live with is peculiar to that approach, and that this is so because the person-centred approach draws its energy and derives its vision from the archetype of Hermes.

If we limit our worship to a single god we find ourselves enmeshed in that god's pathology. Hermes is a more complex personality than most, and his pathology takes many forms. We might mention groundlessness, irresponsibility, absence of an ethical sense, grandiosity, seduction, the need to be constantly on the move, deception, manipulation, opportunism, the lack of interest in work and productivity, an indiscriminate eclecticism, the unwillingness to stand up for anything, the obsessive eagerness to sell or barter, the tendency to see market value as the only criterion of quality, and an obsession with 'spin'. The god of disguise can even be seen in the current use of the expression 'client-centred' in the health professions to indicate a focus on customer satisfaction. I suggest that there is a lot of Hermes pathology around in the culture of late capitalism, though I am aware that in making such a suggestion I am speaking from the perspective of Zeus, Hera and Apollo, to whom such things matter. If we have no god but Hermes, we are likely to harbour a clutch of such pathologies in our personalities and therapies. On the other hand, if we neglect to give Hermes the acknowledgement due to him, we will miss out on the flexibility, playfulness, grace, intuition, imagination, curiosity, magic, poetry and sense of the sacred which are peculiarly his. I suggest that the value of the person-centred approach lies largely in its ability to make just this acknowledgement to Hermes, the 'dispenser of favours, guide, giver of good things' (Boer, 1970: 59).

An archetypal analysis such as I have been attempting itself represents a postmodern way of thinking or, if you prefer, a Hermes consciousness. From this perspective it must be clear that my basic intention is to explore an image, not to propound a truth. For me the image is a rich one, and its exploration gives me a means to deal with my own felt meaning of the person-centred approach, which I am not at present able to set out with proper Apollonine rationality. The myth of the infant Hermes which shows us Zeus sending the two squabbling brothers, Apollo and Hermes, left brain and right brain, off together to seek the cattle of the gods, reminds us that there are two complementary ways of approaching reality, and that they don't negotiate an agreement and become friends until the end of the journey.

2

HEALING THE PLANET

When we reflect on the condition of the planet and what might be done about it, we find our imaginations easily slip into the medical metaphor and diagnose the planet as a patient. We see all sorts of sickness, much of it apparently terminal: advanced environmental degradation; stockpiles of deteriorating nuclear weapons waiting for terrorists or a computer bug to detonate them; widespread starvation, famine and disease; corruption of political life, where even leaders of intelligence and goodwill are unable to make the decisions which desperately need to be made; savage ethnic wars; the collapse of ethics; an out-of-control financial system which no one really understands; and so on. We can pursue the medical metaphor, formulate a treatment and set out to cure the disease, or at least alleviate the symptoms. We know that there are many people doing that already: engineers, agronomists, economists, medical researchers, ecologists and the rest. We may even designate a role for counsellors in this.

However, I suggest that this is a fantasy. It does not represent an objective truth about the planet and our relationship to it. Rather, it represents a way of imagining it. The notion that we can treat the planet as an object, see what is wrong with it, and fix it, has to be set against other fantasies. The use of the word fantasy does not imply that this is not a legitimate way of imagining it, only that it is imagination that we are talking about – not ultimate truth. There are many ways of looking at the planetary crisis, and if we cannot view it from all perspectives at once we can at least try not to be trapped in a single fantasy.

One such fantasy is the fantasy of the Many. It is the fantasy at the root of most of the psychological models of human life. In this fantasy, the universe consists of many separate things which, though they may have connections with each other, are essentially separate. Human beings are essentially individuals, existing in a world of differentiated objects. The centre of experience is the individual ego. Human beings exist as separate, encapsulated egos which communicate by passing information across the spaces between them. For those whose work as therapist is embedded in this fantasy, it is the individual who is healed, or adjusted, or stimulated to grow, or allowed to emerge, or who continues the journey. The individual relates to his or her environment (human and non-human) as subject to object. The environment itself is composed of many different 'things'. Even the psychological environment is composed of such 'things' as consciousness, empathy, communication, memories and the unconscious.

A contrasting fantasy is the fantasy of the oneness of all things. In this fantasy, human beings are not terribly important. We do not have a separate existence. We are not individuals living within an environment; the environment is us. We are part of a larger system, which will continue to live and renew itself when human beings cease to exist. The given universe does not exist for human beings, for all our arrogant assumption that there is something special about us. The universe exists, and we may or may not be a significant part of it. Or, more poetically, the earth is our mother and we live in symbiotic union with her, and have no existence except in this union. There are no separate 'things', only the flow of life. Healers who work within this fantasy do not separate the health of the individual and the health of the earth.

I keep using the word fantasy because I am not concerned here with the facts of our situation, not concerned with what is 'objectively true' about it, but with the ways we imagine it. I use the word fantasy where I could perhaps talk about narratives or discourses or even paradigms, because it carries the sense of a world experienced imaginally. I am interested in the stories we tell ourselves, particularly the 'big stories', the myths and fairy tales which are worked over and modified and passed down in every culture as representations of our experience of the world and our attempts to make sense of it. Jungians are inclined to the view that the tendency to imagine or construct the world in specific ways is hard-wired in our physiology. Whether or not we accept this notion, it seems that the myths of the great classical cultures still reflect our psychological experience of the world. We tend to think of myths as stories which we have at our disposal, to hear or tell and be affected by. We would do better to think of myths as narratives within which we live our lives. Mircea Eliade (1971) argued that in the mythical consciousness characteristic of pre-scientific societies, everything has already happened in the Dreamtime. We have not outlived our mythical consciousness. We still relive the stories of the gods. They provide what Whitehead calls the 'secret imaginative background' which colours our philosophies.

For the archetypal psychologist the gods are more than colourful metaphors. They represent deep structures in our individual and collective psyche. Archetypal psychologists may argue about whether these deeply embedded patterns of instinct, imagination and behaviour represent primordial Platonic forms or evolutionary adaptations, but they agree that human behaviour is patterned in certain ways and that the mythologies of the great classical civilizations provide a rich source of insight into these patterns.

The ancient Greeks had many gods, but there are three in particular that I want to address here. We find them powerfully at work in our culture and in the person-centred approach to counselling.

We find the fantasy of the Many represented in classical mythology in different versions of the Hero story, in which the Hero struggles against fate, faces dangers, fights monsters and saves people from the bad guys. The hero is an individual with tasks to perform, a mission to fulfil and a journey to complete. He (almost always *he* in the myths of the patriarchal Greek society) may have humble and obscure beginnings, but sometimes he gets to be accepted among the gods in the end.

We find the fantasy of the One personified in the goddess Gaia, the earth goddess. In classical times we find a cluster of goddesses representing different aspects of the original Great Mother: Gaia, Demeter, Maia, Artemis, Hestia, even Aphrodite and Athena. The Great Mother is not only the source of our life. She is the womb from which we emerge and to which we return, the container in which we feel safe.

Alongside these we find the image of Hermes, the anti-hero, the trickster son of the Great Mother, who warns us that we will not find ultimate meaning either in the Gaia story or the Hero story. He suggests that one story is as good as another and that if we want to find ultimate meaning we need to hear all the stories at once.

MOTHERS AND HEROES

In Greek mythology there is always some tension between the Mother and the Hero, mirrored in every mother's anxiety as her adolescent children resist her care and try to find their own way. The child's growth into independence reflects our species' growth into independence (of sorts) from the earth. Our earliest ancestors spent their lives within the container of earth and sky, without much ability to experience themselves as separate from their environment. Over the millennia our species gradually became aware of being separate from the earth, and individuals became aware of being separate from the container of their clan. We have reached the point in the past few centuries where 'civilized' human beings imagine themselves to be distinct not only from the earth but of a different nature from all other living beings, and individuals pride themselves on their independence and uniqueness. Whether we look at species or individuals over history we will see humans breaking away from their identity with earth or tribe and becoming conscious agents who act upon the objects in their world.

Anthony Stevens (1999) argues that the archetypal patterns we see in our behaviour have become hard-wired in our brains through evolutionary adaptation. Some of the earliest humans discovered that it was safer to be inside the cave than outside it. Those who didn't discover this were less likely to survive and have descendents. So here we are some millions of years later with a tendency to feel that 'inside' is safer than 'outside' and constantly seeking containers (nations, cultures, groups, clubs, professions, the therapeutic relationship) so that we may have a barrier between inside and outside and feel more comfortable inside.

We find a parallel way of thinking in developmental psychology. Jean Knox (2003) argues that when are born we have already had the experience of being in a container, and for most of us it is a safe container. We are born knowing the difference between a blissful 'inside' and an uncomfortable 'outside'. We spend our lives going from the container of our mother's womb to the container of our mother's arms to the container of our family to the containers of all the relationships and clubs and institutions and belief systems which give us a sense of security and belonging.

The difference between inside and outside is not the only thing we experienced at birth. We have also experienced the difference between here and there; we have made a journey, and the notion of path towards separation from mother is also hard-wired in our brains. The beginnings of our tendency to imagine and experience life as a journey and a struggle appear to be embedded in our physiology.

The Roman poet Ovid tells the story of Erysichthon, a would-be hero who failed to give proper respect to the goddess.

Erysichthon is a chieftain in northern Greece, a warlord if you like, who takes his gang of thugs on raiding parties into the neighbouring lands to collect whatever loot they can carry. On their return from a raid, they eat and carouse until they run out of provisions and have to go out and plunder some more. It occurs to Erysichthon that it would be much more congenial if they had a decent banquet hall in which to have the regular feast. Accordingly, he embarks on a building program. He takes his men out into the forest and orders one of them to start chopping down a tree. The man begins to chop, but when the tree starts bleeding he throws down his axe and refuses to go on. Erysichthon picks up the axe, kills his servant and sets to felling the tree himself. The tree nymph who is the soul of the tree cries out in fear. She is heard by the other tree nymphs in the forest, who call on the mother goddess to help. (Ovid gives her the Roman name, Ceres. She is identical with Demeter, goddess of the nurturing earth.) When Ceres arrives, disguised as a priestess, she tells Erysichthon that he must stop what he is doing, for when the tree dies her nymph will die. Erysichthon, of course, is not going to let anyone stop him from carrying through a major development project, and takes no notice. Ceres tells him that he may as well continue, as a banquet hall is exactly what he is going to need, but warns him that he will regret it.

So while Erysichthon and his men continue with their construction, Ceres sends one of her nymphs to the frozen north to find Penia, goddess of hunger. She and Penia do not usually have much to say to each other, but Penia happens to owe Ceres a favour. She rides the north wind down to Greece and enters into Erysichthon. He is overwhelmed by an insatiable hunger. He sends his men out time and again to bring him more food, but it is never enough. He sells his beloved daughter into slavery so that he can buy more food, but still cannot satisfy his hunger. He sits in his banquet hall eating everything in sight, including the tablecloth and cutlery. Still hungry, he sucks his finger, then bites it. He doesn't finish till he has eaten himself.

27

Joseph Campbell (1968) distinguishes four functions of myth. We can see them all at work in this story. The *metaphysical* function is to tell us what sort of a universe we live in. This story tells us, among other things, that the world belongs to the gods, and we must be careful not to think that we are in control. Through its *cosmological* function the story did for its hearers what science does for us nowadays. It explains that huge ancient tree stump in the forest and the ruins of the banquet hall on the hill. It tells us that feast and famine alternate with the uneasy relationship between two goddesses. Through its *social and moral* function, the story tells us how we must behave, respecting the forest as the outward expression of an inner divinity. The *psychological* function causes us to reflect on the way that the conflict between the nature goddess and the Hero is played out within our own personality and behaviour.

The Greeks did not have an environmental movement. They had myths which told them: This is the way the world is – inner and outer. Ignore it at your peril.

PROMETHEUS

Prometheus is not your ordinary hero. He is not a human but a Titan, one of an older race of gods who ruled the cosmos before Zeus and his family took it from them. In the battle between the Titans and the Olympian gods, Prometheus switched sides and helped the gods to win. He expected to be rewarded when the spoils were divided. When this failed to eventuate, he set about making the lives of the gods less pleasant. His key strategy in this was the creation of men. Having created these nasty little beings, he had to protect them from Zeus's attempts to wipe them out. He set about providing them with the possibility of a civilized life.

Prometheus is the scientist and technician, the hero who liberated human beings from the power of the gods, who stole the gods' fire to bring light and warmth to humanity, who taught men how to take control of their worlds by technology, who refused to allow women a place in the scheme of things, who set out to improve the lot of humanity and was punished for it by Zeus. The culture of the scientific-industrial era has worked itself out within the Promethean fantasy of individuality, autonomy, control of nature, 'masculine' rationality, progress, liberation, and salvation through technology, in spite of accumulating evidence that science and technology do not inevitably make people freer and happier. It is only now, when it is becoming apparent that the Promethean project of controlling and improving the planet has got us into a state of crisis, that there is serious challenge to the Promethean version of truth.

Counselling psychology, whether seen as a science, an art or a craft, has from the beginning been framed by the myth of the Hero. There are many variations on the Hero myth, different ways of representing what it means to become an individual, to fulfil our responsibilities and find our own way in the world. Prometheus' story is only one of these, but it has special significance for those of us who are prepared to intervene professionally in the lives of others. We hear in the story of Prometheus our conviction that we can free ourselves and our clients from the arbitrary and unpredictable power of our instincts and use technology to make a world where we can be happy and in control of our lives. We find the Promethean project in developmental psychology, in psychiatry, psychoanalysis, ego-psychology, cognitive behavioural therapy, solution-focused counselling and the humanistic existential therapies, and in the assertion that counselling psychology is a science rather than one of the creative arts.

Counselling as a profession starts with the assumption that both therapist and client live in a world which is essentially distinct from them, a world which must be dealt with as 'other'. Individuals act in and on this world as separate and distinct identities. They may be linked by empathy and relationship, but their separateness is not challenged. The therapist takes on the mission of Prometheus, using her skills (including the skill of relationship) to liberate her client from the power of impulse and compulsion, from conditions of worth, from a poor self-concept, from self-destructive habits, from inappropriate self-talk, from dependence on the therapist, or whatever. The therapist supports the client on a hero's journey, past beasts and barriers, out of darkness into light, from powerlessness to empowerment.

The centre of this psychological world is the heroic ego, as Freud asserted so confidently: 'Normally there is nothing of which we are more certain than the feeling of our self, of our own ego. The ego appears as something autonomous and unitary, marked off distinctly from everything else' (Freud, 1961: 14).

For Freud it was obvious enough that the differentiation of self from environment was a necessary and significant achievement for the species and for each individual infant.

> *One comes to learn a procedure by which, by deliberate direction of one's sensory activities ... one can differentiate between what is internal – what belongs to the ego – and what is external – what emanates from the outer world. In this way one takes the first step towards the introduction of the reality principle which is to dominate future development. (Freud, 1961: 14)*

No more 'participation mystique' with mother or nature. No more infantile sense of undifferentiated oneness with the world. The self stops at the skin. We are on our own in an alien world of objects. The clearer the boundary we build between self and other, the more heroic the ego, the less miserable we will be.

When we are enmeshed in a particular myth, it tells us that: This is the way the world is; it can be no other way. Assumptions that are taken for granted are mistaken for unassailable truth. The enmeshment of Western culture in the Promethean myth in the nineteenth and twentieth centuries carried with it the assumptions that human beings could and should use science and technology to control the planet and make themselves healthy and prosperous. The enduring enmeshment of counselling in the Promethean myth is manifested not only in the individualistic values of conventional therapy but also in the modernist privileging of technique. We find the Promethean fantasy powerfully present in the skills orientation which emerged from Carl Rogers' 'necessary and sufficient conditions', and has come to dominate conventional counsellor education. This orientation owes its development largely to the Hero-stance of Carkhuff and Truax.

Carkhuff's writing is manifestly Hero literature. Not only did he write within a fantasy of intellectual control over the messy field of human communication and personality change, but he assumed technical control over input and outcome and over the process of bringing people to 'higher functioning' and enabling them through their increased 'effectiveness' to take responsibility for social and political change. He focused on the impact which the behaviour of one individual (the helper) has on the behaviour of another individual (the helpee) and on finding a measurable relationship between cause and effect. There is a vast difference between this way of writing about client-centred therapy and Rogers' own writing, even when he was at his most empirical, and it is certainly in contrast to Rogers' later writing about the person-centred approach. We do not hear so much of Carkhuff now, yet the technique-centred, skills-based practice typified by Carkhuff and Egan still represents a certain type of orthodoxy in the field, and for good reason. There are many useful ways of thinking about therapy. Prometheus is not interested in what something *means*, but in whether it *works*.

If we *see through* Rogers' early writings on client-centred therapy, looking for the god hiding behind them, we will detect Prometheus in Rogers' search for a method that works. We will find Prometheus also in Rogers' confidence in the capacity of science to solve human problems and make a better world. Person-centred counsellors who find in themselves a sense of mission, a desire to liberate people from anxiety and powerlessness, the simple wish to make things better for people, even the hunger to be the best counsellor they can be, are acting out of the energy of Prometheus. Our lives are pretty deeply embedded in the Hero narrative.

The problem with this, which is only gradually being recognized, is that when we look at the bigger picture, it seems as though it is our collective domination by the Hero narrative which is responsible for the plight of the planet and our personal pathology. We can no longer assume as a matter of course that science and technology will inevitably produce a better world, or even stop us destroying the world we have, just as we can no longer assume absolutely that a 'strong ego' is the most appropriate personal goal. From this perspective our focus on the Hero narrative begins to seem not just problematic but pathological. James Hillman is by no means alone in referring to the 'ego-pathology' of our 'normal' ways of being in the world. Jung suggests that, 'We are beset by an all-too-human fear that consciousness – our Promethean project – may in the end not be able to serve us as well as nature' (Jung, 1979, CW 8, para. 750). And again: 'In spite of our proud domination of Nature we are still her victims as much as ever and have never even learned to control our own nature, which slowly and inevitably courts disaster.' (Jung, 1979, CW 18, para. 597).

Though Promethean values are no longer so much a part of mainstream thinking that they are unchallengeable, we still resist letting them go. We are still inclined to assume that we ought to be

31

able to understand and control our world and we have some nostalgia for the days when we dwelt happily in the fantasy that one day we would be able to do so. In so far as we practise our profession within this culturally approved narrative we take certain things for granted. Our notion of successful therapy is built on the images of progress, emancipation and technique. We are inclined to assume that understanding leads to liberation. In our counselling we tend to behave as though healing comes from the effectiveness of our intervention, that our skills matter more than relationship, wisdom, personality, moral integrity or anything else that might distinguish one counsellor from another. We readily conclude that if our counselling is not effecting any change in the client it is because we are not doing it right. We overlook the latter part of the Promethean narrative which tells us that our emancipation from the power of the gods is illusory and that every technical solution brings new problems. On the global scale we fear for the future for, as Jung says: 'Our progressiveness, though it may delight in a great many wish-fulfilments, piles up an equally gigantic Promethean debt which has to be paid off from time to time in the form of hideous catastrophes' (Jung, 1979, CW 9, para. 276).

The old stories are true. Otherwise we would have stopped telling and believing them long ago. Our dwelling in the Promethean story for the past couple of centuries has brought us benefits which we would be very loath to abandon. We are not going to save our planet for our grandchildren if we set aside the promise of technology. We are not going to be effective counsellors if we do not care to perfect our skills. The Promethean story is true. But, like the other old stories, its truth is incomplete.

GAIA

When James Lovelock first challenged the conventional scientific understanding of what sort of thing our planet is, arguing that it makes more sense to talk about the earth as a living organism rather than as a machine, his ideas did not receive much public attention. It was only when, on the advice of the novelist William Golding, he presented his ideas under the title *Gaia: A new look at life on earth* (1979) that he caught people's attention. Gaia was recognized as the ancient Greek name for goddess Earth and with this title he plugged into a collective inclination to imagine the earth as alive and mothering. His book became a best-seller and a significant influence on our thinking about the planet.

In European mythology the Gaia story is the oldest story of all. Gaia is the personification of the earth, the Great Mother from whom we are all born and to whom we all return. Ecopsychology is framed within the Gaia fantasy. It challenges the anthropocentric assumptions on which most therapies are based. It does not perceive a boundary of 'difference' between humans and the rest of the planet. In such a perspective, adequate human functioning demands a congruence not just between one's behaviour and one's self-concept, or between one's self-concept and one's 'real self', but a congruence between self and nature. The planet is not a machine but a living organism. We are cells of her body and have no existence apart from her.

Stephen Aizenstadt asks the question that I am attempting to address here: 'What would a psychology look like if it is based on an ecocentric worldview rather than an egocentric one?' (Aizenstadt, 1995: 98). He suggests that we might, for instance, view depression as a natural response to the manic condition of the world. We might see the condition of the world being projected in the behaviour of human beings, rather than human beings projecting their pathology onto the world. We might give up the notion that psychological health is solely a function of individual wholeness and nurturing human relationships, and imagine rather that that both physiological and psychological illness is connected to our damaged relationship to nature. Theodore Roszak develops the essentially Jungian argument that we are deeply implicated in nature, that the integration and emergence of the whole self, conscious and unconscious – a process which Jung called individuation – is simply harmonizing oneself with the natural world. Ecopsychology, as he understands it:

> *holds that there is a greater ecological intelligence as deeply rooted in the foundations of the psyche as the sexual and aggressive instincts Freud found there. Or rather, the psyche is rooted* inside *a greater intelligence once known as the* anima mundi, *the psyche of the Earth herself.* (Aizenstadt, 1995: 16)

Whether Gaia is for us a goddess, an organism animated by soul, or a biocybernetic universal system, we are in the mother story as soon as we shift our focus of significance from *ego* to *eco.*

On first reflection, there does not appear to be much connection between the conventional individualistic theorizing of counselling practice and the great web of life. There are plenty of people prepared to argue that the care of the worried well and even the mentally suffering is an indulgence and an irrelevance in the current ecological emergency. If we do not do something quickly we are doomed (Lovelock, 2006: 2010). Our efforts should be spent on saving the planet. After that we can worry about whether we are happy or not.

When Rogers developed his notion of an actualizing tendency, a tendency to become 'that self which one truly is' (Rogers, 1961: 181), he did so within the Hero narrative of independence and autonomy. However, by the time he wrote *A Way of Being* (1980) he had developed a transpersonal notion of growth and communication and he described his group experiences in phrases like 'participating in a larger universal formative tendency' (p. 128) and 'an awareness of together being part of a broader universal consciousness' (p. 197). He suggested that there might be a non-anthropocentric base for theorizing growth and change.

> *I hypothesize that there is a formative directional tendency in the universe. This is an evolutionary tendency towards greater order, greater complexity, greater interrelatedness. In humankind, this tendency exhibits itself as the individual moves from a single-cell origin to complex organic functioning, to knowing and sensing below the level of consciousness, to a conscious awareness of the organism and the external world, to a transcendent awareness of the harmony and unity of the cosmic system, including humankind. (Rogers, 1980: 133)*

Rogers came to see client and therapist as together caught up in a process of becoming which includes everything in the universe. The drive to maintain and enhance the experiencing organism is not something operating within the client or within the client–therapist encounter. Rather, the 'unfolding process' is something bigger than them, and they are inside it. As Hillman suggests, we are always in one archetypal fantasy or another, and this is the fantasy of Gaia.

Our psychology has trouble in expanding the notion of empathy beyond the one-to-one interaction between humans. We think we can talk about empathy with human beings well enough, but what could we possibly mean by empathy with the planet, empathy with animals, empathy with rocks and stones and trees? And are we really capable of unconditionally valuing the rainforest (mosquitoes and all) for its own sake, rather than because it serves us in some way?

Those whose basic assumptions are grounded in the Mother story have no problem with such questions. The systemic ecologist whose world is a wholly material web of life, sees the oneness of the system in which human beings are intrinsically connected with all material existence, and she may have no interest in the meanings which individuals attribute to their experience of this. The pan-experiential philosopher sees subjectivity as the essence of all being, and deep empathy with the planet as the natural condition of human beings. The nature mystic cherishes and celebrates the experience of transcending the boundary between the part and the whole. From such perspectives, the sense of separateness which turns empathy into a deliberate act of cognition or imagination is an aberration, and the notion that empathy only exists in relationships between two human individuals is a nonsense.

Yet we cannot be seduced into giving all our worship to Gaia. We are both one and many. To be carried away by the regressive wish for symbiotic union with the Great Mother is no solution for the planet's condition. To mistake the 'unity-consciousness' of infantile regression for transpersonal experience is no less pathological than to deny altogether the transpersonal dimension of human life. To approach Gaia with the mantra that 'Mother loves us' is to ignore both the myth and the evidence that mother both nurtures and devours.

The Earth Mother has many names. As Demeter, her preferred name in classical Greece, she is domesticated as the goddess of motherhood and agriculture. As Themis, goddess of cosmic order, she is mother to Prometheus, who does much to destroy that order by championing human beings, but is reconciled to her at the end. As Maia, she is mother to Hermes, another god who is particularly friendly to humans. It is Hermes that I wish to discuss next, not only because his narrative appears to be the dominant narrative of late capitalism, but because he warns us that all the gods must be worshipped. We cannot adequately address the pathology of the planet by replacing the total and uncritical worship of Prometheus by the total and uncritical worship of Gaia.

HERMES

The myths of Gaia and Prometheus have shaped scientific and philosophical thought since science and philosophy first emerged. On the one hand, we have the story of progress, the story of humanity's heroic struggle out of primitive darkness and ignorance into the brightness and knowledge of the modern world. On the other, we have a story of loss and alienation – the loss of our sacred unity with *all that is* and our alienation from our true being. In one story we rejoice in the triumph of reason. In the other we blame the emergence of reason and ego for our separation from the original state of oneness with nature – and the ecological collapse and spiritual barrenness which have followed from it. Currently, however, we find ourselves immersed in a third story. Just as we can find the ancient worship of Gaia flourishing anew in many New Age communities, and just as it makes some sense to argue that the modern, industrial era has been inordinately devoted to the worship of Prometheus, we can look at postmodern, post-industrial society and find evidence of a very different god at work. The Age of Prometheus may be as good as over. The Age of Hermes may be just beginning.

In the past 40 years we have had numerous cultural philosophers pointing out that the sensibility of the late twentieth and early twenty-first century is quite different from that of the era preceding it. They point to the explosion of information, the commodification of knowledge, health, happiness and anything else for which a market can be found or invented, the dominance of image, the collapse of the 'grand narratives' and the consequent relativization of truths, the challenge to the fantasy of control and the fantasy of progress, the shift from a focus on substance to a focus on image, an all-pervasive experience of illusion and deception. Jacques Lyotard (1983) coined the phrase 'the postmodern condition' as a label for this state of things. I suggest that if we manage to *see through* these phenomena to the image and god behind them, we will find Hermes.

David Ray Griffin (1989) distinguishes three worldviews which we now find competing for our allegiance. He calls these 'the modern worldview', 'the deconstructive postmodern worldview' and the 'constructive postmodern worldview'. The modern, materialistic, mechanistic worldview has been dominant for 300 years or more. In this worldview the world is understood to be built up from its smallest parts (atoms) to construct machines, a category which includes both trees and humans. The parts exist independently of each other – they do not require relationships with other parts to maintain their existence. As it happens, the world now revealed by physics and biology no longer looks like a machine, but the worldview persists, with its assumption that we can find the objective truth about reality if we look hard enough.

By contrast, the deconstructive postmodern worldview 'deconstructs' all notions of truth, purpose and meaning, arguing that they have no substance. If we explore any idea or value deeply enough and take it apart we will find that there is nothing there. Nothing is more real, more meaningful or more valuable than anything else. The deconstructive worldview naturally rejects the notion that science can uncover any ultimate truth about reality. Any statement we try to make about the world will be found, on examination, to be groundless.

The constructive postmodern worldview, on the other hand, acknowledges the ability of science to tell us something valid about reality, but rejects the notion that only science is capable of doing this. In this worldview, aesthetic and religious experiences also tell us something about reality. Constructive postmodernists are deeply interested in notions of meaning and purpose. They argue that the parts cannot be understood except in relation to the whole; indeed the parts only exist through their relationship to the whole. They do not imagine the universe to be composed of 'things' at all, but suggest that the basic core of the world's being is 'life' or 'creativity'. Griffin himself is a process philosopher, strongly influenced by the ideas of Alfred North Whitehead who argued in *Modes of Thought* (1938) that science deals only with half the evidence available to human experience. By restricting themselves to the 'objective facts' scientists cannot find enjoyment, intention or creativity in nature. Yet we can find them in our experience. He also argued that truth is partial and plural and observed that both scientists and sceptics were falling for what he called 'the fallacy of dogmatic finality'. He urged us to avoid one-sided seeing, for 'There are no whole truths; all truths are half-truths. It is trying to treat them as whole truths that plays the devil' (Whitehead, 1953: 14).

Mythologically, the modernist worldview is represented by the narrative of Prometheus, the strong-minded individual who sets us free and teaches us to take control of our world. Likewise, we find both the constructive and deconstructive postmodernist worldviews represented symbolically in the myth of Hermes, the god of both truth and lies, whose feet never touch the ground. In the myths as the ancient Greeks told them, Prometheus is alienated from Mother (Themis) until his eventual reconciliation. Hermes, on the other hand, claims to be 'doing it all for Mother (Maia)'.

We found in the late twentieth century a general abandonment of the heroic fantasy of the control of nature. This is reflected in contemporary psychologies which challenge the notion of egoic control of personality and behaviour. Promethean, positivist science is being supplanted by a Hermetic, postmodern science characterized by incomplete information, catastrophe and chaos, indeterminacy, paradox, discontinuity, and a tendency to uncover new questions rather than new answers. We seem to be deeply embedded in the myth of the 'bringer of dreams', the god of the marketplace, of fast footwork and smooth talking.

Archetypal images have both negative and positive aspects, and this is manifested in the personalities of the gods. The destructive or nasty or pathological aspects of behaviour were shared out among all of them. Zeus is both punitive and benevolent. Ares engages in passionate activism as well as mindless violence. Prometheus is the arrogant and sexist saviour of humanity. Gaia both nurtures and devours her children.

Hermes is no exception. He is the god of deceit and manipulation and groundlessness. He is also the god of magic and dialogue and transformation. At best the postmodern counsellor is imaginative, tolerant, pluralistic and flexible. At worst she is superficial, nihilistic, eclectic and slippery.

In so far as our assumptions are embedded in the Hermes story, we will find in our personalities and professional practice a tendency to privilege image over substance, seeming over being. We will find a reluctance to commit ourselves to structures, ideas or relationships. We will be inclined to see ourselves as companions in the client's journey, rather than as healers, advisers or nurturers. We will 'facilitate' or 'manipulate' rather than direct or even, guide. We will be hesitant to face and declare our own values, to fight for our beliefs, or to pass judgement on anyone's behaviour. We will be pluralistic in theory and technique. Perhaps this will be manifested in a groundless eclecticism. On the other hand, perhaps it may indicate that we are genuinely polytheistic in our values, perceiving truth to reside, not in either

Prometheus or Gaia or Zeus or Eros, but in all of the gods at once and together, in the whole polyphony of voices, in the discords as well as the harmonies.

Rogers may have flirted with Prometheus in his early career, when he was striving to give client-centred therapy credibility within the culture of applied psychological science, but the mindset he brought to *On Becoming a Person* (1961) and the writing which followed it clearly encompass a Hermes 'mode of apprehension'– to use one of Jung's many definitions of archetype. We see the god of process and constant movement in Rogers' confrontation of conventional notions of personality, and his adoption of a process conception of the self. He challenged the notion of a substantial, enduring self, seeing his clients as moving from defining themselves as a 'self' who thinks and feels in predictable ways to 'living subjectively in the experience, not feeling about it ... The self, at this moment, is this feeling ... The self is, subjectively, in the existential moment. It is not something one perceives' (Rogers, 1961: 147).

In the first decades of the twenty-first century we find health professionals using the expression 'apocalyptic nihilism' to label the state of young people whose response to the present planetary emergency is to see nothing to commit to, nothing to hope for and nothing to live for. If nothing is to be valued above anything else, then nothing is to be valued at all. This is one form of Hermes pathology. The counter to this is the message of Hermes' myth that all the gods are to be worshipped, that the squabbles between them, the conflict of values and the clash of perspectives, are to be accepted simply as manifestations of the way the world is. Unfortunately, when one god lets us down we tend to redirect all our worship to another, not realizing that our problem may derive not from our worship of a particular god but from our unwillingness to worship all the gods at once. An obsessive, monotheistic worship of Hermes or Gaia is no more a solution to the problems of the planet than the monotheistic worship of Prometheus.

Yet we need a Hermes consciousness to confront the urgency of our situation. When Prometheus is punished by Zeus, bound to a rock in the outer reaches of the universe, it is Hermes who challenges his claim to be the true saviour of mankind, and argues that he should take a more humble stance towards the eternal order. It is Hermes who connects with us as the guide of souls, the messenger of the gods, the healer. It is Hermes who subverts and destabilizes the patriarchal order when he steals the cattle of the gods. When Maia, the earth mother, scolds her child for causing such trouble, the infant Hermes replies: 'Mother, I did it for you'. It is Hermes who tells us to carry our truths lightly, an admonition that we need to take seriously in a culture that is still committed to the dogma of unending 'progress' and 'development' in spite of the logic that tells us that our planet's resources are limited, and the clear evidence that uncontrolled 'progress' is destroying the planet's capacity to sustain human life. It is not enough to turn Prometheus' energies towards sustainable technologies. We need to give up the basic assumptions that have supported the Promethean project over the past three centuries – the assumption that we have a right to exploit the earth without concern for the future; the assumption that science will eventually find a way to rescue us, the assumption that we are active and the planet is passive; the assumption that our individual benefit is more important than the state of the earth. We cannot take on new beliefs and attitudes until Hermes, 'the loosener' enables us to let go of those we already have.

There are echoes in the Hermes myth of Hermes' origins as a god of an oppressed rural people whose land has been taken from them by invaders, and who do not have the means to challenge their oppressors except through theft and trickery. There are echoes also of the oppression of the native earth-worshippers by the worshippers of the sky father, who had seized political and religious power and who have had it ever since. In Hermes' assertion that 'I did it for you, mother,' there is a suggestion that mother will have her day of honour once again, and that it is her son, the trickster and rogue, who will bring this about. The global financial crisis of 2008 certainly had Hermes' signature. There is as yet no indication that Hermes' hand has been removed from the controls of the international financial system. Perhaps we have had a foretaste of the catastrophic collapse which will destroy our capacity to hurt Gaia/Maia in the ways we currently take for granted. Lovelock has recently written on *The Revenge of Gaia* (2006) – maybe Hermes will have a hand in this.

MANY GODS, MANY TRUTHS

The Hero stories of the great classical mythologies and of modernist science and psychology depict the struggle for egoic consciousness to emerge from the darkness of unconsciousness, the chaos of nature and the tumult of uncontrolled energies. By contrast, the mother stories of religious traditions, nature philosophies and ecological science do not see chaos, darkness and tumult, but an order which may be beyond our comprehension. The Hermes story tells us that the way forward is not to assert the legitimacy of one of these stories and belittle the other, but to hold the two in tension.

The mythologies of the great classical cultures represent a world where each god has his or her distinct truth, and all must be acknowledged. I am not suggesting that we can live in the kind of symbiotic union with the planet which seems to have been experienced by our Stone Age ancestors, any more than I am suggesting that a focus on personal development and technological progress will find us a way out of our present social and environmental predicament. However, I do believe that we must learn to acknowledge both the primacy of the individual and the primacy of the planet. We have to learn to live simultaneously in both the Prometheus fantasy and the Gaia fantasy, and to do this we need a Hermes consciousness.

When Lovelock gave us the image of Gaia in 1979, it was largely rejected by his fellow scientists, but welcomed by New Age Gaia worshippers and the emerging Green movement – an association which did it no good in scientific circles. Lovelock found himself sharing the 'green' assumption that the survival of our species cannot be achieved without a massive shift in our sense of connection with the earth, for 'until we all feel intuitively that the Earth is a living system, and know that we are part of it, we will fail to react automatically for its and ultimately our own protection' (Lovelock, 2010: 128). However, he was dismayed by the 'woolly thinking' and 'unreasoning fear' which would rely on the minimal impact of technologies like wind power and photovoltaic cells rather than accept technologies like nuclear power, which he maintained are more reliable and which alone can buy us time to adapt to the menacing reality of climate change (Lovelock, 2010: 68*ff*; Gribbin & Gribbin, 2009: 151). Likewise, when we come to counselling we should not assume that it is enough to focus romantically on our organic relationship with the planet and ignore the reality of our client's egoic, decision-making experience in a world populated by other egos. Empowerment is not a dirty word.

Each archetypal image represents a distinct 'mode of apprehension'. In attempting to address the pathology of the planet we can apprehend the task intellectually, emotionally and imaginatively in a number of ways. From the Promethean perspective we can deal with the planet as a machine of which we are (potentially at least) in control, just as we deal with ourselves therapeutically as machines of which the ego is (potentially at least) in control. From the Gaian perspective we deal with the planet as a living organism, and our therapy is directed at restoring the union between the individual and the greater organism. From the Hermetic perspective, we deal with the planet and our place in it as flux and process, not seeking to ground ourselves in any truth as absolute, but opening ourselves to the possibility of transformation through the immediacy of experience.

This involves being open to the paradoxical nature of our relationship with our planet. As E.O. Wilson argues in *Biophilia* (1984):

> *Natural philosophy has brought into clear relief the following paradox of human existence. The drive towards perpetual expansion – or personal freedom – is basic to the human spirit. But to sustain it we need the most delicate, knowing stewardship of the living world that can be devised. Expansion and stewardship may appear at first to be conflicting goals, but they are not ... The paradox can be resolved by changing its premises into forms more suited to human survival, by which I mean protection of the human spirit. (Wilson, 1984: 140)*

The reader will readily *see through* the assumptions and argument of this chapter and find there a reiteration of the Hermes myth. I have no apology for that. I am stuck in it, as our global culture is, and risk the pathology that goes with it. There are many things which excite me in a postmodern consciousness, and many things which worry me deeply. However, they all belong to the same story. We need to follow Hermes' own advice and example and dwell very lightly in his world. He's a friendly god, but he can't always be trusted.

3

THE CLIENT-CENTRED ECOPSYCHOLOGIST

Carl Rogers' psychology and therapy are not enmeshed in a fantasy of control, and he did not identify the person with the rational ego any more than Jung did. He preferred the Gaian language of biology (the organism, growth) to the Promethean language of mechanics (energy, structure) in discussing the 'what' and 'how' of personal development. He acknowledges the influence of Otto Rank's 'relationship therapy' on his early thinking and practice. However, there has been, and remains, a stream of thinking in client-centred therapy which can well be called Promethean.

Rogers' early empiricism contributed to this, as did his early ambition to develop a technique that was better than other techniques. His theory of personality and behaviour as developed in *Client-Centered Therapy* (1951), and developed further in his paper 'A Theory of Therapy, Personality and Interpersonal Relationships as Developed in the Client-Centered Framework' (Rogers, 1959), is radical in the context of the positivistic assumptions which framed American academic psychology for most of the last century. Nevertheless, we can now see in this systematic exposition of his theory of personality some reflections of the same Cartesian and positivist biases as the behaviourist theory he found so unsatisfactory. It is mechanistic and materialistic, which is exactly how a 'proper' scientific theory is supposed to be. Rogers systematically explores cause and effect within the boundaries of sensate knowledge and modernist logic. It is clear from Rogers' later writing that by the time he produced *A Way of Being* (1980), this sort of thinking had lost its attraction for him. Nevertheless, it has remained an important thread in the theory and practice associated with client-centred therapy.

It is not my purpose here to expand on the ways in which client-centred therapy, through its focus on subjective experience, individuality, choice and personal power, reflects the images of the Hero fantasy. What I am concerned with here is an attempt to explore another truth, albeit another partial truth, about client-centred therapy. I want to examine what client-centred therapy looks like when it is framed within the mother fantasy.

BOUNDARIES OF THE SELF

Ken Wilber (1996) deals with the individual versus planet problem, the Hero versus Mother conflict, by calling on Arthur Koestler's word 'holon', by which he means something which is both a part and a whole. An atom is an entity in itself; it also exists as a part of a molecule. A molecule exists as an entity in itself; it also exists as part of a cell. And so on, all the way up the 'holarchy'. We seem to have no problem with applying this notion to everything smaller than us in the 'holarchy', and even to everything larger than us, but we have some resistance to applying it to ourselves. We like to see ourselves as top of the heap, rather than as cells of a larger organism.

One reason why the writings of Carl Jung have some appeal for psychologically oriented ecologists and ecologically oriented psychologists is that his therapy of the individual was grounded in a notion that our individuality is a secondary phenomenon. For Jung we are momentary manifestations of a greater reality. Rogers, by contrast, developed a theory of personality which conceived individuality as the primary phenomenon. In this view, each of us exists separately in a world of experience on which we act and which acts upon us. For client-centred therapists working within the framework of Rogers' theory of personality, it is the subjectivity of this individual existence which is the focus. They deal with the world as object, as experienced by the client–subject, rather than dealing with the self–client relationship as an expression of the world–subject.

In *Client-Centered Therapy* (1951), an exposition of a theory of personality and personal behaviour, Rogers makes the point that he is not fully satisfied with current explanations, including his own, of how a portion of a child's experiential world gradually becomes differentiated as the self. He points out that the self is not necessarily co-existent with the physical organism. Following Andras Angyal, he argues 'that there is no possibility of a sharp line between organism and environment, and that there is likewise no sharp limit between the experience of the self and of the outside world' (Rogers, 1951: 497). His way of dealing with this question in 1951 was to call on the Promethean image of control: 'Those elements which we control are regarded as part of self' (Rogers, 1951: 497). Indeed they are, as long as we are embedded in the Hero story. However, from the tentativeness of his language we might conclude that Rogers was, even at this date, reserving his decision on where the self ends and entertaining the notion, which Gregory Bateson and other systems cyberneticians have strongly argued since, that any boundaries we set to the 'self' are arbitrary. Moreover, the boundaries we put on the ecosystem are clearly as arbitrary as the boundaries we put on the self.

For a deep ecologist like Warwick Fox (1990), the 'self' is identified with 'all that is', in a 'deep realization that we and all other entities are aspects of a single unfolding reality' (Fox, 1990: 252). He is careful to point out that this realization does not imply that all multiplicity and diversity is reduced to homogeneous mush, but rather 'the fact that we and all other entities are aspects of a single unfolding reality means neither that all entities are fundamentally the same nor that they are absolutely autonomous, but rather simply that they are relatively autonomous' (Fox, 1990: 252). Such ideas can sit comfortably enough with a client-centred framework, and we can argue that in the healing relationship of one-to-one therapy we are engaged in the healing of the planet just as deeply as those whose concern for the planet leads them into social and political activism.

Once we relativize the atomistic individualism which has characterized conventional modernist understandings of therapy, client-centred practice takes on an extra dimension. We find, for instance, that Rogers' proposition that a condition of successful therapy is that the client must be anxious or at least vulnerable to anxiety, has implications outside the domestic problems of the client. At one level we have personal anxieties; at a second level we have collective anxieties – family, workplace, profession, society, nation, culture; at a third level we have species anxiety; at a fourth level we have a suffering planet, which is itself an element in a larger system. Client-centred therapists and other practitioners of the person-centred approach have shown an increasing awareness of the second of these levels. It appears in the work of those whose client-centred practice is influenced by systems thinking. It appears in suggestions that, when practising our craft in a multicultural society our empathy must extend not only to the client but to the client's culture. It appears in the increasing awareness of the politics of the person-centred approach. It found a further expression in the cross-cultural forums initiated by Rogers. However, it is not the second level which interests me here, but the third and fourth.

It seems to be a given that we are currently experiencing a massive collective anxiety about the incomprehensible danger we are in. We repress this anxiety both personally and collectively, but it manifests itself in collective pathological behaviour. It seems to me that it is the essential work of therapy to challenge the lies we tell ourselves, not just the personal ones but the shared ones. The counsellor who attends fully to the client as holon will be listening not only to the private pain but also to the pain of the species and the plight of the world. The unconditional caring which comes with this attention will go 'all the way down' the holarchy (and all the way up). James Hillman comments on his experience as therapist attending to the pathology of the world:

> *I find today that patients are more sensitive than the worlds they live in ... I mean that the distortions of communication, the sense of harassment and alienation, the deprivation of intimacy with the immediate environment, the feelings of false values and inner worthlessness experienced relentlessly in the world of our common habitation are genuine realistic appraisals and not merely apperceptions of our intra-subjective selves. My practice tells me that I can no longer distinguish clearly between neuroses of self and neuroses of world. (Hillman, 1982: 72)*

SELF-REALIZATION AND THE FORMATIVE TENDENCY

One of the key concepts in deep ecology is self-realization, a concept borrowed from Spinoza. It is a loose translation of Spinoza's term 'conatus', by ecophilosopher Arne Naess, by which he meant the basic motivation which can be considered the essence of all things, i.e. the tendency to persist in their own being. For people working in the client-centred framework, such a notion resonates strongly with Rogers' statement that the organism has 'one basic tendency and striving – to actualize, maintain, and enhance the experiencing organism' (Rogers, 1951: 487). However, it is absolutely central to

Spinoza's understanding that this self-realization is realization of the whole, since there is only one substance, of which we are, individually and collectively, specific expressions. For Spinoza our self-realization is not the realization of a separate autonomous self, but of a more and more expansive and non-egoic sense of self, a self which is to be identified with 'all there is'.

When Rogers expands on his notion of an actualizing tendency he originally does so within the Hero narrative, asserting that the organism 'moves in the direction of greater independence or self-responsibility [and] ... in the direction of an increasing self-government, self-regulation, and autonomy, and away from heteronomous control, or control by external forces' (Rogers, 1951: 488). However, he adds that 'the self-actualization of the organism appears to be in the direction of socialization' (Rogers, 1951: 488). That is to say, increasing autonomy and independence do not imply separateness and alienation, but rather increasing interest in, empathy with and compassion for others. For Naess, on the other hand, it is the expansion of the sense of self (and abandonment of a sense of being autonomous) which brings a deeper and broader identification with and, consequently, compassion for others.

It is clear from Rogers' earliest formulations of his theory of personality that he is more comfortable with an organic image of humanity, individually and collectively, than with a mechanical one. He reiterates, over and over again, that experience is 'organismic', that human existence is 'growth', and that the successful outcome of therapy is for the client to become in awareness as well as in experience 'a complete and fully functioning human organism' (Rogers, 1961: 104).

Keith Tudor (2010) argues that Rogers' work comes within the 'lost tradition' of organismic psychology, and comments on the fact that this aspect has been largely neglected even by those writing within the person-centred framework.

> *Given how much Rogers referred to the experiencing organism and related concepts – its tendency to actualize, the organismic valuing process, and the wisdom of the organism ... I am surprised by how little attention the organism attracts in person-centered and experiential literature, especially when we contrast this with the coverage of his concept of the self. (Tudor, 2010: 58)*

Tudor argues here and elsewhere (2006) that organism is the 'root metaphor' of person-centred psychology, reminding us that this has significant implications for our notion of the self, for:

> As organisms, human beings have an interdependent relationship with our environment, and cannot be understood outside of that environmental context. (Tudor, 2010: 61)

Van Belle (1990) argues very convincingly that it was the centrality of the growth image in Rogers' formulation of client-centred therapy which led him towards his later 'mystical' thinking. It led him to propose that growth is something that happens to people rather than something they do; that growth is a universal process in which people exist; that growth shapes the individual rather than the individual determinining or controlling the nature of growth. For Van Belle, given Rogers' adherence to this notion of growth, there is an inevitability in Rogers' movement over time from his early formulations of theory and methodology to what he terms 'mystical universalism'. By the time he wrote A Way of Being (1980) Rogers had, through his experience in encounter groups, developed a transpersonal notion of growth and communication, and he describes his experiences in phrases like 'participating in a larger universal formative tendency' (Rogers, 1980: 128) and 'an awareness of together being part of a broader universal consciousness' (Rogers, 1980: 197).

For many client-centred theorists and therapists, including Van Belle, this shift from a focus on individual subjectivity to a focus on cosmic consciousness was not a particularly welcome development in Rogers' thinking. Client-centred theorists and therapists have tended to stay with Rogers' earlier formulations. These provide a framework, a purpose and a methodology which enable effective one-to-one therapy to be undertaken. 'Mystical universalism' seems more problematic in this respect. However, I believe that our approach to the task (a Hero image) will be richer and more fruitful (a mother image) if we appreciate that in these early formulations there is already a tension between the two narratives, and if we take seriously Rogers' suggestion that the formative tendency is not an individual – nor even a specifically human – phenomenon, but something which characterizes both human and non-human existence.

It should be noted that Rogers justifies his fairly tentative statements of cosmic identification by starting from his experience of identification with 1, 10, 100 or 1,000 individuals and expanding it to embrace the universe. For a deep ecologist like Fox, this is misguided. This sort of personally based identification, starting with the people who are closest to us (partner, family, tribe, species) and spreading outwards is as likely to lead to the oppression, exploitation and destruction of those parts of the human and non-human world which we do not include in the 'us' as it is likely to bring us to greater harmony with them. From the ecologist's point of view we ought to start at the other end – we should identify first of all with a universe which contains all entities impartially, and through this identification bring an attitude of 'steadfast friendliness' to each being we encounter, for 'cosmologically based identification means having a lived sense of commonality with all other entities (whether one happens to encounter them personally or not)' (Fox, 1990: 257).

Fox is at pains to point out that identification means:

> the experience not simply of a sense of similarity with an entity but a sense of commonality ... What identification should not be taken to mean, however, is identity – that I literally am that tree for example. What is being emphasized is the tremendously common experience that through the process of identification my sense of self (my experiential self) can expand to include the tree, even though I and the tree remain physically 'separate'. (Fox, 1990: 231)

Rogers from the start preferred to imagine personality as process rather than as structure, and not simply as an individualistic process. He came to see client and therapist as being together caught up in a process of becoming which includes everything in the universe. The drive to maintain and enhance the experiencing organism is not something within the client or something within the client–therapist encounter, but rather, the 'unfolding process' is something they are within. This position differs little from that of many deep ecologists.

This is not to deny the significance of individual human life and experience. Alfred North Whitehead 1929/1978 whose 'process philosophy' has had some influence on the way the deep ecological position has developed, took the view that all aspects of the universe are moving towards the realization of ever greater richness of experience. Murray Bookchin (1980) argues that evolutionary processes strive towards the realization of ever greater degrees of individuation, freedom and selfhood. The same perspective is behind Rogers' notion that organismic choice is 'guided by the evolutionary flow' (Rogers, 1980: 127).

> *Thus, when we provide a climate that permits persons to* be *– whether they are clients, students, workers or persons in a group – we are not involved in a chance event. We are tapping into a tendency which permeates all organic life – a tendency to become all the complexity of which the organism is capable. (Rogers, 1980: 134)*

Eugene Gendlin, who was associated with Rogers in the development of the person-centred approach and went on to develop the approach known as focusing-oriented psychotherapy, has another way of expressing this. He writes of the bodily sense as the link between the conscious person and 'the deep universal reaches of human nature where we are no longer ourselves' (Gendlin, 1984: 81) and he writes of pathology as frustration of the life process.

To work as client-centred therapists within such a framework may not make a significant change in what we do, but it may enlarge our perception of its significance.

ECOCENTRIC VALUING

Some 50 years ago, Rogers developed the notion that unconditional positive regard is one of the necessary and sufficient conditions for therapeutic growth. At that time, his theory and methodology were sufficiently embedded in the Promethean fantasy for him to argue only that such an attitude is therapeutically effective (i.e. it 'works') and that he could provide an adequate theoretical explanation of how it 'works'. However, if we can get out of the Promethean mindset we may become interested in other aspects of this question, as he did. Is our interest in people egocentric and utilitarian? Do we value them only because they contribute to our income, our sense of competence, our professional advancement, our emotional satisfaction, our need for relationship? Or are they innately worthy of respect? Is the attitude of unconditional positive regard (non-judgemental acceptance, respect, caring, prizing, non-possessive love) something that we ought to bring to our relations with other human beings? Or is our entertaining such a moral imperative an indication that we are dominated by particular 'conditions of worth' supplied by a professional or religious subculture? Or does 'to be that self whom one truly is' mean being someone who no longer suppresses the organismic sense of unity with others, so that not to care for others would be incongruent with our true nature.

In ecopsychology similar questions arise. Is our interest in the planet egocentric and utilitarian? Do we adopt an environmentally sensitive attitude and work to raise other people's environmental awareness simply because 'it works' to save the human and non-human world from catastrophe? If I put my energy into saving the planet is it enough to do so because in doing so I save myself, my children and grandchildren, my species? Or is the planet of value for its own sake, regardless of its usefulness to human beings? Is there a cosmic purpose that provides a moral imperative to environmental activism? Is concern for the planet simply an expression of our true nature, relieved of its egocentric distortions?

Caring for our client and caring for our planet may be not so much an expression of our morality as they are an expression of our identity. If we can occasionally get out of the Promethean mindset which asserts our autonomy and defines both our client and the rainforest as 'other', if we can set aside the Cartesian–Newtonian fantasy that the observer and the observed are different phenomena, we may find that accepting that we are our world has inevitable consequences in how we treat it/us – in all its/our human and non-human manifestations. Arguments about the necessity, sufficiency and unconditionality of 'positive regard' take on a different aspect within the Gaia fantasy.

ECOCENTRIC EMPATHY

In conventional discussions of therapeutic empathy, the separate identities of the therapist and client are taken for granted. However, if we cease to assert this essential separateness as axiomatic, our notion of empathy can change somewhat. If, moreover, we allow ourselves to abandon the modernist assumption that all knowledge originates in seeing, hearing, tasting, smelling or touching objects outside the boundary of our skin, we can contemplate the possibility that we can know another person's subjective experience directly. Alvin Mahrer (1978) has argued along similar lines in his description of experiential psychotherapy. Alison Talbot (1997) has provided evidence that the somatic sharing of a client's internal experience is not uncommon among therapists. Rogers himself suggests in his later writing that we recognize a transpersonal, boundary-crossing experience of empathy.

He cites with approval a participant in one of his workshops:

> ... I felt the oneness of spirit in the community. We breathed together, we felt together, even spoke for one another. I felt the power of the 'lifeforce' that infuses each of us – whatever that is. I felt its presence without the usual barricades of 'me-ness' or 'you-ness' – it was like a meditative experience when I feel myself as a centre of consciousness. And yet with that extraordinary sense of oneness, the separateness of each person present has never been more clearly preserved. (Rogers, 1990: 148)

It has often been pointed out that the assumption that the observer and the observed are separate phenomena has long been abandoned in quantum physics but is sedulously maintained in the social and behavioural sciences which look to the 'hard sciences' for their validation. I suggest that the separation of therapist–observer–subject and client–observed–object in Rogers' early formulation of empathy is a manifestation of this powerful, but challengeable, assumption. However, we are not compelled to understand empathy according to Rogers' early formulation, which makes it a cognitive act by which we enter the perceptual world of the other and thereby understand it as if it were our own. We can, by contrast, think of empathy as the dissolution of the boundaries by which we assiduously maintain our sense of self, in order to let the experience of the client be our own experience. We can think of empathy not as communication but as identification, not just with a particular client but with the 'unity in process' which is manifested at this moment in this client. In this we would be following the vision not of the scientist, who needs an objective world to work on, but of the poet and artist who trusts that her subjective experience is the world's subjective experience and understands that, if she lets herself be open to the pathos of the world, she can find in her own internal experience an enduring statement of how the world is.

Rogers remarks in more than one place that the more intensely personal and individual a communication is, the more universal it is. In *A Way of Being* (1980) he comments on the peculiar satisfaction to be found in really hearing somebody:

> *It is like listening to the music of the spheres, because beyond the immediate message of the person, no matter what that might be, there is the universal. Hidden in all of the personal communications which I really hear there seem to be orderly psychological laws, aspects of the same order we find in the universe as a whole. So there is both the satisfaction of hearing this person and also the satisfaction of feeling oneself in touch with what is universally true. (Rogers, 1980: 8)*

Our psychology, even the fairly radical psychology of client-centred therapy, has trouble in expanding the notion of empathy. We think we can talk about empathy with human beings well enough, but what could we possibly mean by empathy with the planet. Martin Buber has many sympathetic commentators, who embrace with enthusiasm his distinction between I–It relationships and I–Thou relationships, but they are inclined to stop taking him seriously when he suggests that the two kinds of relationships exist not only in our encounter with other human beings, but in our encounter with the non-human world.

ECOCENTRIC CONGRUENCE

Rogers developed a model of therapy in which the means and the end are identical – congruence. We are used to dealing with this idea on the individualistic level. If, in my interaction with my client, I am 'all of a piece', if my thinking and feeling and talking and behaviour are all coming from the same place, if I am not telling lies to myself or my client, even lies I am not aware of telling, the chances are that my client also will begin to function more congruently. We can push this a little further. Both I and my client need to be congruent not only in thinking and feeling and behaviour, not only in our awareness and our unconscious processes, and not only within our own organism. We need also to be congruent with what we call the 'natural world'. We need to be in harmony with the rhythms of nature. So does our culture, and so does our species. We are ready enough to accept that the separation of

53

mind and body is pathological. We need to be equally aware of the deep pathology that has come from the modernist separation of culture and nature. The incongruence between who we as individuals imagine we are and who our total organisms know we are can be perceived as an expression of the incongruence between our culture and nature. The client-centred therapist can both offer and invite 'deep congruence', just as she can both offer and invite 'deep empathy' and 'deep acceptance'. Not only can but must, if she is not to be irrelevant.

Client-centred therapy works at the client's point of discomfort, the point of incongruence between the client's organismic experiencing and his symbolization of this experiencing. In Rogers' early formulations he depicted culturally imposed 'conditions of worth' as largely responsible for this incongruence and asked us to trust in the client's actualizing tendency to provide the energy and direction for change. Personal change in the perspective of client-centred therapy means becoming what we already are. Or rather, expressing in our surface behaviour and awareness what we already are at depth. A shift of focus from individual to planet enables us to entertain the notion that our emerging awareness is the planet's emerging awareness of itself. The place of culture in this is problematic.

Culture can be thought of as mediating between planet and individual. From the Hero perspective the cultural group is simply a collection of individuals who through an ongoing process of communication end up sharing much the same thoughts, attitudes and assumptions about the world. From the Mother perspective, the group is primary: it gives birth to the individual as a particular manifestation of its life and its truths. Whichever way we think of it we must admit that culture and individual consciousness are entirely interdependent. A culture depends on the aggregation of the subjective worlds of all the individuals within it. On the other hand, the individual's survival depends on absorbing the taken-for-granted beliefs and values held in the culture, so as not to have to invent or discover them all from scratch – a task which would take a lifetime. Cultures themselves may be congruent or incongruent with the planet. It is plausible to suggest that our current global predicament is a consequence of the incongruence between the Western-dominated global culture and the planetary environment in which it exists. Indigenous cultures which have been congruent with the planet for thousands of years have been or are being rapidly destroyed.

We might posit an ideal world in which there is no conflict between the formative tendency of the individual, the conditions of worth imposed by the culture, and the maintenance of the total ecological system of which both the individual and the cultural group are elements. There would be no need for therapy in such a world. In the world in which therapy does have a place there are aspects of culture which are ultimately dysfunctional and which have predictably catastrophic consequences. In such a world, certain aspects of culture are an impediment to the individual's proper relationship to the planet, as a disease might be an impediment to an organ's (or a cell's) proper relationship to the body. In such a world, the process of client-centred therapy inevitably involves the client in focusing on himself. 'Not only is there movement from symptoms to self, but from *environment to self* and from *others to self* (Rogers, 1951: 135). In such a world, the client-centred therapist pursues the point of discomfort in the client's subjective experience on the understanding that as the nature of the client's incongruence comes into his awareness and as he finds the feelings which are congruent with his organismic experiencing and the words and images which are congruent with his feelings, he will be reborn as the person he 'naturally' is. Or, to switch from the Gaia images of birthing and growth to the Promethean image of emancipation, she will emerge from the prison of her culturally embedded prejudices, introjected values and 'conditions of worth' as a free and autonomous person whose freedom and autonomy are totally compatible with the nature of the larger world.

We need not limit this model of change to our thinking about the increasing congruence of the individual. We can postulate that the formative tendency functions in a similar way in the cultural collective, that the same progress from vulnerability to anxiety to awareness of anxiety is potential in the cultural collective as it strives (in spite of its distortions) to become congruent with the 'becoming' of the ecosystem as a whole. The uneasy emergence of environmental, feminist and communitarian movements in recent decades within the dominant individualistic–competitive global culture can perhaps be understood is just these terms. Therapists can be agents of change for their cultures or subcultures, not only through their work with individuals but by approaching the cultural collective as a whole – with the same empathy, congruence and unconditional positive regard as they bring to their individual clients. There is a need to reframe political and environmental activism in this way, as Rogers himself began to do in his most mature work. As long as the cultural group is collectively 'vulnerable to anxiety', and as long as the therapist can find an opportunity to establish contact and communication with it, the principles of client-centred therapy may provide a means to facilitate its transformation.

CONNECTING

Neils Bohr, the founding father of quantum physics, proposed the axiom that opposites are not contradictory but complementary.

A focus on the uniqueness of the client need not inhibit our awareness of a cosmic order in which the individual is entirely insignificant. A conviction that 'all is one' does not have to cancel out an appreciation of separateness and diversity. On a cosmic scale, the unfolding of the universe is manifested in two opposing processes which work together; one process *creates* by separating out the richness and diversity of the many, the other process draws into *unity* the divisions that are so created, so the cosmic balance is maintained.

Any act of creation involves a separation from the primal matrix, or from the human mother, or from undifferentiated experience. On the human scale, we can describe the drive to relationship, whether manifested in lust, loneliness or the therapeutic conditions, as grounded in a drive to union not just with a specific other but with Gaia, mother of us all. Otto Rank, whose ideas were influential in Rogers' early efforts to develop a consistent theory and practice, saw our basic anxiety as coming from our separation from mother (both human and cosmic) in the trauma of birth. For Rank, our search for relationship comes from the anxiety of separation and the desire to re-experience the primal unity. In such a perspective, the relationship offered by the therapist has, in itself and regardless of technique, the potential to be healing – a healing which is manifested in an increasing capacity for choice.

From Rogers onward, the counsellor–client relationship has been understood as fundamental in person-centred counselling. Conventionally, we have imagined relationship as an artefact of the communication between two persons. In the first place there is a counsellor and a client who are communicating. As a consequence of this, a connection develops between them. However, we can imagine this quite differently. If we look at the counsellor and client communicating we might imagine that the connection is primary. A counsellor and a client just happen to be on the opposite ends of it. Because we can see the individuals, because they are concrete 'things', we assume them to be more 'real' than the relationship which connects them. We should acknowledge that this is an assumption. In a process cosmology such as that developed by Alfred North Whitehead, or in other models of reality which have emerged, like his, from twentieth century physics, the universe does not consist of 'things' at all. It consists of connections between events. Furthermore, in such a vision of reality, each momentary event or 'occasion of experience' (Whitehead's term) involves the whole universe. Everything is connected. The notion that counsellor and client are fundamentally isolated individuals communicating through words and gestures across the space between them is an illusion.

Rogers' focus on individual subjectivity in the 1940s and 1950s was radical enough in the context of a psychological science which was obsessed with objectivity and determinism. However, he did not at the time permit himself to take the more radical stance of challenging the primacy of the individual. In the time and cultural context in which client-centred therapy was developed, such a notion was unlikely to occur to him. In spite of Rogers' modification of this stance in his later writing, person-centred theory has in general been conservative in adhering to Rogers' early formulations. Counselling is still perceived to be an interaction between one individual and another.

Nevertheless, for a decade or more, this assumption has been challenged within person-centred theory. The emergence of systems approaches in counselling theory has led to an acknowledgement that the experience of both the counsellor and the client is necessarily enmeshed in the social worlds in which they exist. The political contexts and implications of client-centred counselling have come under increasingly critical observation (Barrett-Lennard, 2005; Proctor et al, 2006). There has been an increasing focus on the 'in-between', the 'we', in the counselling interaction, as in Schmid's focus (inspired by the work of Emmanuel Levinas and Martin Buber) on person-centred counselling as dialogue (Schmid, 2002), and Mearns and Cooper's (2005) revisioning of good practice in terms of relational depth.

Godfrey Barrett-Lennard has for a decade or more put relationship at the centre of the counselling process, asking such questions as 'Human relationship: Linkage or life form?' (see Barrett-Lennard, 1998, 2003, 2005, 2007, 2009).

Ecopsychology suggests that we take this thinking a step further. The 'in-between' is not confined to the physical and psychological space between me and my client. The 'we' is not confined to the two of us, or even the social and political worlds we bring with us to our interaction. We both speak to and for a larger, unfolding organism. We speak to and for something we call 'life'.

As Rogers puts it:

When I can relax and be close to the transcendental core of me then ... it seems that my inner spirit has reached out and touched the inner spirit of the other. Our relationship transcends itself and becomes a part of something larger. (Rogers, 1980: 129)

CONCLUSION

Rogers was able to express the cosmic paradox in human terms. He was convinced that human beings have a natural tendency to care for one another, to submerge ego in the oneness of relationship. Paradoxically, he was convinced also that a caring relationship fosters creativity and diversity. He placed a high value on creativity and diversity, on the uniqueness of the individual's response to her world when no longer constrained by fear; yet his experience and observation of this uniqueness convinced him that it is grounded in the universal.

I am not suggesting that abandoning our focus on individual development and resting in a sense of cosmic unity will give us a way out of our present social and environmental predicament. Neither am I arguing that we have to follow Rogers into the language of 'spirituality' and 'mysticism'. We should, of course, note that in *A Way of Being* (1980) Rogers seeks validation for his ideas not in mystical writings, but in science.

However, I do believe that we must learn to acknowledge both the primacy of the individual and the primacy of the planet. We have to learn to live simultaneously in the fantasy of the Many and the fantasy of the One. We have to recognize that both the Hero story and the Mother story tell us not how it used to be in this world or how it ought to be, but how it is. The mythologies of the great classical cultures represent a world where each god has his or her distinct truth, and all must be acknowledged. For Rogers, also, reality was multiple (Rogers, 1980, Chapter 5).

The literature of ecopsychology is growing but is still somewhat limited. To this point, those who have entered the field have been more inclined to call on Jung and Abraham Maslow than on Rogers for eco-compatible insights into psychological processes (e.g. Fox, 1990; Roszak, 1995; Wilber, 1996). This is not surprising. Both professional and popular perceptions of Rogerian theory perceive it as entirely individualistic. I suggest that a better understanding of person-centred theory and practice might give ecopsychologists an appropriate way of dealing, both theoretically and practically, with human psychopathology. Andy Fisher (2002) has made a move in this direction by including Rogers' insights in his development of a 'radical ecopsychology' and acknowledging Eugene Gendlin's substantial contribution to ecopsychological thinking. Might I suggest, also, that an increased openness to an ecological perspective might enable client-centred therapists to demonstrate the relevance of their work in a situation of global emergency.

4

ROGERS, WHITEHEAD AND
THE EVOLVING UNIVERSE

Person-centred counsellors have no trouble accepting Carl Rogers' proposition in *A Way of Being* (1980) that there is a directional process in all human beings, that 'the substratum of all human motivation is the organismic tendency toward fulfillment, ... toward actualization, involving not only the maintenance but also the enhancement of the organism' (Rogers, 1980: 123). However, some person-centred counsellors manage to carry on without thinking twice about the other 'foundation block of the person-centered approach' (Rogers, 1980: 114): a formative tendency in the universe. They ignore the implications of this statement about the cosmos; they tend to ignore Rogers when he talks seriously about the growth of client and counsellor being 'a part of something larger' (Rogers, 1980: 129), of 'tapping into a tendency which permeates all organic life – a tendency to become all the complexity of which the organism is capable' (Rogers, 1980: 134).

When Rogers came to write on 'the foundations of a person-centred approach' he was putting his ideas about counselling into the context of a particular way of understanding the universe. The universe he is writing about in *A Way of Being* (1980) is not a huge machine, as Newton and mainstream science would have us believe. Rather it is alive, a universe in which 'there is in every organism, at whatever level, an underlying flow of movement towards constructive fulfillment of its inherent possibilities' (Rogers, 1980: 117).

It should be noted that while Rogers' rejection of the 'clockwork' image of the universe is overt in *A Way of Being* (1980), and while he uses the language of organism throughout his work, he was not entirely consistent in this. Though we find him referring to the formative tendency as early as 1951 in the introduction to *Client-Centered Therapy*, he was content as a researcher to work within the conventional mechanistic cause–effect model. His 1959 paper 'A Theory of Therapy, Personality and Interpersonal Relationships Developed in the Client-Centered Framework' (pp. 84–256), which stands as a key statement of his theoretical position on personality and therapy, is written within this framework. After a long career he was obviously still satisfied with its logic and precision (Rogers, 1980: 59). He was able to carry two contradictory notions of human nature in his head at the same time. As Karl Popper observes:

> *Common sense inclines, on the one hand, to assert that every event is caused by some preceding event, so that every event can be explained or predicted ... On the other hand ... common sense attributes to mature and sane human persons ... the ability to choose freely between alternative possibilities of acting. (Popper, 1982: xix)*

Rogers was radical in his conviction that human beings are 'choosing' rather than 'caused', free rather than determined. Though this kind of thinking in psychology in the 1950s was regarded as unscientific, Rogers took life and choice seriously. In this he was at the forefront of a shift in scientific thinking which occurred in the latter part of the twentieth century. While he was doing 'proper science' and establishing the credibility of client-centred therapy, his deep assumptions about life were incompatible with the mechanistic fantasy of modernist science.

Ilya Prigogine, who spent a lifetime as physicist searching for a way of understanding the universe which accounted for both causality and chance, suggests that:

> *What is now emerging is an 'intermediate' description that lies somewhere between the two alienating images of a deterministic world and an arbitrary world of pure chance. (Prigogine, 1997: 189)*

Prigogine, who won the Nobel prize in 1977 for his work on 'dissipative structures', was himself influential in the emergence of this 'intermediate' description of the world. His research and speculation have been critical in the development of the image of the universe as a self-organizing complex system – an organism rather than a machine.

IMAGINING THE UNIVERSE

Ivan Ellingham has pointed out the dissonance between organicist and mechanistic concepts to be found in the literature of the person-centred approach. He argues that:

> The critical flaw intrinsic to person-centred theory has to do, I contend (cf. Ellingham, 1997), with its being a mix of concepts deriving from two disparate paradigms, two fundamentally different guiding visions of the world: on the one hand, the Cartesian–Newtonian (C–N) paradigm which underlies Newtonian physics and our contemporary commonsense understanding of reality; on the other, a paradigm which is still in the process of emerging from the Cartesian–Newtonian, a paradigm variously labelled holistic, organismic, process, and from which has arisen field theory, general systems theory and ecopsychology (cf. Capra, 1982: 196). A simple measure of the contrast between these two paradigms is that the former employs the machine as its root metaphor, the latter uses the living organism. (Ellingham 2001: 96)

Ellingham highlights the concept of congruence as a particular illustration of the cognitive dissonance apparent in person-centred theory. He argues that Rogers' characterization of congruence 'is couched in Newtonian–Cartesian terms derived from Freud' (Ellingham, 2001: 109). When Rogers expands on his notion of congruence (e.g. Rogers, 1961: 61–62, 182–183), his thinking appears to be embedded in a 'hydraulic' image, an image of energy exchange – Freud's particular variant of Cartesian–Newtonian imagining. He is thinking of the person as an organism, certainly; but he is imagining the organism the way mechanistic science (including conventional biology) does – as a machine. At the same time he rejects the mechanistic assumption of his contemporaries and their intellectual heirs that the therapist's task is to diagnose the patient's condition, determine its cause and fix it. He is striving, like Prigogine, to find a description that lies between the two alienating images of a cause–effect determinism and pure chance.

Rogers was more comfortable with organic metaphors than mechanistic ones. He suggests that the actualizing tendency is something we share with potatoes, recalling a boyhood memory of potatoes sprouting in the basement of the family home, sending up sad spindly sprouts which 'were, in their bizarre, futile growth, a sort of desperate expression of the directional tendency I have been describing' (Rogers, 1980: 118).

However, we must be careful not to imagine that Rogers' use of the term 'organism' was merely metaphoric. He was seriously committed to the notion that human beings are living, growing and choosing – a notion which is either totally obvious or totally incredible according to our view of what kind of universe this is. Behind his observation of a 'directional tendency' is a particular understanding of the universe. He is placing his formulation of the actualizing tendency within the context of a universe which is alive and directional. In *A Way of Being* (1980) he argues that the actualizing tendency is not just a characteristic of human beings or, indeed, of all human life, rather it is a feature of the universe as a whole. There is, he asserts, 'a formative tendency at work in the universe, which can be observed at every level' (Rogers, 1980: 124). In making this assertion, Rogers aligns himself with a number of twentieth century scientists and philosophers who have rejected the image of the 'clockwork universe' which modern science inherited from the Enlightenment. He cites in particular Jan Smuts, Henri Bergson, Alfred North Whitehead, Albert Szent-Gyoergyi, Lancelot Whyte, Ilya Prigogine, Magohah Murayama and Fritjof Capra, all of whom have adopted a 'holistic' or 'organic' image as better representing the kind of universe we inhabit (Rogers, 1980: 124*ff*).

These thinkers do not all emphasize the same ideas, but it is a set of ideas that belong together. They suggest that life is not the accidental product of random combinations of atoms but an essential aspect of the universe, that the universe does not consist of an enduring substance called 'matter' but is better thought of as 'emerging process'. They suggest that it makes sense to think of the universe as a complex whole in which everything is connected in an unbroken and undivided movement, a whole which is emerging or evolving rather than running down.

To many of the philosophers of the ancient world it seemed fairly obvious that the universe is alive. It was clear enough to Aristotle and his contemporaries that the universe moves itself and moves purposefully. For centuries there was not much dispute about this. In the seventeenth century Isaac Newton and Rene Descartes introduced the notion that the universe behaves like a machine, that trees and animals, and even humans, are simply complicated machines. Though

63

many of Newton's contemporaries such as Baruch Spinoza and Gottfried Leibniz argued that the cosmos is a living organism, and the romantic philosophers and poets of the eighteenth and nineteenth century kept the image alive, it was an image that was totally rejected by mainstream science.

The mechanistic image of the universe has proved so useful for science that it has come to be assumed as unchallengeable fact in the minds of most educated people. We have learned that the universe is a vast machine consisting of a lot of separate 'things' connected by complicated cause and effect relationships. Most of us have grown up with the taken-for-granted understanding that the world is made up of a lot of separate, solid 'things'. Some of them have an added component called 'life'. Others do not. We think of ourselves as consisting of a physical 'thing' called a body with a not-so-physical 'thing' inside us which we call a mind or (maybe) a soul. We use all this to observe and assess other 'things', which constitute what we call reality, and we make choices about how we are going to treat them.

Keith Tudor and Mike Worrall (2006) point out that in person-centred theory and psychoanalytical practice the organism has been largely sidelined in favour of the more popular notion of the self. They argue that:

> Whilst Rogers' contribution to the development of self theory may be better known, we view his contribution to organismic theory and psychology as more significant in that it marks person-centred psychology as one which consistently views the organism as a whole, and as the source of subjective experience ... Organismic psychology also emphasizes the indissolubility of organism and environment and, therefore, the inevitability of interpersonal relationships. The organism cannot be understood outside its environment. (Tudor & Worrall, 2006: 47)

In this context they cite Andras Angyal (1941: 89) who makes the point that 'any attempt to make a morphological separation of organism and environment fails and necessarily leads to endless hair-splitting dialectic'. It is worth noting that as early as his 1951 book *Client-Centered Therapy*, Rogers was acknowledging the influence of Angyal on his thinking.

THE NEW SCIENCE

While Rogers was writing *A Way of Being* (1980), the biologist Rupert Sheldrake was writing *A New Science of Life* (1981) in which he argued that the cosmos seems more like a growing and developing organism than an eternal machine. He proposed that the idea that the universe is machine-like, governed by universal and immutable laws, is no longer consistent with the evidence we get from science. Certainly, there are some aspects of the universe which are machine-like, but we find more and more ways in which it is not. He suggests that the universe revealed by science is characterized not by laws but by 'habits' (his version of archetypes). Ten years later he was arguing vigorously that we must recognize nature as alive, a recognition which has profound social and political consequences:

> As soon as we allow ourselves to think of the world as alive, we recognize that a part of us knew this all along. It is like emerging from winter into a new spring. We can begin to reconnect our mental life with our own direct, intuitive experiences of nature. We can participate in the spirits of sacred places and times. We can see that we have much to learn from traditional societies that have never lost their sense of connection with the living world around them. We can acknowledge the animistic traditions of our ancestors. And we can begin to develop a richer understanding of human nature, shaped by tradition and collective memory, linked to the earth and the heavens, related to all forms of life; and consciously open to the creative power expressed in all evolution. We are reborn into a living world. (Sheldrake, 1990: 188)

Like Sheldrake, Rogers appears to take 'life' seriously as an essential quality of the universe – not an accidental one. In imagining the universe to be alive and emergent he connects with understandings of the world which are as old as civilization.

Rogers' acknowledgement of scientists and philosophers who have influenced his image of the universe includes the physicist Fritjof Capra. He cites Capra's *The Tao of Physics* (1975), in which the latter points out the parallels between the image of the universe provided by twentieth century physics and that of the Eastern mystics. Capra went on to argue in *The Turning Point* (1982) and *The Web of Life* (1997) that science in the twentieth century had been undergoing a paradigm shift, away from the materialistic, reductionist, mechanistic worldview to something new – to an image of reality as a complex organic system which conventional scientific ways of thinking had no capacity to comprehend. Sally Goerner argues similarly in *After the Clockwork Universe* (1999) that the science of the Enlightenment, regardless of how useful it has been in the past, is no longer able to deal with the problems which it has created. It has given us a mentality that encourages competition, control and exploitation in our relations with nature and with each other, individually and collectively. She underlines the need for a science which is aware of the pitfalls of rationalist thinking and can help us find a way through the complex problems which beset us.

One of the conclusions that has been readily derived from the dominant, mechanistic image of the universe is that the universe is subject to entropy, leaking energy, wearing out and running down. Darwin's theory of evolution had challenged that conclusion, suggesting that nature is becoming more complex, producing 'higher' forms of life from 'lower' ones. For 100 years or more scientists were content to live with this contradiction. However, assumptions began to change in the 1960s. When Rogers proposed in *On Becoming a Person* (1961) that the 'actualizing tendency' was grounded in a 'directional trend which is evident in all organic and human life – the urge to expand, extend, develop, mature' (Rogers, 1961: 351), he was making an observation which was beginning to be taken seriously in the physical sciences. Nobel Prize winner Albert Szent-Gyoergyi was arguing that there is 'a drive in living matter to perfect itself' (Szent-Gyoergyi, 1966: 153). He proposed that evolution is no longer to be imagined as an essentially blind and mechanical process, but rather a natural consequence of a dynamic inherent in all living beings 'through which forms tend to reach higher and higher forms of organization, order and dynamic harmony' (Szent-Gyoergyi, 1966: 154). His argument was based on the mounting evidence for the existence of a principle opposite to entropy, a principle which he called syntropy.

In *Order Out of Chaos* (1984) Ilya Prigogine and Isabelle Stengers attempted to resolve the entropy/syntropy contradiction, developing the idea that under certain conditions order emerges from disorder. Prigogine argued that because of their focus on closed systems, and their assumption that order, stability, uniformity and equilibrium are the normal state of being, scientists have overlooked the evidence that most of reality is not stable at all. It is the moments of stability which are 'abnormal'. Reality is more generally characterized by disorder, uncertainty, disequilibrium, and non-linear relationships. Under certain conditions, order emerges spontaneously from this chaos. The universe is self-organizing.

James Lovelock published *Gaia: A new look at life on earth* in 1979, arguing that we need to stop imagining the earth as a machine and imagine it/her rather as a living body. The notion aroused a great deal of emotional opposition in scientists. Thirty years later it has become fairly conventional for scientists to accept Lovelock's image of the earth as a dynamic, self-regulating system consisting of physical, chemical, biological, social and psychological elements, and to view humans as components of the system rather than simply observers of it (see Lovelock, 2010).

Lovelock thought it necessary to point out that in referring to the earth as Gaia, and even in arguing that the earth behaves like a living organism, he was speaking metaphorically. He does not wish to persuade us that the earth is literally a goddess, but rather that it makes more sense, and is more consistent with the available data, to imagine the planet as a living organism than it does to imagine it as a machine.

The scientists cited by Rogers do not claim to be stating the ultimate truth about the universe. They are more inclined to approach reality in the manner of physicist David Bohm, who argues that our theories are essentially ways of imagining the world:

> ... *there is evidently no reason to suppose that there is or will be a final form of insight (corresponding to absolute truth) or even a steady series of approximations to this* ... *[T]his means that our theories are to be regarded primarily as ways of looking at the world as a whole (i.e. worldviews) rather than as absolutely true knowledge of how things are (or a steady approach towards the latter). (Bohm, 1980: 5)*

It is an idea with which Rogers was familiar:

> *I think that men and women, individually and collectively, are inwardly and organismically rejecting the view of a single, culture-approved reality. I believe they are moving inevitably towards the acceptance of millions of separate, exciting, informative, individual perceptions of reality. (Rogers, 1980: 106)*

Like Rogers, Bohm was attempting to bridge the gap which had developed between science and meaning-making. One of his key concerns was to attack the prevailing tendency in science to think in terms of a fragmentary self–world view. The way of thinking promulgated by conventional science gives us a picture of the universe as consisting of nothing but an aggregate of separately existent atomic building blocks. Bohm argues that this fragmentary way of looking and thinking has implications in every aspect of human life, dividing mind from matter, science from art, dividing us from each other and from the non-human world (Bohm, 1980, ch. 1; 1996, ch. 2). His solution is not to seek a unifying and fixed worldview that is just as absolute as the fixed worldview of positivist science. He argues that what we must do is seek the meaning of wholeness, which involves discovering that the measurable and immeasurable 'are but different ways of considering the one and undivided whole' (Bohm, 1980: 21).

Behind Bohm's argument is a concern that his ideas not be hijacked by Gaia worshippers and other proponents of New Age thinking, who can be just as dogmatic in their conviction that they have found the ultimate truth as the materialists they are reacting against. From his perspective, neither the image of the organic universe nor the image of the mechanical universe represents the 'facts' about the universe; they simply represent different ways in which we can imagine it.

About this time the biologist E.O. Wilson contributed to the argument by introducing 'the biophilia hypothesis'. He proposed that evolutionary adaptation has given us an organic relationship to 'nature' which needs to be manifested in our attitudes and behaviour, for:

> *we are human in good part because of the particular way we affiliate with other organisms. They are the matrix in which the human mind originated and is permanently rooted, and they offer the challenge and freedom innately sought. (Wilson, 1984: 139)*

One of the key influences on the development of the new science has been systems theory, which had its beginnings in the 1920s. More recently, complexity theorists have found new evidence and arguments to support the notion of an organic, evolving universe. This involves re-thinking evolutionary theory to account for the evidence that there are sources of order in the universe which include both selection and self-organization. Stuart Kauffman, for example, argues that, rather than being the result of chance, human beings were 'expected', that life and human consciousness began 'as an expected emergent property of the kinds of organic molecules that almost inevitably were formed on the early earth' (Kauffman, 1995: 304). Ervin Laszlo (2003, 2004) points out that while this evolution is not haphazard, it is not entirely predictable. Nevertheless, it has an underlying direction: the basic evolutionary dynamic is towards greater and greater structural complexity.

While Rogers was writing *A Way of Being* (1980), Murray Bookchin, who initiated a way of thinking which he called social ecology, was arguing that:

> [there is] a drive or tendency in evolution toward greater complexity, culminating in the almost unbelievable complexity of the human mind – the development of consciousness. Humanity is not only part of evolution but is its leading edge, imbued with the power to influence the very process that shapes it. Evolutionary processes strive towards the realisation of ever greater degrees of individuation, freedom and selfhood. (Bookchin, 1980: 78)

He argues, like Sheldrake, that evolution is enabled not by ruthless competition but by mutually beneficial co-operation between species. Increasing individuation, freedom and selfhood emerge only in the context of an emerging whole.

Bookchin represents a radical ecological perspective, attacking the assumption that the planet exists for human beings to dominate and exploit. He attacks the mindset which has us becoming 'environmentally aware' only because of the danger our current treatment of the planet presents to us and our descendents. He argues that the earth is to be valued for its own sake – not because it is useful to humans. In the bigger picture, human survival does not appear to be terribly important. A self-organizing planet may have to get rid of us in the interests of its own survival. For 30 years Arne Naess, the founding genius of the deep ecology movement, attacked our anthropocentric image of the planet and argued that human individual 'self-realization' is simply one manifestation of the 'self-realization' of the universe (see Naess, 1973; Witoszek & Brennan, 1999).

'New science' is not particularly new anymore. We might argue that it has never been really new but represents an alternative stream of scientific thinking several centuries old. Wolfgang Pauli, who joined Jung in his attempt to integrate archetypal theory with the understandings we gain from science, wrote to Emma Jung in 1948 bewailing the current situation in his own speciality, quantum theory:

> *My branch of science, physics, has got somewhat bogged down. The same thing can be said in a different way. When rational methods in science reach a dead end, a new lease of life is given to those contents that were pushed out of time consciousness in the seventeenth century and sank into the unconscious. (Pauli, cited in Miller, 2009: 196)*

Since the 1980s there has been significant historical analysis of the 'radical enlightenment', a cultural movement which originated in the seventeenth century and took a different trajectory from both the mainstream 'moderate enlightenment' and Christian orthodoxy (cf. Jacob, 2006; Israel, 2009; Gare, 2006). The moderate enlightenment was grounded in belief in a clockwork universe supervised by a transcendent deity (who was later found to be superfluous); in contrast, the radical enlightenment did not separate creator from creation – nature simply *is* and everything that exists is part of this greater *all*. The proponents of the radical enlightenment were demonized as 'freethinkers', harassed and imprisoned by both church and state, and variously labelled as pantheists, deists, pagans and atheists. While the philosophers of the moderate enlightenment supported monarchy and the protection of property, the radical philosophers sought to bring about democracy, tolerance, the liberation of women and the abolition of slavery. Where the moderate enlightenment proclaimed its newly discovered ability to reach truth through propositional logic, the radical enlightenment understood the value of imagination, intuition and dialogue. The key seventeenth figure in this tradition is Spinoza, whose influence is still dominant in the thinking of the deep ecologists (Lloyd, 1996). Through the eighteenth and nineteenth centuries we can see the worldview of the radical enlightenment shaping the thinking of a significant minority of political theorists, as well as poets, philosophers, theologians and scientists. We find this alternative scientific tradition represented in the first decades of the twentieth century by Alfred North Whitehead, William James and

Henri Bergson, and more recently by Rogers' contemporaries in a wide range of disciplines, from astrophysics to cybernetics (see Waddington, 1961; Lovelock, 1979; Bateson, 1980: Bohm, 1980; Jantsch, 1980; Maturana & Varela, 1980; Sheldrake, 1981; Prigogine & Stengers, 1984). We can find the same trajectory being followed at the present time by physicists and biologists who are exploring the mysterious relationship between the physical world, consciousness and a transcendent reality (see Davies, 1992; Laszlo, 2003, 2004; Haisch, 2006; Rosenblum & Kuttner, 2006; Lanza & Berman, 2009; Birch, 2008).

Christian de Quincey (2002) takes an even longer view in documenting the background to 'new paradigm' science, and the recent assertion of a 'pan-experientialist' or 'pan-psychist' understanding of the universe. The breakdown of Newtonian–Cartesian worldview began in earnest in the early twentieth century, but the philosophical consideration of 'mind-in-matter' and an organic, 'feeling', universe has a much longer history, going back through the neoplatonists and Pythagorus to Orphism in the European tradition and to Taoism in the East. Complexity theory now tells us that we are participants in nature and that our participation counts. Paracelsus, Giordano Bruno, Gottfried Leibniz, Samuel Taylor Coleridge, Johann von Goethe, Alfred North Whitehead, Albert Einstein and countless others would have agreed.

We can argue that Rogers' thinking as represented in *A Way of Being* (1980) fits fairly comfortably within this philosophical and scientific tradition – a tradition in which a preference for democracy, a commitment to social justice and a desire that all humans may be enabled to develop their full potential, are grounded in an organic image of the universe.

When Capra wrote *The Turning Point* in the early 1980s he was arguing that the revolution in modern physics is an expression of a much broader revolution, one which goes beyond the sciences and involves a transformation of worldviews and values. The proponents of the new science may disagree on a lot of things, but they do agree that their science points to the necessity of a revolution in our worldviews, our attitudes and our connection with the planet and the universe beyond it.

BEING AND BECOMING

Ilya Prigogine and his co-author Isabelle Stengers locate their worldview in the context of the 'central problem of Western ontology: the relation between Being and Becoming' (Prigogine & Stengers, 1984: 310). A key figure in this discussion in the early twentieth century was Alfred North Whitehead. He has strongly influenced such 'hard science' thinkers as David Bohm, Rupert Sheldrake, Ilya Prigogine and Ervin Laszlo. He has also had an important, albeit indirect, influence on the person-centred approach.

Rogers acknowledges Whitehead's part in developing the particular understanding of the universe which he brings to his discussion of the foundations of the person-centred approach (Rogers, 1980: 132). His tenure at the University of Chicago in the 1950s and 1960s coincided with the position of that university as the energetic centre of Whitehead's process philosophy in the US. The key figure in this was William Hartshorne, and there were numerous others in philosophy, theology and the sciences who used Whitehead's process thought as a framework for research and teaching in their disciplines. It would be surprising if Whitehead's influence did not extend as far as the counselling centre. Though we do not find much reference to Whitehead in their writings, Rogers, Eugene Gendlin and Seward Hiltner put process at the centre of their thinking about counselling in the books that emerged from this place and time (Rogers, 1951, 1961; Gendlin, 1962; Hiltner, 1949). Whether or not Rogers was conscious of the impact of Whiteheadian philosophy on the development of his own thinking in the Chicago years, there are traces of Whitehead's process philosophy to be found throughout his work.

WHAT SORT OF UNIVERSE?

Alfred North Whitehead began his scientific career as a mathematician and physicist and ended it as a philosopher trying to work out what sort of universe we are part of. He was passionately engaged in constructing a way of thinking about the universe which was based on human experience and which applied equally well to the subatomic world, the human world and the intergalactic world. He started with the notion that if the picture of the universe revealed by subatomic physics is an accurate one, the universe must be like that 'all the way through'. Thus, there is no substance, only process; no 'things', only possibilities becoming events.

There are strong similarities between Whitehead's idea of the process by which nature unfolds and the ideas of quantum theory. Whitehead says that the world is made of 'actual occasions', each of which arises from potentialities created by prior actual occasions. These actual occasions are 'happenings' or 'events', each of which comes into being and then perishes, only to be replaced by a successor. These experience-like 'happenings' are the basic realities of nature, according to Whitehead, not the persisting physical particles that Newtonian physics took to be the basic entities.

Though Whitehead may have been most immediately influenced by what physicists were discovering about the nature of the universe in the early decades of the twentieth century, his philosophy comes in direct line from the insights of Heraklitus in the West and Buddha in the East.

In the seventh century BCE Heraklitus, a guru-philosopher who lived in western Asia, used the image of fire to address the question of what 'stuff' the cosmos is composed of. In so doing he was coming as close as he could to our own notion of energy. Fire (or energy), he supposed, was not simply one 'thing' among others in the universe, but was what gave everything form and kept the universe in existence: 'This universe, which is the same for all, has not been made by any god or man, but it always has been, is, and will be, an ever-living fire, kindling itself by regular measures and going out by regular measures' (in Burnet, 1930: 138). In the fragments that we have of his writing, he expands this image, pointing out the potential for everything to turn into fire; how fire is a process of continual exchange; how fire seeks satisfaction; how fire advances and withdraws; how fire catches all things by surprise. Paradoxically the everlasting fire that creates the 'flow' of the universe also secures its stability. For the same 'measures' of fire are always being kindled and extinguished. There must be a continual cycle of energy exchange, for it is impossible for fire to continually consume its nourishment if it is not at the same time giving back what it has consumed already. When Heraklitus shifted his image from fire to water (another image of flowing energy) he pointed out that not only can we not step twice into the same river, but also that we are not the same person stepping into it in two successive instants.

Another image, equally ancient, comes from Hua-yen Buddhism. It is the image of Indra's net.

Far away in the heavenly dwelling of the great god Indra hangs a wonderful net which stretches out infinitely in all directions. At each node hangs a glittering jewel and since the net is infinite in size the number of jewels is infinite. In each jewel we can see the images of all the other jewels reflected. Each jewel contains an image not only of every other jewel but of itself reflected in every other jewel, and so on ad infinitum. Each jewel's reflections are what make it a jewel, so that without them it would not exist. Every jewel is part of every other and contains every other. When any jewel in the net is touched, all other jewels are affected.

Whitehead's theory is a 'bootstrap' theory. Each of us in our moment of aliveness is connected to every other experience of aliveness in the universe and it is this connectedness which holds us in existence. Through our connections we each contain the whole universe, and every other entity in the universe contains us. Everything we do has an impact, however slight, on the whole universe. Take away the connectedness and there is nothing left.

EVOLUTIONARY FLOW

Whitehead took the view that all aspects of the universe are moving towards the realization of an ever greater richness of experience. The same perspective is behind Rogers' notion that organismic choice is guided by the evolutionary flow. Like Whitehead, he perceives the universe as a living, evolving organism.

> *Thus, when we provide a climate that permits persons to be – whether they are clients, students, workers or persons in a group – we are not involved in a chance event. We are tapping into a tendency which permeates all organic life – a tendency to become all the complexity of which the organism is capable. (Rogers, 1981: 134)*

Growing, for both Rogers and Whitehead, is not something we do. It is not even something that happens to us. Rather, it is a cosmic event in which we participate.

Whitehead imagines the cosmos to be involved in a 'creative advance'. Rogers shares this view:

> *Some of my colleagues have said that organismic choice – the nonverbal, subconscious choice of [a] way of being – is guided by the evolutionary flow. I agree: I will go one step further. I would point out that in psychotherapy we have learned something about the psychological conditions that are most conducive to this highly important self-awareness … The greater this awareness, the more surely the person will float in a direction consonant with the directional evolutionary flow … Consciousness is participating in this larger, creative, formative tendency. (Rogers, 1980: 129)*

According to Whitehead human beings are no different in this respect from everything else in the universe. The entire universe is in a constant process of becoming. In my own becoming I am, in the present moment, an 'occasion' or 'drop of experience' which 'prehends' (grasps, feels) all my previous moments of experience and identifies this community of past 'occasions' as 'me'. This present moment of experience immediately 'dies' and becomes part of this remembered (or prehended) 'me'. All the past 'occasions' shape the way I respond to the world in the present moment, but they do not determine it. In the present moment of subjectivity I can choose between repeating myself and being new.

When Rogers first proposed the notion that the best vantage point for understanding the client is from within the client's own frame of reference it made little sense to conventional psychologists. In the dominant behaviourist worldview the client's subjective experience of making choices was seen to be an illusion, as behaviour is determined by environmental stimuli. In the world of psychoanalysis behaviour was likewise thought to be determined – by unconscious motivation. Rogers may not have been directly influenced by Whitehead's thinking, but it forms part of the intellectual background for his notion that the client-as-subject is not simply determined, but is always busy constructing meaning from experience, and his conclusion that the best thing the counsellor can do is accompany and support him or her in the process.

When we focus on our clients as persons to be observed, remembered and 'managed', we are focusing on them as objects. When we look at them and listen to them, we are looking at and listening to their past selves. (Though it may take only micro-seconds for our consciousness to register the sensory input, everything we see and hear is nevertheless in the past.) Yet in the moment of experience we share with them they are not objects at all. They are alive, self-conscious, choosing, creating and becoming. When we manage to focus on our shared moment of experience, on the 'we' in the interaction, we and our clients and our counselling are alive and capable of transformation.

BEING CONNECTED

When we look at a therapeutic interaction between counsellor and client, we are inclined to see two individuals and imagine that there is a relationship of some sort between them. In Whitehead's view, we have it back to front. In each moment of experience it is the relationship which holds the two experiencing subjects in being, not two individuals who make a relationship happen. They are directly connected, as aspects of a single cosmic moment of experience. For Whitehead, the universe is not made of people or chemicals or atoms. It is made of relationships which bring people and atoms and chemicals into being.

When we observe and hear a client we are probably most aware of the external visual and aural data we are receiving. However, we are also 'prehending' our client through a much more basic and primitive mode of perception, which Whitehead called 'causal efficacy' – an immediate, direct, non-sensory connection with our client in a universe in which all things are interconnected. The whole past experience of the evolving universe flows into us in the present moment. We recognize this in our 'gut feelings', in our intuition, in emotions which don't seem to be related to anything we can observe in the present moment, in occasional experiences of knowing more than our senses can tell us. Through this mode of perception, which has been seriously undervalued and denied by modern science, we experience our client directly and internally, and acknowledge that indistinct, fuzzy, tugs on our awareness may be meaningful.

In his early writing Rogers understood empathy to be an essentially cognitive process. He argued that human behaviour, no matter how bizarre it may appear to the observer, is always rational and purposive 'in response to reality as it is perceived' (Rogers, 1951: 494). He takes the perfectly rational view that while it would be desirable 'to empathically experience all the sensory and visceral sensations of the individual', this is impossible. Throughout his discussion the client's world is clearly the client's and the counsellor's world is clearly the counsellor's. By contrast, his later thinking about empathy includes the sense of direct knowing, a sense that he and his client are elements of a greater whole.

> *When I am at my best, as a group facilitator or as a therapist, I discover another characteristic. I find that when I am closest to my inner, intuitive self, when I am somehow in touch with the unknown in me, when perhaps I am in a state of slightly altered consciousness in the relationship, then whatever I do seems to be full of healing ... At those moments it seems that my inner spirit has reached out and touched the inner spirit of the other. Our relationship transcends itself and becomes a part of something larger. Profound growth and healing and energy are present. (Rogers, 1980: 129)*

Rogers left us the notion that empathic understanding is a 'necessary and sufficient condition' for the particular kind of transformation that can take place through the interaction between counsellor and client. Whitehead had taken it further, proposing that there is actually no space between counsellor and client. We do not sit in our particular capsule of individuality and exchange messages with a client who sits in his or her individual capsule. We are all aspects of each other. If you cease to exist, so do I. Physicists who care to explore the implications of quantum theory beyond the subatomic world cannot avoid the conclusion that it is consciousness that creates the world. To put it crudely, I do not see you because you exist. Neither do you exist because I see you! We both exist because we see (or at least prehend) each other. (Even when I seem to be alone I continue to exist because I am prehended – however faintly – by you and every living being.)

For Rogers, it is the acknowledgement and enhancement of the connection between counsellor and client which enables the actualizing tendency. Within the therapeutic relationship as Rogers imagines it, client and counsellor are caught up in 'the creative advance', participating in each other's becoming and the becoming of the cosmos.

A PROCESS PSYCHOLOGY

When clients talk of the need to discover themselves, they assume that there is something there to find, that if we help them peel away the layers they will find their authentic self. They rarely talk about wanting to create themselves. Conventional psychology, academic as well as popular, maintains that each of us has an independent, enduring self which is the agent of our behaviour, conscious and unconscious. It is something we seek to protect and sustain, even if we find it less than ideal.

Whitehead argues otherwise. Everything, including ourselves, is constantly coming into and going out of existence. We are not objects that endure through time while things happen to us. We are rather a cluster of experiences, creating and experiencing ourselves anew in every moment.

The notion of ongoing process is likewise central to Rogers' understanding of life and therapy. In his model of therapeutic process we see our clients moving from defining themselves as a 'self' who thinks and feels in predictable ways (being determined by all their past moments of experience) to 'living subjectively in the experience, not feeling about it … The self, at this moment, is this feeling … The self is, subjectively, in the existential moment. It is not something one perceives' (Rogers, 1961: 147). As Whitehead puts it: 'My present experience is what I am' (1938: 163).

This is a far cry from the images of self that clients generally bring to counselling. Simone is a chain smoker; Philip is habitually violent; Sally is an alcoholic; Reg has been overwhelmed by anxiety for years. They tell us that they do not like being like this and want to change. Yet often they are simultaneously saying: 'This is who I am. That's just the way it is.' They may imagine that they have a true self which might emerge if they could get out of this prison, but they are not likely to see their task as creating themselves. Yet they have the chance to create themselves in every moment. As Brizee puts it: 'Freedom is the issue … Is one a smoker or has one created oneself as a smoker 4,593,210 times? The manner in which reality is defined is crucial' (Brizee, 2000: 154).

The notion that there is a substantial, enduring self waiting to have its specific potentials actualized is as foreign to Rogers as it is to Whitehead. He was no fan of the notion of 'self-actualization' – a term which carries this implication. He preferred to talk about the 'actualizing tendency'. In this view, a therapy based on the notion of preserving the client's personal self is misguided. We live in a universe which provides other possibilities and makes other demands.

THE RHYTHM OF LIFE

In describing what happens when he is 'close to what is going on in me' in his interaction with a client, Rogers writes about the feelings which 'rise up in me' and their transmutation into an image, and then into intuitive knowledge and articulation of an idea. Similarly, Eugene Gendlin's experiential focusing technique starts with an awareness of what is going on in the body, invites this to manifest itself in an image and eventually transmutes into articulation of something which was previously below the level of awareness.

When Rogers comments that his experiences of deep connection with clients give him a sense of being 'in tune with the pulse of the world' (Rogers, 1980: 313) he is echoing Whitehead's notion that life is essentially rhythmical. Whitehead points out that:

> *our bodily life is essentially periodic. It is dominated by the beatings of the heart, and the recurrence of breathing. The presupposition of periodicity is indeed fundamental to our very concept of life. (Whitehead, 1911/ 1982: 122)*

We now know more than Whitehead did about our biological rhythms. We know that our organisms cycle from a state which can be imagined as dark, slow, vague, blunt and physical to a state which appears to be at the opposite pole, namely, light, fast, precise, sharp and mental. We experience an annual cycle, a monthly cycle, a daily cycle and an ultradian (90-minute) cycle. We know that our brainwaves cycle between the high frequency beta waves of our 'thinking' state, through alpha and theta to the delta waves of deep sleep and back again. We find cycles in our cells and cycles in our lives.

Whitehead understood the ongoing life of the world to consist of 'throbs of experience' (1929/1978: 190), each of which includes the whole world. From the microscopic level, through the level of individual experience, to the level of the cosmic 'creative advance' there is a movement from physical experience through subjective

79

awareness to an integration of the two in a new concrete reality. Following Whitehead, Franz Riffert writes of 'pulsating micro-processes that stretch through the universe and become especially obvious in the living organism' (Riffert, 2005: 90), arguing that the rhythmic pulsations that characterize processes at the microscopic level must pervade reality at all levels. If we accept Whitehead's view that the universe does not consist of things but of 'throbs of experience' we can argue as Whitehead does that the rhythm of life which is manifest at the level of the electron or quark is manifest in each moment of our experience, manifest in the rhythm of learning, manifest again in the rhythm of a human lifetime, and manifest also in the rhythm of our species' existence.

Whitehead was particularly interested in the implications of this for learning. He was convinced that there was a rhythmic dimension within each instance of learning – a movement from physical to mental to an integration of the two. He gives us an image of cycles within cycles within cycles, or eddies within eddies within eddies, as he writes, 'the development of mentality exhibits itself as a rhythm involving the interweaving of cycles, the whole process being dominated by a greater cycle of the same general character as the minor eddies' (Whitehead, 1911/1982: 27).

We can usefully think of therapy as a learning experience, involving cyclic moments of experience and insight, within a larger cycle of the therapeutic interaction, within the larger cycle of the client's lifetime. Implied in this is the notion that the therapeutic process as a whole, and the therapeutic process in each moment, starts in the physical, whether the physical is acknowledged or not. It is, as Rogers asserts 'a total, organismic, frequently non-verbal type of thing' (Rogers, 1961: 86). In writing about education, Whitehead described a cyclical process from 'romance' to 'specificity' to 'generalization', that is, from bodily feeling and emotional involvement in an experience, to curious inquiry and a grasp of concrete detail, to the construction of principles and behaviour which become the felt starting point for a new cycle. We can posit the same micro-cycle, within a larger cycle, within therapy. The process starts in experience and moves through reflection to a larger sense of 'what it is all about'. This then frames our next moment of experience.

A notion such as that is basic to Gendlin's thinking. The focusing process begins with a 'directly sensed bodily experience' (Gendlin,

1996: 16). The 'border zone' between the conscious and the unconscious 'occurs *bodily,* as a physical, somatic sensation. It is sensed in the viscera or the chest, or the throat, some specific place, usually in the middle of the body' (Gendlin, 1996: 18). Gendlin is careful to point out that this is not simple physical sensation, divorced from thoughts, feelings, memories, and desires. Rather, it is experienced as an intricate whole: 'One can sense that it includes many intricacies and strands. It is not uniform like a piece of iron or butter. Rather it is a whole complexity, a multiplicity implicit in a single sense' (Gendlin, 1996: 20). Focusing on this felt sense – exactly as it is, without the presuppositions and assumptions embedded in the constraints of language – leads to symbolization and 'felt meaning'.

Gendlin sees felt sense and the subsequent emergence of felt meaning as a step in the direction of growth. We may take up Whitehead's suggestion and see this immediate experience and insight as a pulse within the greater pulse of a particular life event, within the pulse of a lifetime's growth from infancy to maturity. And this pulse is subsumed within the greater pulse of human evolution, all driven by the 'formative tendency' (Rogers), 'lifeforces tending towards resolution' (Gendlin) or the 'creative advance' (Whitehead) of the universe.

We do not need to take a cosmic perspective to appreciate Gendlin's insight that understanding and meaning emerge not from outside our body's boundaries, but from within. In his theory of personality and behaviour, Rogers attributes psychological maladjustment to the denial of both sensory (external) and visceral (internal) experiences, the consequent lack of symbolization, and the tension which results from this denial (Rogers, 1951: 481–533). It is only when all the sensory and visceral experiences are integrated that 'the tendency towards growth can become fully operative and the individual moves in the direction normal to all organic life' (Rogers, 1951: 514). He speculates that visceral experience is sourced in subliminal perception or 'subception'. He is arguing here, as Gendlin does, that mentality begins in somatic experience. Significantly, it is not only the client whose learning begins in bodily experience. This is equally true of the counsellor, whose felt meaning of the interaction and empathic understanding of the client is felt in her or his body before it ever finds images, thoughts or words.

Theodore Reik, who was a student of Freud, tells how he once met his teacher on the street in Vienna and took the opportunity to ask his advice about a couple of decisions he needed to make: what profession he ought to follow and whether he should marry a certain girl.

> 'I can only tell you of my personal experience,' he said. 'When making a decision of minor importance, I have always found it advantageous to consider all the pros and cons. In vital matters, however, such as the choice of a mate or a profession, the decision should come from the unconscious, from somewhere within ourselves. In the important decisions of our personal life, we should be governed, I think, by the deep inner needs of our nature. (Reik, 1948: vii)

When Freud recommended that Reik go with his instincts, his 'gut feelings', he did not know, as we do now, how consciousness is distributed throughout the body, and that, after the brain, the gut is the part of our body which is most able to process information. The enteric nervous system, which is embedded in the lining of the gastrointestinal system, contains some 100,000,000 neurons. In view of its autonomy and complexity, it is sometimes referred to as the 'second brain'. Through its connection with the central nervous system it picks up sensory information (the sound of screeching brakes, the sight and smell of attractive food) and responds with an immediate reflex reaction (tightening of muscles, salivation). Awareness comes a moment later, and may not come at all if the signals are faint, or we are 'out of touch with our bodies'. Until fairly recently the complexity of the gut was not understood, the wisdom of the gut was not appreciated, and there was no research evidence for kinesthetic intuition. Descartes' spirit/matter distinction had morphed into a mind/body distinction and then into a brain/body separation. Yet for most of human history (and all of pre-history) such distinctions did not exist. Knowledge, for our pre-literate ancestors, was an organismic felt sense. We should appreciate that this knowledge is still available to us.

In this regard, Gendlin reminds us that our bodies only exist in interaction, and that they interact with all other being: 'as bodies, not just through what comes through the five senses. Our bodies do not lurk in isolation behind the five peepholes of perception' (Gendlin, 1992: 342). We have no existence apart from the greater organism in whose life we participate.

When Rogers asserts that the human beings have one basic tendency: 'to maintain, actualize and enhance the experiencing organism' (Rogers, 1951: 487), and later explicitly extends this notion not only to the species collectively but to the universe, he assumes that we understand that organisms are alive and experiencing, and that experience precedes symbolization.

> *In therapy a person adds to ordinary experience the full and undistorted awareness of his [sic] experiencing – of his sensory and visceral reactions. He ceases, or at least decreases, the distortions of experience in awareness … In this sense the person becomes for the first time the full potential of the human organism, with the enriching element of awareness freely added to the basic aspect of sensory and visceral reaction. The person comes to be what he is, as clients say so frequently in therapy. What this seems to mean is that the individual comes to be – in awareness – what he is – in experience. He is, in other words, a complete and fully functioning human organism. (Rogers, 1961: 104)*

Where Rogers speaks of 'experiencing' as the first phase of learning, Whitehead refers to 'prehension' – the influx of data from numerous actual entities in the past world. (Everything we experience is in the past, even if that past is only a micro-second away.) This is the necessity of 'causal efficacy' which shapes, but does not determine our reaction. The second phase, facilitated by the counsellor in this case, is a creative and critical response to all of this material. Lastly comes the phase of generalization, which is a synthesis and harmonization of the physical prehensions of the first phase and the conceptual prehensions of the second. In Whitehead's language, the 'actual entity' thus 'achieves satisfaction' and provides the starting point for the next 'throb of experience'.

Whitehead's universe is a fractal universe. The rhythm of each actual entity's becoming and being at the microscopic level is replicated at the level of human experience and replicated again in the life of the universe. When we are being 'truly human', our lives, our counselling interactions, and the moments of experience from which insight emerges, are 'in tune with the pulse of the world' (Rogers, 1980: 313).

BEING CREATIVE

Rogers puts creativity at the centre of his model of therapeutic growth. In *On Becoming a Person* (1961) he asserts that the mainspring of creativity is the actualizing tendency and states in *A Way of Being* (1980) that personal transformation occurs through participation in a 'larger, creative, formative tendency'. Here, Rogers echoes Whitehead's way of imagining personal transformation, though he has not thought it through as thoroughly as Whitehead. Whitehead does not see human development as the emergence of something that is already latent in us. He imagines it rather as a response to the lure of something beyond us. He suggests that there is a central organizing force that actively seeks to realize the qualities of intensity, harmony, beauty, complexity, enjoyment and peace. Every moment of becoming, whether at the atomic level, the cellular level, the individual human level or the level of the entire cosmic organism is an expression of this same dynamic source and is attracted towards the fulfilment of its greatest possibilities. In us and our clients, each new moment is a moment of creation in which we may either allow ourselves to be drawn towards the goal of beauty and complexity and become more than what we have been, or we allow ourselves to be trapped by past habits and reactions into repeating ourselves once more. Furthermore, this creative moment that we experience is not just our private moment. It does not exist apart from the creative moment that the whole universe is experiencing.

FACING NEW HORIZONS

Every attempt to develop a 'big theory' runs the risk of settling into a stable pattern of dogma that true believers take for truth and non-believers dismiss as nonsense. Whitehead had a horror of 'inert ideas'. When we are putting Rogers' ideas into practice, we must likewise beware of turning his creative process into 'inert ideas'. His own ideas were constantly in process. He challenges the notion that we can find any ultimate truth and suggests that we must base our search for truth 'on the assumption that there are as many realities as there are persons'(Rogers, 1980: 105). This is not a statement of radical relativism. He is not suggesting that we are condemned to be isolated from each other's worlds of experience. Rather, his suggestion is that we take each other's worlds more seriously, enter and explore them, and delight in their diversity. The universe may be too complex to describe without ambiguity and paradox, but it is not too complex to experience and not too complex to enjoy.

It would be foolish to assert that Alfred North Whitehead's writings were a direct and major influence on Rogers' development of person-centred theory and practice. I imagine that he would have become extremely impatient with the abstraction and metaphysical hair-splitting of *Process and Reality* (Whitehead, 1929/1978) if he had ever bothered to read it. However, I suggest that his psychological writing is underpinned by a 'philosophy of organism' not unlike Whitehead's. I suggest that the Chicago context in which he developed his radical notions of what works in counselling may have provided the intellectual background which shaped his thinking along these lines.

Alongside his attempts to establish the credibility of his theory and practice through research carried out within the conventional empirical framework, we find that Rogers maintained a commitment to what William James termed 'radical empiricism', a readiness to take 'the immeasurable' seriously as evidence, which enabled him to recognize his fellowship with the proponents of the 'paradigm shift' when they emerged in the latter part of the century. Ilya Prigogine, in acknowledging Whitehead's contribution to making the universe intelligible for us, suggests that 'we face new horizons at this privileged moment in the history of science' (Prigogine, 1997: 189). We should appreciate our good fortune in having Rogers point us and our profession towards those horizons.

5

COUNSELLING
THE FIVE-MINDED ANIMAL

In 1931, following unpleasant confrontations with Adolf Hitler's Brownshirts, Jean Gebser left Munich and fled penniless to Spain. Within five years he had sufficient Spanish to write poetry in his adopted language and serve in the Republican Ministry of Culture. In 1936 he had to flee again, leaving just a few hours before his Madrid apartment was bombed by General Francisco Franco's forces. This time he fled to Paris, where he joined the circle of cultural radicals around Pablo Picasso. In 1939 he managed to escape the Nazis by fleeing to Switzerland and got across the border two hours before it closed. In 1951 he became a Swiss citizen.

During his years as a refugee Gebser had the privilege of meeting with some of the best minds of Europe. His conversations with them stimulated his research into the big idea which was pestering him. He was convinced that Western consciousness was being 'restructured'. His evidence for this came firstly from the natural sciences, where he noted that the old assumptions of materialistic determinism no longer made any sense, and where conventional logical, dualistic thinking could no longer cope with the research data. His observations of cutting-edge science led him to wonder whether he would find a similar shift of consciousness in the arts and social sciences. All of this fed into his great work *The Ever-Present Origin* (Gebser, 1949/1986).

The context for Gebser's research and writing was a sense of emergency. Gebser was lucky to escape alive from the chaos of European tribal warfare. However, 1945 did not bring tranquillity. It brought a new emergency, with the Cold War and the nuclear arms race. As a refugee in Europe in the 1930s and 1940s, he had seen the collapse of rationality and the overwhelming dominance of the magical and mythical thinking generally associated with pre-scientific societies. Now he became convinced that a mere return to rationality could not save humanity from disaster. Rationality and its twin offspring – science and technology – seemed to have got humanity into a mess. The kind of thinking which had produced the planetary emergency was not likely to be the kind of thinking which could save us from it. The world was facing a crisis.

> We must soberly face the fact that only a few decades separate us from that event. This span of time is determined by an increase in technological feasibility inversely proportional to man's sense of responsibility – that is, unless a new factor were to emerge which would effectively overcome this menacing correlation. (Gebser, 1986: xxvii)

Gebser wrote these words in 1949 when he was taking on the task of describing this 'new factor'. For the best part of 400 years, people who cared about such things had taken it for granted that educated European men represented the pinnacle of God's creation or – once Darwin's followers had rethought creation – the triumphant culmination of evolutionary progress. Gebser did not have the same respect for mere rationality, and he did not accept the notion of inevitable progress. He insisted that he was not making an assumption of 'progress' or even 'development'. There is no 'continuous improvement' in human consciousness. To his way of thinking, the rational structure of consciousness which had dominated European culture since the Enlightenment was not a higher form of consciousness. It had not emerged from simpler and 'lower' forms of consciousness through an inevitable evolutionary progression, but was actually a deficient form of consciousness, cut off from its magical and mythical roots; an evolutionary dead end.

Gebser's focus was on culture, not individual psychology. He was interested in what he called the 'structures of consciousness' as they manifested in human history and human experience. He distinguished five such structures: the archaic structure which characterized the earliest humans; the magic structure of the early Stone Age; the mythical structure which emerged after the ice ages; the mental–rational structure of the great classical civilizations, the European Renaissance and the Enlightenment; and the 'new factor' – the integral structure which he saw emerging in the mid-twentieth century, against the background of a disintegrating mental–rational world.

In *The Ever-Present Origin* (1949/1986) Gebser describes each of the structures, from archaic to integral, as a series of mutations of awareness. In doing so he makes it clear that this kind of historical sequencing is characteristic of mental–rational consciousness. The magical and mythical structures of consciousness do not bring with them a capacity for logical, sequential thinking, and integral consciousness transcends it. The structures do not follow one another inevitably, but each appears in and through the others. While a particular structure of consciousness will be dominant in a particular culture at a particular time, the other structures are never left behind. Scientists and philosophers in Nazi Germany could think logically and scientifically within the narrative constraints of a toxic myth. Magic and myth keep appearing amid the evidence-based rationalizations of a modern, technological society.

Gebser points out that the structures can take either an 'efficient' or 'deficient' form. For instance, in pre-scientific societies ritual magic held the clan together and had an essential place in healing. However, sorcery and superstition are grounded in the same magical consciousness. They are 'deficient' manifestations of it. Likewise, while the scientific thinking which emerged in the European Renaissance was a manifestation of mental consciousness, the narrow materialistic rationality which became characteristic of mainstream modern science represents this structure in its 'deficient' form.

Integral consciousness, the 'new factor' which Gebser claimed to see emerging in the arts and sciences in the mid-twentieth century, involves, as the name implies, an integration of the four simpler structures, but is not simply an aggregation of the others. It is something new.

FIVE-MINDED ANIMALS

Gebser's is not a model of evolution as this is generally understood, but is a model of 'unfolding' or 'emergence'. In any case it is not historical or evolutionary development which interests us when we are looking for the implications of 'five-mindedness' for counselling. Rather it is the way these minds push and pull against each other in a counselling interaction, for:

we must first of all remain cognizant that these structures are not merely past, but are in fact still present in more or less latent and acute form in each of us.'(Gebser, 1949/1986: 42)

Or, as Jung puts it:

We keep forgetting that we are primates and that we have to make allowances for these primitive layers in our psyche. (Jung, 1977, vol 1: 119)

Within the mental structure of consciousness, which has been dominant in Western societies since the Enlightenment, we see ourselves as individuals and are interested in consciousness as something which belongs to each of us separately. This was not Gebser's focus. He says little about individual psychology. In his discussion of the emergence of the structures of consciousness he does not find a place to mention Jean Piaget, whose work must have been familiar to him and who was developing a theory of child development which paralleled Gebser's theory in significant ways. Piaget saw cognitive development proceeding through four stages: the sensorimotor stage (infancy), the pre-operational period (early childhood), the concrete operational stage (later childhood) and the formal operational stage (adolescence and adulthood). Piaget's description of these stages comes close enough to Gebser's descriptions of archaic, magic, mythical and mental consciousness to have at least aroused his curiosity.

Piaget's thinking was limited by his commitment to a hierarchical notion of stages of development. Gebser's idea of the different kinds of consciousness is not hierarchical at all. Some structures are more complex than others, but they are not an advance on them. The notion that they appear in sequence from most 'primitive' to most 'advanced' is a construction of our mental consciousness, which measures and calculates. Reality, for Gebser, is not constrained by our notions of time and space. Everything is present in the present moment, though our mental consciousness does not experience it in this way.

Kieran Egan's (1997) model of cognitive development echoes Piaget's, but Egan, like Gebser, is much more aware of the impact of culture on individual consciousness, and he is not constrained by Piaget's notion that we leave behind the infantile and childhood stages as we mature. In expounding his model of psychological development in *The Educated Mind* (1997), he suggests that we are 'five-minded animals':

> *We have, you might say, a fivefold mind, or, more dramatically, we are a five-minded animal in whom different kinds of understanding jostle together and fold on one another, to some degree remaining 'somewhat distinct'. (Egan, 1997: 80)*

The parallels between Egan's five minds and Gebser's structures of consciousness are obvious enough. Like Gebser, he lays them out in sequence: the somatic mind of infants, the magic mind of early childhood, the romantic mind of late childhood and early adolescence, the philosophic mind of late adolescence and early adulthood, and the ironic mind of the mature individual. He also sees them as 'jostling together' rather than sequentially replacing one another. Robert Kegan (1983, 1998) likewise distinguishes five stages in psychological development, which he labels the five 'orders of consciousness'. Egan and Kegan want us to understand that as we develop new ways of thinking and understanding through the course of childhood and adolescence we do not entirely outgrow and leave behind our earlier ways of understanding.

Gebser's focus on culture reminds us that we do not do our thinking as entirely autonomous individuals. We may be inclined to think of a culture as the aggregation of the thoughts, attitudes, assumptions and behaviours of a particular group of individuals. We need to remember that group mind (group consciousness) is not the sum of the minds of the members of that group. On the contrary, individual consciousness has grown out of, and is grounded in, group consciousness.

Merlin Donald (1991, 2001) argues that cognitive evolution has from the beginning been tethered to culture. We may live more or less comfortably in what he calls 'the myth of the isolated mind', yet it is the advantage of having a collective consciousness that has made us successful as a species. In his history of the evolution of cognition and culture, Donald points to three major transitions which changed the nature of human consciousness. The consciousness of our primate ancestors was episodic. They had awareness, sensitivity to events and the capacity to react to them, but no capacity for conscious, purposeful action. The first transition, a couple of million years ago, was to mimetic consciousness. The early humans had this new cognitive capacity which their primate ancestors had lacked, a capacity which involved body language, imitation, gesture and intentional vocal sound. These enabled the development of a group mentality and a human culture. The second transition, to mythic consciousness, came with the emergence of *homo sapiens sapiens* about 125,000 years ago. Spoken language produced oral culture, and ritual and spoken language held the clans and tribes together and gave them an advantage over competing subspecies. By Donald's reckoning the third transition, to theoretic consciousness, came about 40,000 years ago with the emergence of technologies which made it increasingly possible to externalize memory. No longer did humans have to rely entirely on their brains to remember. No longer did they have to work out everything for themselves.

> *Mimetic consciousness gave us self-conscious control over our actions, mythic consciousness enabled us to accumulate knowledge more quickly and accurately through the use of speech, theoretic consciousness enabled us to have a powerful and abstract reflective culture.*
>
> *Thus modern culture contains within it a trace of each of our previous stages of cognitive evolution. It still rests on the same old primate brain capacity for episodic or event knowledge. But it has three additional, uniquely human layers: a mimetic layer, an oral linguistic layer, and an external-symbolic layer. The minds of individuals reflect these ways of representing reality. (Donald, 2001: 262)*

Both Piaget and Donald miss the crucial insight that is central to the work of Gebser, and is shared by Kegan and Egan – that logical, rational thinking is not the most we can do. Our minds can also handle paradox, irony, ambivalence and mystery. And we live in a world where we need to use all of our minds.

ARCHAIC MIND

In archaic consciousness, the therapist and client do not inhabit separate worlds. Nor are they separate from the planet and the cosmos. Gebser compares it with 'the original state of biblical paradise: a time where the soul is yet dormant, a time of complete non-differentiation of man and the universe' (Gebser, 1949/1986: 43). Gebser describes the earliest humans' 'unperspectival' experience of the world as an experience where there is no 'I' to stand in a specific spot and see the world from a specific direction, no capacity to distinguish between earth and sky, between self and other, inner and outer. He declares that it involves 'the perfect identity of man and universe' (Gebser, 1949/1986: 45).

We still slip back into our archaic unity consciousness in deep sleep, or enter it voluntarily or involuntarily through trance, drugs or certain kinds of meditation. Our archaic minds have a very dim awareness, which is bodily, pre-reflective and pre-lingual. A great deal of our behaviour – maybe most – is unconscious, even robotic. We experience the world and react to its stimuli without awareness. We can actually do quite complex things while our brains are either asleep or focused on something else. Our bodies are enmeshed in a physical world. For a few million years they functioned adequately in this world without the need for conscious attention. They continue to do so now, when our attention is absent. We all have our 'inner zombie'.

We can, if we choose, change our ordinary state of consciousness to this less complex state through auto-suggestion or deep relaxation. Or we can let ourselves be put into trance by hypnosis, chanting, music, dancing, or drumming. Or we can stop all mental activity for a time and let ourselves slip into a much simpler state of being. If we just sit, cease doing anything – no thoughts, no images, no feelings, no intentions – we may find that we can enter a state of trance in which our sense of our individual reflecting ego, our sense of the boundary between our internal and external worlds, becomes greatly diminished. We can enter a state in which we and the universe are comfortably one. In the language of developmental psychology or evolutionary psychology this simplest form of meditative trance, like the trance induced by repetitive chanting or dancing, is a regressive experience, a return to 'primitive' or intra-uterine experience through the shutting down of individual awareness. Through our pre-reflective, archaic consciousness we experience ourselves, however dimly, as continuous with the physical universe. There is no 'I'. There is no 'other'. There is no 'environment'. There is no reflection. There is only experience and instinct. There is evidence that it is desirable and healing to enter this state from time to time.

It is now common enough for meditation to be recommended as a means of countering adverse stress and its consequent damage to the immune system. However, when Ainslie Meares decided to abandon his psychiatric practice in the 1970s and become a 'non-medical consultant in mental relaxation' (McKinnon, 2012: 20), it was a radical and apparently reckless thing for a doctor to do. Meares had found that teaching his patients a simple form of stillness meditation had a profound impact on their mental and physical health (Meares, 1967). He developed the Atavistic Theory of Mental Homeostasis, convinced that the body is equipped to heal itself when favourable circumstances are in place, and had found that he could facilitate the process by inducing in his patients a state of 'atavistic regression'.

> *From the biological point of view, the function of logical critical thinking is a recently acquired ability of man [sic]. At an earlier period in our evolutionary development, before logical critical ability had evolved, the mental process of man must have been more primitive. I shall refer to this simpler level of integration as atavistic regression, because this mode of regression is toward a mode of function of remote ancestors ...*
>
> *It seems that it is slipping back to a more primitive mode of mental functioning that provides the conditions that allow the natural restorative processes of the mind to function more effectively and so to establish psychic homeostasis. (Meares, cited in McKinnon, 2012: 15)*

Gebser argues that the archaic structure of consciousness is the ground of all the others. Empathy is, for Gebser, utterly basic to the human condition. The experience of oneness with the universe is the ground of our empathic experience of other people. We do not have separate lives, either as individuals or as a species. The life in us is the life which is in everything. The relationship between counsellor and client is based in an identity of being, not simply with each other, but with a universe in which time, space and ego are illusions. We identify with the conscious mind through which we know ourselves as autonomous, decision-making beings, but all the while we are connected to the universe through an archaic mind which is neither autonomous nor decision-making. Consciously we experience our own anxiety and, through empathy, the pain of those close to us. Unconsciously we experience the pain and stress of the planet.

Our connection with the universe is a physical one. Behaviourist psychology, for all the narrowness of its vision, had one crucial insight.

There is a level of human behaviour for which self-awareness is entirely irrelevant. Though we imagine ourselves to be self-aware beings, most of our behaviour is unconscious. We do lots of complicated things without any awareness of doing them. We react to a stimulus physically and emotionally and our awareness catches up after the event. There is evidence that even when we consciously choose to act our body starts to move in the chosen direction before we are aware of making the choice. We are entirely entangled in our human and non-human world. Classical behaviourism imagined this to be a matter of simple cause–effect relationships between separate objects. It is becoming more conventional now to imagine our behaviour as reacting within, and acting upon, a vast complex system of relationships. Gebser suggests, more radically, that in our pre-reflective, archaic consciousness we do not have separate identities. We are parts of a bigger system in which we interact without awareness. It is our mental consciousness which constructs the arbitrary boundaries between self and other.

Person-centred counsellors are inclined to overlook the 'zombie' dimensions of human behaviour. Rogers' focus in describing therapy was on subjective experience, on the individual's capacity for choice. Not only does the therapist offer empathic understanding; the client must be aware that empathic understanding is being offered. Classical behaviourism suggests that this is nonsense, that there is only stimulus and response. For instance, the client-centred counsellor values emotional expression. The client deliberately or inadvertently expresses emotion. The counsellor reacts to this stimulus with a smile. The client's behaviour is reinforced; he continues to talk about his feelings. The counsellor is content with the knowledge that she is in no way influencing (or manipulating, or controlling) the client's behaviour. The client has no awareness of being manipulated. Yet the counsellor is manipulating the client – unconsciously – just as her own behaviour is being manipulated by the client. This is not all that is happening, but there is little point in pretending that it is not.

Robert Carkhuff (1969) challenged Rogers' assumption that the therapeutic conditions are not effective unless they are communicated to the client, arguing that empathy, congruence, acceptance and the other therapeutic conditions are of themselves instrumental in effecting the client's healing, whether or not the client is aware of them being offered. Rather than try to settle this argument, we should consider that there is more than one mind in each of us, and that one of these minds works in just this way – with minimal awareness and no reflection. Our archaic minds are not dependent on verbal or visual communication. Our bodies may appear to be separate, but our embodied archaic minds are not, nor are they separate from the greater organism of which we are cells. Our empathy does not have to leap across the space between us. Our congruence involves living as the kind of beings we are at depth – one with the universe.

Whitehead argued that every 'drop of experience' of which the universe is constituted is bipolar. It has both a physical and a mental pole. In a molecule or a cell, the physical pole is dominant. In human experience the mental pole is generally dominant. However, in our archaic consciousness, in those moments of experience where awareness is dim, it is the physical pole which dominates. The mental pole becomes dominant as we experience life through the more complex structures of consciousness.

MAGICAL MIND

Our archaic minds experience instinct and stimulus and act on them automatically. Our magical minds bring awareness and emotion to our impulse. We have no sense of individual selfhood, but experience 'the vegetative intertwining of all living things ... in the egoless magic sphere of every human being' (Gebser, 1949/1986: 49). This sense of 'vegetative entwinement' which we share with our earliest human ancestors is spaceless, timeless and egoless. Identity belongs to the group, not the individual. Though intertwined, we are no longer in a state of undifferentiated unity with nature. Rather, we are one with the clan, bound to it by our emotions. It is this shared consciousness that Gebser labelled 'magical'. It may be the shared consciousness of the football crowd, who collectively feel the fatigue, despair and delight of the heroes with whom they identify and who engage in various rituals to ensure a propitious outcome; it may be the community of knowing and feeling of the religious gathering, involved in a ritual which allows them to relive the creative moment; it may be the *participation mystique* of mother and newborn child, the phenomenon of sympathetic illness or sympathetic pregnancy, the unity of experiencing of two persons who are deeply in love, the uncanny coincidences in the experiences of twins. In such circumstances there can be an immediacy of communication through body-sense and emotion. Our magical mind does not have, and does not need, words. A rational, scientistic culture ignores the phenomenon, or labels it 'telepathy' and tries to find an explanation for it within the conventional communication paradigm. Pre-scientific cultures accept such phenomena as a matter of course, along with all the magical phenomena which we now label 'parapsychological'. For Gebser, these experiences are perfectly normal.

In my own experience of intensive group work I have sometimes found myself in a 'non-ordinary' state of consciousness, in which I have experienced feelings, even physical tensions or pains, which 'belong' to others in the group. I have found myself and others uncannily 'intuitive' even precognitive, sensing others' internal states without doubt or hesitation. I have found people sharing simultaneous images and sharing dreams. Rogers (1980) refers to the same kinds of experience.

Many counsellors will admit to experiencing physical sensations, tensions or pains while counselling their clients, sensations which seem to belong to the client rather than themselves. The counsellor feels a pain in the shoulder, a tightening in the stomach, a cold shiver down the spine, an overwhelming nausea, which does not seem to relate to the words the client is saying or the thoughts the counsellor is thinking. Or the counsellor has an experience of fear, or despair, or depression, and with it a sense that it is not her own response of fear or despair or depression to something the client has said, but is somehow a direct experience of what is going on in the client. This phenomenon has been reflected on much more within the analytic tradition than elsewhere. Andrew Samuels (1989) examines the various ways by which Freudian and Jungian writers explain such phenomena, considering such labels as 'projective identification' (Melanie Klein), 'syntonic countertransference' (Michael Fordham), 'reflected counter-transference' and 'embodied countertransference' (Andrew Samuels). Samuels argues that 'the analyst's body is not entirely his or hers alone and what it says to him or her is not a message for him or her alone' (Samuels, 1989: 164).

Likewise, the client may have a direct experience of what is going on in the counsellor, may feel in his or her body the counsellor's stress or calm. Indeed, the counsellor may be directing the client towards well-being through her non-verbal communication of her belief in the client's actualizing tendency. This does not have to be intentional on the part of the counsellor. It does not have to reach the client's awareness. It happens below awareness through their 'vegetative intertwining'.

Magical consciousness does not need, indeed does not have, words.

Not all counsellors experience these phenomena, but they are too common to be ignored. In mainstream writing about the therapeutic interaction the phenomena seem not to exist, or are belittled as 'merely projection', evidence of therapists' lack of adequate ego boundaries. In New Age writing it is more generally viewed as evidence of a higher, or more evolved, consciousness. I want to argue, with Gebser, that the world of magical consciousness knows no ego boundaries, that we have access to a mode of consciousness which deals with reality in just this way. And in doing so I want to avoid either romanticizing or disparaging magical consciousness which, as Gebser asserts, can be either efficient or deficient.

From the viewpoint of our ordinary rational consciousness we are inclined to view such phenomena as the transmission of a sensation or image from one self-contained person to another, in time and across space. We are also inclined to see a cause and effect relationship between the client's communication of his experience and the reflection of it in the therapist. Gebser's notion of a consciousness which experiences an ego-less, time-less, space-less, unitary world 'in which each and every thing intertwines and is interchangeable ... [and] which operates without a causal nexus' (Gebser, 1949/1986: 48) challenges us to look at these experiences somewhat differently. If we drop our egocentric assumptions we can imagine a reality in which everything is connected, in which the shared somatic or imaginative experience of client and therapist are not transmitted from one to the other, but are literally co-incidental. This may not be the world as we rational, sophisticated people imagine it, but it is the real world nonetheless, and we usually experience it unconsciously.

I may have learned to ignore my vague hunches and faint gut feelings, but if my awareness was subtle enough, and not inhibited by my rational consciousness, I might accept them as the signals of my organic connection with every living being, especially with those close to me. Many counsellors have learned from experience that one way of accessing the emotional state of their client is to check what is going on within their own body.

When the thoughts and feelings of counsellor and client are in tune it is 'almost like being in love'. Indeed, being in love is a magical phenomenon. Two people experience a relationship in which 'my thoughts are your thoughts and your feelings are my feelings' and are unable to notice any evidence to the contrary. This is different from a mature loving relationship, in which each acknowledges that the other has thoughts and feelings that are independent. In the psychoanalytic tradition falling in love is understood to be an experience characterized by projection and transference, dynamics that also drive the therapeutic relationship. The phenomena of projection and transference arise from magical thinking, when we confuse similarity with identity or the part with the whole. Projection and transference do not figure much in person-centred theory, which is more interested in subjective experience than unconscious processes, but we should not ignore the power of magic.

The tribal community controls instinct and impulse by developing rituals and taboos. As individuals, we think of emotion as something we have. It may be difficult to control at times, but it is ours. However, for our magical mind it is the emotion that has us. Our rage, lust, depression or exhilaration are not initiated by us, rather, they happen to us. They are energies that take possession of us, dominate us for a while, and leave us when it suits them. Magical behaviour (ritual, incantation, spells) was quite adequate as a way of dealing with the world in the well-functioning tribal community and there are still aspects of our experience that we should attribute to magical consciousness. Our ability to heal ourselves by means of placebos, and the power of group religious ritual to heal and transform, attest to magical consciousness being a valid response to the world.

The world experienced by our magical minds is one in which 'things happen'. We use magic to make good things happen and protect us from bad things happening. This is most evident in our superstitions. Our Stone Age ancestors tried to gain some control over the transcendent power of nature through magic and sorcery, ritual, totem and taboo, experiencing this magical world through a group ego, sustained by the clan. It is in the magical structure that empathy, considered as an experience of the primal sensing and feeling states of other members of the clan, is first a distinguishable phenomenon. Magical consciousness is found in therapies in which the healer is envisaged as a conduit for a transpersonal, palpable, healing energy (called chi, for instance, or reiki, or orgone energy, or the Holy Spirit) rather than as someone whose personal intervention heals the patient, or even as someone who facilitates the patient's self-healing. It is found in traditional healing ceremonies where healer and patient enter a common psychic space through ritual.

Even the conventional counselling interaction is surrounded by ritual. The display of the counsellor's qualifications on the office wall, the furniture, the dress (whether fussily formal or carefully casual) are designed to directly influence the client. Magic labels such as 'Dr' and 'psychologist', are used to predispose the client to a positive outcome. The exchange of money has ritual significance; the more expensive the consultation, the greater the expectation of healing. In this, the individual client is, likely enough, not thinking about such things but rather is carried along by the shared assumptions of his cultural group. Person-centred counsellors are probably less inclined to engage in magic and ritual than counsellors of some other persuasions, but magic is not easily avoided, even if that were totally desirable.

We cannot escape magic. We fill our lives with ritual: the morning cup of coffee, the favourite chair, the favourite jacket and the way we greet our clients, all function to keep us safe and keep the world turning smoothly. We may not do a rain dance to make it rain, we may not do the fire dance to ensure that the sun rises the next morning, and we may have perfectly good, rational explanations for why we sit in a particular chair, talk in a particular way, decorate our room in particular colours, but there is magic involved in all of this. Last time I did X, Y happened; if I do X again, Y will happen again. There may be perfectly sound theoretical reasons for doing X, but the magic mind simply bypasses them and does it because 'it works'. We may think that we are making our own decisions about our professional practice, but our actions are embedded in the ways of behaving of the particular professional clan we belong to. 'This is the way we do things around here. If we do things differently *something terrible will happen!*'

Rogers found that if he constantly checked that he was understanding the client correctly, if he helped the client to find words for something felt but inadequately said, he got to understand what was going on in the client and was able to support him or her in their exploration. Somehow this was transformed into something called 'reflective listening' and counsellors were trained in this 'technique'.

Where the ritual reflection of content and feeling (or any other technique) is assumed to be therapeutically effective in and of itself we are talking about magic. It is not what Rogers had in mind. What he did have in mind was the healing power of the truly empathic relationship. In his early theorizing of client-centred therapy he was certainly not imagining empathy as the fusing of the separate identities of the counsellor and client. He was busy being a 'proper psychologist'. Yet in his theory lay the germ of the idea that relationship of itself is healing, because non-relationship is a toxic attack on the essence of who we are. Congruence is at the centre of process and outcome in the person-centred approach, and to be congruent is to be who we are at depth – relational beings.

MYTHICAL MIND

In mythical consciousness, the therapist experiences the client's world imaginatively. While the magical structure of consciousness is sensate, pre-rational and pre-verbal, the mythical structure is imaginal, irrational and verbal. It maintains the collective identity of the magical along with a limited sense of individuality. The mythical mind does not give me a direct experience of how you are and feel. Rather, it enables me to imagine how you are and feel. And it enables this because our separate stories are a common story.

Mythical thinking is characterized by image and narrative. Its time is rhythmical or circular time, a continuous reiteration of the basic narratives of our relationship to the world. Mythical empathy involves the counsellor entering into the client's story, recognizing its universality as well as its uniqueness, being in the story with the client.

The mythical mind has a limited sense of separate self. The magical structure does not distinguish self from not-self; the mythical structure knows self and not-self as a polarity, a 'complementarity'. In our mythical consciousness we are both one and separate. I know your story by knowing my own; I know my story by knowing yours. The more intensely personal your story is, the more universal it is, and the more it is intensely mine. However, I do not assume, as I might in my magical consciousness, that your story and my story are indistinguishable. For Robert Kegan (1998), writing about the transition from the 'second order' consciousness of childhood to the 'third order' consciousness of adolescence, the critical distinction is that through our third order consciousness we understand that other people have thoughts and feelings independent of our own.

Rogers also saw the relationship as something which includes yet transcends these separate identities:

> *In terms of the therapeutic situation, I think this feeling says to the client, I have a real hunger to know you, to experience your warmth, your expressivity – in whatever form it may take – to drink as deeply as I can from the experience of you in the closest, most naked relationship we can achieve. I do not want to change you to suit me; the real you and the real me are perfectly compatible ingredients of a potential relationship which transcends, but in no way violates, our separate identities. (Rogers, 1951: 164)*

However, in our mythical, third order consciousness, the thoughts we have are not strictly our own. We do our thinking within narratives that we have been born into, or have adopted to replace inherited narratives that we have found inadequate. Most of our beliefs and values are tribal. They have been absorbed from our culture – from our families, our education, our peers and the media. We have generally absorbed them at a young age, accepted them without reflection as 'the way the world is'. We do our thinking within the taken-for-grantedness of a shared story about who we are and what sort of a world we live in.

The counsellor and client, in so far as they are functioning at the level of what Kegan (1998) calls 'third order mind', bring their myths to the interaction. The client is living within a narrative which defines appropriate roles, values and behaviours. These may be taken completely for granted. Or the issue may be that there is tension between these roles and a different set of roles, values and behaviours which belong to a different narrative and which are currently forcing themselves on the client's attention. Counsellors also come with a narrative which defines appropriate roles, values and behaviour, both for themselves and for the client. As long as counsellor and client continue to operate in third order/mythical consciousness the only available outcomes are either confirmation of the client's old or emerging value package (whichever best matches the counsellor's narrative) or an unsuccessful attempt to shake the client free of a narrative which the counsellor does not share.

Whereas the magical mind works through emotion, the mythical mind works through image. The construction of images is a right-brain activity. The right brain processes in image what the left brain can only process in words. Obviously the two often work together. The right brain is good at sensing the big picture in all of its complexity, but needs the words to express it. The left brain is good at the detail, but may miss the big picture. A lot of what we call thinking might be better called imagining. It can be argued that all our language is based on metaphor, and that even the most sophisticated theories are grounded in our imagination. They are ways of imagining the world at least as much as they are ways of thinking about it.

Right brain therapies such as Jungian active imagination and Assagioli's psychosynthesis depend on the ability to engage with mythical consciousness. The therapist enters the imaginal world of the client and stays with the client's images, not interpreting, not rationalizing, being an affirming presence in the imaginal world, helping the client to carry on telling the story. In hearing the client's story we need to note also that the client's story does not belong to the client alone. Jung and James Hillman have taught us that our individual stories are all versions of the 'big stories', the great myths. In mythical consciousness the boundary between the individual and the collective is permeable. So is the boundary between self and other. Many person-centred therapists utilize the mythical structure when they cease reflecting and responding, and simply tune into the client and wait for their felt sense to deliver an image, keeping in mind Rogers' observation that what is most intensely personal in the client's experience is likely to be most universal.

Eugene Gendlin's notion of the 'felt sense' has been influential in the way many person-centred counsellors go about their work. Gendlin suggests that we trust our somatic experience, and rest in this fuzzy, wordless 'felt sense', waiting for an image to emerge from it and patiently interrogating this image until we find words for our experience. The counsellor can recommend this process to her client and guide him through it. More powerfully, counsellor and client together can stop talking and listening and rest in the felt sense of their being together in this transformational moment, allowing their felt sense to deliver images which may help them articulate the meaning of their experience, each understanding that the images belong to both of them. Often enough they find themselves sharing the same image or dreaming the same dream.

Counsellors conventionally maintain the assumption that the therapist and patient are two separated, intact entities who are constrained to relationships to one another within an objectively real world. If we are sharing the images or dreams of our client, there must be some kind of communication passing between us. However, this is not the only way of thinking about it. Classical Jungians discuss such phenomena as expressions of a collective or objective psyche. Post-Jungians like Hillman (Marlan, 2008) take seriously the notion of the *mundus imaginalis*, a level of reality located between the material, sensate world and the world of ideas or spirit. Commenting on this notion, Samuels argues that 'the mundus imaginalis functions as a linking factor between patient and analyst' and that 'some of the analyst's countertransference may be regarded as visions and hence part of this imaginal world' (Samuels, 1989: 164).

For most of us, most of the time our experience of the mythical world is diluted by reflection, abstraction and pre-conception. The mythical world is far more unitary than the conceptualized world of mental–rational consciousness. It does not manifest the either/or of dualistic, rational thinking, rather, its world is bipolar, taking the rational mind's oppositions (body/mind, conscious/unconscious, self/other, health/pathology, goodness/badness, subject/object, female/male, spirit/matter, one/many, even truth/falsehood) as complementary manifestations of a unitary reality. The mythical world is not a world of 'dead matter' like the world of rational, mechanistic science. It is ensouled, alive and replete with divinity (or divinities).

Jung refers to the sense of being in rational control of our lives as 'the superstition of modern man in general' (Jung, 1979, CW 18, para. 555). He goes on to say:

In order to maintain his credo, he cultivates a remarkable lack of introspection. He is blind to the fact that, with all his rationality and efficiency, he is possessed by powers beyond his control. The gods and demons have not disappeared at all. They have merely got new names. They keep him on the run with restlessness, vague apprehensions, psychological complications, and invincible need for pills, alcohol, tobacco, dietary and other hygienic systems – and above all, with an impressive array of neuroses. (Jung, 1979, CW 18, para. 555)

Julian Jaynes (1976) argued, from his examination of Homer's *Iliad*, that when these stories were first told the Greeks had no sense of being individuals who reflected on their situation and made decisions. They just did what the gods told them to do. They heard the gods' voices inside their heads and acted on them. Their behaviour was governed by messages from the right cerebral hemisphere. However, by the time the stories in the *Odyssey* were first told, they were able to reflect on their behaviour and make conscious, rational (left brain) decisions. If Jaynes is right, the shift from right brain dominance to left brain dominance in the second millennium BCE marks the breakdown of the mythical structure of consciousness in Greek culture and the emergence of the mental structure. Now we find them 'jostling together'.

MENTAL–RATIONAL MIND

Our mythical mind allows us to live our lives within narratives which give meaning to what we do and meaning to whatever happens to us. However, we have a mental mind which enables us to check these narratives against the 'facts' of our experience.

Our mental–rational consciousness is at work when we look at the world objectively, assess the facts, see connections, count, estimate, calculate and plan. Mental consciousness is self-conscious, individualistic, and proactive. However, we are often under the illusion that our mental consciousness is at work when we are actually imagining the world rather than engaging with it objectively. And indeed, the ways we imagine the world are borrowed from our culture rather than created by ourselves.

Robert Kegan, in distinguishing between the third order mind characteristic of traditional cultures and the fourth order mind which adults need if they are to cope adequately in the modern world, suggests that in third order consciousness we identify with the contents (mostly inherited) of our mind. In fourth order consciousness, however, we are able to think about our thoughts, to judge whether they match up to the evidence of the world as we experience it. We objectify and quantify time and space, think of ourselves as self-contained and categorize the objects of our experience as either true or false, right or wrong.

In his critique of the limitations of client-centred and other humanistic therapies, Alvin Mahrer sets out the three assumptions on which he believes the approach is based:

(a) Therapist and patient are assumed to be two fundamentally separate and intact entities.

(b) Their relationship is predominated by the patient's frame of reference. The patient has this frame of reference, and the therapist acknowledges and uses the patient's frame of reference.

(c) Both therapist and patient are assumed to exist within an encompassing world of objective reality upon which the patient's frame of reference is but one perspective. (Mahrer, 1986: 143–145)

In Rogers' early theorizing about the nature of empathy he was clearly concerned to develop a logical, systematic and abstract way of explaining the phenomenon and its implications for therapy. He accepted the assumption that counsellor and client are existing in separate, rational worlds, assumed that one can look only from one direction at a time, that while the therapist knows the client's frame of reference, he does not experience any confusion of identity, or become engulfed in the client's experiencing. The therapist's value to the client depends on the latter's determination to maintain his distinct separateness. Rogers expressed this idea with some emphasis:

Am I strong enough in my own separateness that I will not be downcast by his depression, downcast by his fear nor engulfed by his dependency? Is my inner self hardy enough to realize that I am not destroyed by his anger, taken over by his need for dependence, nor enslaved by his love, but that I can exist separate from him with feelings and needs of my own? When I can freely feel this strength of being a separate person, then I can let myself go much more in understanding and accepting him. (Rogers, 1958: 15)

In *Client-Centered Therapy* (1951), Rogers is consciously and deliberately working within a mental–rational framework. Take his reflections on the proposition: 'The best vantage point for understanding behaviour is from the internal frame of reference of the individual himself' (Rogers, 1951: 494). He argues that human behaviour, no matter how bizarre it may appear to the observer, is always rational and purposive 'in response to reality as it is perceived'. He takes the perfectly rational view that while it would be desirable 'to empathically experience all the sensory and visceral sensations of the individual', this is impossible. Admitting that a great deal of the client's experience of the phenomenal world is not brought to the conscious level, he argues that on the one hand it is unsatisfactory to try to understand the client's unconscious experiencing through an external interpretative framework, and on the other that to stay with the client's awareness gives us an incomplete picture. He acknowledges that the counsellor's understanding of the client's phenomenal world will be at least partly derived by inferences from elements of that world that belong to the counsellor and client's common experience. Throughout his discussion, the client's world is clearly the client's and the counsellor's world is clearly the counsellor's and the contents of one can pass to the other only by communication and (less accurately) by observation.

Moreover, Rogers sees the aim of therapy as helping the client 'to perceive himself as the evaluator of experience, rather than regarding himself as existing in a world where the values are inherent in and attached to the object of his perception' (Rogers, 1951: 138). He wants the client to move from the taken-for-granted world of third order consciousness to the critically observed world of fourth order consciousness – to emerge from the discomfort of living within a myth that does not match his experience, so that he can take responsibility for his own beliefs and values. In discussing this dynamic, Kegan uses the example of Rogers and Gloria in the film *Three Approaches to Psychotherapy* (Shostrom, 1986). Towards the end of an interview, in which Gloria has been unable to get Rogers to tell her what she should do, we find the following interaction:

> *Gloria: (After a pause) I do feel that you have been saying to me – you are not giving me advice but I do feel like you are saying, 'You know what pattern you want to follow, Gloria, and go ahead and do it.' I sort of feel a backing up from you.*
> *To which he responds:*
> *Rogers: I guess the way I sense it, you've been telling me that you know what you want to do and yes, I do believe in backing up people in what they want to do. It's a little different slant than the way it seems to you.*
> *(In Kegan, 1998: 245–6)*

When Gloria expresses confusion Rogers points out that there is little point in her doing something that she has not actually chosen to do, and that what he has been trying to do is help her find out what her 'inner choices' are.

Gloria is clearly stuck in a narrative which includes both the assumption that there is a right answer to her question and the assumption that a wise and compassionate older man like Rogers, the famous psychotherapist, will know what that answer is. Rogers also has a narrative, which involves the notion that Gloria's 'actualizing tendency' will enable her to move from the conditions of worth of third order/mythical mind to the independent action of fourth order/ mental mind. Kegan does not appear to share this assumption, and argues that Gloria may currently be incapable of fourth order consciousness, in which case she will simply not be able to understand what he is talking about. She may not have attained the psychological development necessary to take on the role of 'author' of her own life, which is a function of mental consciousness.

The mental–rational mind seeks clarity, both in demanding a coherent theoretical framework within which to work, and in pursuing the fantasy that once we see clearly the causes and consequences of our self-destructive behaviour we will cease to act in this way. Change comes through insight. In this context, empathy is essentially an act of intellection. The counsellor strives to understand what the world of the client is like. It has no necessary connection with feeling, and is certainly not to be mistaken for sympathy. There is no losing of boundaries. What is yours is yours and what is mine is mine, and there must be no confusion. Nevertheless, though 'cool', rational therapy might have been consistent with the theoretical constructs out of which Rogers was working when he first described client-centred therapy, his experience of what worked drew him to suggest that this was not enough. Like Jung, he was 'beset by the all-too-human fear that consciousness – our Promethean conquest – may in the end not be able to serve us as well as nature' (Jung, 1979, CW 8, para. 750).

Our mental–rational minds imagine that self-actualization is something we do, rather than something which we allow to happen. In Rogers' thinking about the both the actualizing tendency and the formative tendency – the 'two foundations of the person-centred approach' – he has no doubt that growth, by whatever name we call it, is not our personal, Promethean achievement, but a consequence of our enmeshment in 'the directional trend which is evident in all organic and human life' (Rogers, 1961: 351). In this he is on the same page as Jung who, in an interview with Ira Progoff in 1952, was asked if individuation did not always involve consciousness. He replied that such a notion was an 'overvaluation of consciousness', and explained that individuation is the natural process by which a human being becomes a human being, the same process as that by which a tree becomes a tree (Jung, cited in Sabini, 2002: 10).

INTEGRAL MIND

Rogers points out in *Client-Centered Therapy* that there is considerable agreement that therapeutic growth takes place as a result of experiences which have 'an emotional rather than an intellectual meaning for clients' (Rogers, 1951: 165). He argues that the therapist must be touched by the experience of the client:

> *I think clients are very much aware of the difference between the counsellor who listens and understands, and simply does not react, and the one who understands and in addition really cares about the meaning to the client of the feelings, reactions and experiences which he is recording. (Rogers, 1951: 165)*

Mental mind is not enough. Our capacity to be reasonable needs to be integrated with our (magical) emotions and our (mythical) imaginings and meanings.

Gebser argues that our contemporary consciousness is multi-structured or, to change the metaphor slightly, multi-layered. Even when we are acting 'rationally', our magical and mythical consciousness is shaping our thinking. The complexity of human behaviour comes out of the interplay of these several 'layers' or 'levels' of consciousness in whatever we do. Gebser suggests that the acknowledgement and appreciation of these discrete structures is a step towards their integration with the mental structure in a more transparent way of experiencing the world.

Three elements stand out in Gebser's analysis of what he calls the *integral* structure of consciousness. The first is time-freedom. Archaic and magical humanity seem to have had no sense of time at all, living in a continuous present. For mythical humanity, time was rhythmical, constantly returning to its beginning. For mental–rational humanity, time became continuous and sequential, and eventually mechanically quantifiable. What identifies an integral sense of time, for Gebser, is the re-owning of pre-rational, magic timelessness and irrational, mythical temporicity alongside mental, measured time. This 'makes possible the leap into arational time-freedom' (Gebser, 1985: 289).

The integral structure of consciousness also has a new sense of space. Archaic and magical humanity lacked all spatial consciousness, because it lacked a defined sense of a self as observer. Mythical humanity emerged from this enmeshment in nature, and became aware of an external world, but self-consciousness was still too weak to experience objective space. It is only in the beginnings of mental consciousness that human beings became able to locate events in objective space. Central to this experience was the discovery of perspective, which demands a point from which the world is viewed and an individual to view it. The mental mind sees reality from one position, gazing in one direction. In the emergent integral consciousness, it becomes possible to view the world without locating the viewer in a particular position in space. Reality can be observed from every direction and every position at once. Gebser refers to paintings of Pablo Picasso and the poetry of Rainer Maria Rilke and T.S. Eliot as illustrations of this.

A third element in Gebser's analysis is the ego. Archaic and magical consciousness were pre-egoic. Mythical consciousness holds only a dim sense of self as distinct from the tribe. Mental–rational consciousness allows the development of separate egoic identity. Integral consciousness is, in Gebser's language, 'ego-free'.

Kegan and Egan have something similar in mind when they carry Piaget's developmental stages into adulthood. Egan's particular take on this, when he talks of the transition from 'philosophic' to 'ironic' understanding, is that ironic understanding embraces the basic, sensorimotor, pre-lingual, somatic understanding that philosophical understanding manages to ignore. In our philosophic consciousness we value the clarity of our perceptions and thoughts. In our ironic mind we value the ambiguity and paradox we experience when our organic sense of reality turns up a different truth from our speculations or taken-for-granted narratives.

Kegan's focus is on subject–object identification. In fourth order mind the subject is the autonomous being who thinks and the object is the contents of his mind. In fifth order mind this autonomous, self-authoring being becomes the object of one's thinking. The fourth order mind engages in the critical thought which constructs the truth from the objective evidence the world provides. The fifth order mind not only looks critically at *what* we think – our (third order) beliefs – which is the specialization of the fourth order mind. It also looks critically at *how* we think. It looks critically at our very rationality. This is in line with Gebser's observation of the twentieth century movement from philosophy to eteology which 'does not merely perceive objects in relation to objects, but perceives thinking itself: a detachment from the mental world without irrationalizing it' (Gebser, 1949/1986: 326).

Where the fourth order, mental mind thinks about counselling within a framework which honours clear, left-brained thinking as the best way to find the truth, the fifth order, integral mind understands that this is only one way to find the truth and that, anyway, there are different kinds of truth. Where the fourth order, mental mind thinks about counselling within a framework which sees the relationship as something created by two separate egos, the fifth order, integral mind understands that the relationship creates the persons engaged in it. In this moment the counsellor is incomplete without this client, and the client is incomplete without this counsellor. (Just as my truth is not complete without your truth, I am not complete without you.) Where the fourth order, mental mind sees the relationship simply as the context in which the client's healing may take place, the fifth order, integral mind values the relationship itself as an opportunity to learn and to 'live out your multiplicity' (Kegan, 1998: 320).

Gebser suggests, logically enough, that just as archaic humanity could not feel what the experience of magical consciousness might be, and just as mythical humanity could not imagine what mental consciousness might be like, modern, rational humanity cannot understand the experience of integral consciousness. Gebser himself claims only to have observed the past and present trajectory of consciousness and on this basis to have guessed at its future direction. I suggest that client-centred theory and therapy is in this trajectory. Whereas the mental mind is dominant in Rogers' early theorizing of personality and therapy, he later acknowledges the impact of magical and mythical consciousness on the therapeutic process. However, he is in no way recommending a regression to the limited awareness of magical and mythical consciousness, but incorporating them in a kind of experience which is highly 'aware'.

In *On Becoming a Person* (1961) Rogers set out his ideas on the nature of the therapeutic relationship. He states:

> *I let myself go into the immediacy of the relationship where it is my total organism which takes over and is sensitive to the relationship, not simply my consciousness. I am not consciously responding in a planful or analytic way, but simply react in an unreflective way to the other individual, my reaction being based, (but not consciously) on my total organismic sensitivity to this other person. (Rogers, 1961: 202)*

In his focus on 'immediacy of the relationship' and his 'total organismic sensitivity', Rogers is echoing what Gebser has to say about integral consciousness, Kegan's understanding of the fifth order mind and Egan's sense that our complex ironic consciousness is grounded in our somatic experience.

He goes on to say:

> *The essence of some of the deepest parts of therapy seems to be a unity of experiencing. The client is freely able to experience his feeling in its complete intensity ... without intellectual inhibitions or cautions, without having it bounded by knowledge of contradictory feelings; and I am able with equal freedom to experience my understanding of this feeling, without any conscious thought about it, without any apprehension or concern as to where this will lead, without any type of diagnostic or analytic thinking, without any cognitive or emotional barriers to a complete 'letting go' in understanding. When there is this complete unity, singleness, fullness of experiencing in the relationship, then it acquires the 'out-of-this-world' quality which many therapists have remarked upon, a sort of trance-like feeling in the relationship, from which both the client and I emerge at the end of the hour, as if from a deep well or tunnel. (Rogers, 1961: 202)*

We can note here that Rogers is neither imaginatively placing himself within the world of the client or constructing that world out of observation and communication. He is not coy about the possibility of being directly in touch with something of the unconscious world of the client. Client and counsellor do not lose their identity, yet there is

111

no sense of counsellor and client being restricted to their separate, egoic space. His view of the relationship is, in Gebser's word, 'aperspectival'. He is not limited to seeing his and the client's shared world from one direction only. He must see it simultaneously from his own position and that of his client.

Rogers refers to Martin Buber's phrase the 'I–Thou relationship', which he calls 'a timeless living in the experience which is between the client and me ... the height of personal subjectivity' (Rogers, 1961: 202). This notion of subjectivity is very different from the ego-based subjectivity characteristic of the rational or fourth order mind.

Rogers is aware that within the mindset of modern materialistic science such experiences simply do not exist. The rational mind has no way of dealing with them.

> *When I am at my best, as a group facilitator or as a therapist, I discover another characteristic. I find that when I am closest to my inner, intuitive self, when I am somehow in touch with the unknown in me, when perhaps I am in a state of slightly altered consciousness in the relationship, then whatever I do seems to be full of healing. Then simply my presence is releasing and helpful. There is nothing I can do to force this experience, but when I can relax and be close to the transcendental core of me, then I may behave in strange and impulsive ways in the relationship, ways which I cannot justify rationally, which have nothing to do with my thought processes. But these strange processes turn out to be right in some odd way. At those moments it seems that my inner spirit has reached out and touched the inner spirit of the other. Our relationship transcends itself and becomes a part of something larger. Profound growth and healing and energy are present. (Rogers, 1990: 137)*

Psychologically, the emergence of the aperspectival, arational, integral world demands a disenchantment with a narrow rational consciousness and a re-owning of the earlier structures. We find in Rogers' statement an acknowledgement of a phenomenon with magical-mythical elements. Magical healing operates through what are for us 'non-ordinary' states of consciousness, is independent of linear space and time, does not know the duality of mind/body and self/other, locates core identity not in the individual but in 'something larger', is felt rather than understood, and does not know the laws of logic. Yet there is more to Rogers' experience than magic. In this experience Rogers is in no way controlled by instinct and emotion. He is fully aware of what he is experiencing. Integral mind takes magic, myth and critical reflection together and constructs something new from their integration.

Those who regard rational consciousness as the peak and culmination of evolutionary progress will see this statement of Rogers as an indication that he 'lost it' in his old age. They will warn us that this honouring of magic and irrationality is regressive, an unfortunate intrusion of magical-mythical New Age consciousness into a perfectly adequate rational-humanistic system of thought. Gebser's response to this would be that the post-egoic states that Rogers is talking about are distinguished from pre-egoic states in that they retain the foundation of ego, rationality and control which they transcend.

In the above passage Rogers is referring to an experience which he cannot justify rationally. We might be inclined to label it irrational. However, Gebser takes pains to distinguish the irrational from the arational:

> It is of fundamental importance that we clearly distinguish between 'irrational' and 'arational', for this distinction lies at the very heart of our deliberations ... There is a fundamental distinction between the attempt to go beyond the merely measurable, knowing and respecting it while striving to be free from it, and rejecting and disregarding the measurable by regressing to the immoderate and unfathomable chaos of the ambivalent and even fragmented polyvalence of psychic and natural interrelation. (Gebser, 1949/1986: 147)

Rogers' reflections are hardly the reflections of someone who has abandoned rationality and slid into an 'immoderate and unfathomable chaos'. Neither has he abandoned his sense of self, but is able to hold the paradox of experiencing self-sense and transpersonal sense simultaneously. In reflecting on his experience he shows an awareness of a paradox, or at least an irony, in finding that a focus on individual experiencing should lead to an experience of oneness, quoting a participant in one of his workshops:

> [I]t was like a meditative experience when I feel myself as a centre of consciousness. And yet with that extraordinary sense of oneness, the separateness of each person present has never been more clearly preserved. (Rogers, 1990: 148)

Rogers notes somewhat apologetically that this account of group empathy 'partakes of the mystical'. What we loosely call 'the mystical' runs all the way from the dimly experienced unity-consciousness of archaic mind to the time-free, space-free, ego-free intense integral awareness of the ever-present origin. 'The mystical' may not be included in conventional scientific discourse, but it is certainly part of human experience.

Through the archaic structure of consciousness we simply experience our identity with 'all that is'. Through the magical structure we experience, still fairly dimly, our entanglement with the universe. Through the mythical structure we identify with our tribe and its stories. Through the mental structure we become aware of ourselves as individuals able to act on the world. The integral structure brings this mental awareness to our experience of unity, entanglement and culture.

BEING IN FIVE MINDS

We are inclined to equate consciousness with the sense of self we experience at the mental level. Yet we constantly shift between this mental–rational consciousness and the older, simpler structures within which it is grounded. Jung disputed the artificial boundary which we set between ourselves and other more 'primitive' forms of life. He frequently reminds his readers that 'we have to make allowances for these primitive layers in our Psyche' (Jung, 1977, vol 1: 119).

Some would argue that these 'primitive layers' have limited value in the modern world. Others would claim that mythical thinking remains a very effective way of dealing with the world, and that it is our capacity for mythical, and even magical, thinking that enables us to find meaning in our lives and gives us a grounding in the concrete world which rational thinking seems bent on destroying. Magical and mythical consciousness can be either 'efficient' or 'deficient', but they are neither better nor worse than mental–rational consciousness. They are simply older and different. Gebser warns us not to try to ground structures of consciousness theory in biological evolution. Nevertheless, there are some interesting parallels with neurobiology.

Neurophysiologist Paul MacLean argued (1973, 1990) that we have not one brain but three. This 'triune brain' is made up of our ancient reptilian brain (brainstem and cerebellum), our paleo-mammalian brain (limbic system) and our neo-mammalian brain (neo-cortex). Each of these brains has its own intelligence, its own subjectivity, its own sense of time and space, and its own memory. Each brain layer has formed upon the older layer beneath and before it, and is connected to the other two. The three brains tend to operate independently, so that we are like a car driven by three drivers (instinct, emotion and cognition) each with its own steering wheel and its own idea of where it wants to go. MacLean is at pains to point out to us that for all our illusion of cognitive sophistication, there are parts of our brains that still think like lizards and horses.

MacLean locates his three-brain model within the framework of biological evolution, seeing a sequential development from the most primitive to the most complex. This has been challenged within his own field of evolutionary biology. He takes for granted the now discredited notion that evolution is progressive, moving from the most 'primitive' to the most 'advanced' life forms. It is now more acceptable to argue that even fish have the beginnings of a neo-cortex and a limbic system and to argue that in any case fish are not lower than horses and apes on some evolutionary ladder. They are highly evolved *as fish*. They just do not happen to be horses or apes or humans. However, MacLean's picture of the brain has proved very useful in helping us explain our behaviour, as long as we set aside the idea that each more 'advanced' brain grew out of the more 'primitive' brain on which it sits.

In *Self Comes to Mind* (2010) Antonio Damasio presents a theory of brain function which parallels MacLean's model in many respects. In discussing how we get a sense of self he distinguishes between the *proto self*, which is generated by the brainstem and which experiences without awareness; the *core self*, generated by the limbic system, which enables us to be aware of our experiences; and the *autobiographical self*, created in the cerebral cortex, through which we have a sense of continuing identity.

When we expand MacLean's model of the brain to include what we have learned from Jaynes' speculations on the 'bicameral brain' and more recent research into brain lateralization (Ornstein, 1997; Dell, 2005) we can suggest that since the cortex and limbic system are split into two – a left brain which processes information atomistically and verbally and a right brain which processes information holistically and imagistically – we may legitimately talk of four interconnected minds – even if the brains associated with them overlap somewhat. We can even speculate about integrating all four in a fifth – 'integral' or 'whole brain' consciousness, and reach the conclusion that there is a neurological basis for the notion that there are all of five minds at work in each of us, five minds which 'jostle together and fold on one another, to some degree remaining "somewhat distinct"' (Egan, 1997: 80).

While there is some interest in mapping these models of mind against each other, it does not really matter whether they fit perfectly, as the people who developed the models were using different criteria for distinguishing one mind from another. They were not asking the same questions and they were looking at the phenomenon of consciousness from different directions. What matters here is the general notion that consciousness is complex and multi-layered, that it ranges from the dim somatic awareness that we share with lizards, through the emotional and imaginative experience that we share with mammals, through a capacity for abstraction that seems to be uniquely human, to what Gebser calls 'the transparency of the whole'. It takes no great stretch of the imagination to see the instinctual, pre-egoic self emerging from the brainstem, or our magical consciousness centred in the limbic system. We should note, however, that Gebser (1949/1986: 37) warns us that the process he is talking about is not biological or historical. Consciousness is not determined by biology. Mind is not simply a function of brain.

Having said that, we should acknowledge the contribution that neuroscience has made to our way of thinking about consciousness. We tend to overvalue our left-brain thinking and undervalue our other mental capacities. Our pre-frontal cortex is pretty useless when it has to read non-verbal or emotional communication. It is the limbic system which processes facial expression, vocal rhythms, scent and posture and lets us know when someone is aggressive, friendly or sexually attracted. We do not usually think this through. We 'just know'. It worked very well for us as infants and can work just as well for us as adults if we do not ignore it. Goleman (1995: 86) argues that it is the limbic system which creates emotional resonance between individuals, so that we can 'tune in' to each other. It is the engine of emotional contagion, whereby we 'lure one another into our own emotional space, revising one another by emotional entrainment, not unlike the way that laughter and yawning are contagious' (Haule, 2011, vol 2: 111).

> *Once we are drawn into the emotional space of another, our own top-to-bottom archetypal structures become activated, hormones dispatched, memories and images evoked, inherited decision biases tapped. This is the causal body-centred chain of events that is opened up by communication between limbic systems, and it is the organic computer that deciphers the information coming from another's meta-mind. (Haule, 2011, vol 2: 111)*

Gebser's exploration of the evolution of consciousness is only a prelude to his main work, which focuses on the nature of the transcendent reality which is manifest in these various structures. What can we say about the 'suchness' of the world, the *itself* which is revealed in the darkness of the archaic structure, the gloom of the magical, the twilight of the mythical, the brightness of the mental and the transparency of the integral? Gebser challenges the privileging of the scientific worldview as the only legitimate window on that reality. He would have it that what we know of reality through our mental–rational consciousness complements what we know, obscurely yet deeply, through archaic, magical and mythical consciousness. It does not falsify it.

Though conventional psychology has no place for such a notion, Jung-oriented therapists have no trouble in accepting it as the framework for their work with clients. Client-centred practitioners who are tied to a rational and individualistic notion of therapeutic growth may have trouble accommodating it within their theory of counselling. Nevertheless, I suggest that those of us who are committed to the person-centred approach need to expand our awareness in order to revision counselling in this way. Gebser reminds us that:

> *Every 'novel' thought will tear open wounds ... Everyone who is intent upon surviving not only the earth but also life with worth and dignity, and living rather than passively accepting life, must sooner or later pass through the agonies of emergent consciousness. (Gebser, 1949/1986: 73)*

Gebser is adamant that integral consciousness is not something to be achieved by us as individuals. It is something which emerges in the collective as a manifestation of the 'ever-present origin'. He thought he could see clear enough evidence that it was in the process of becoming the dominant structure of consciousness in the late twentieth century, but certainly did not see this emergence as inevitable. As individuals we can either be in tune with this emergence or hang on desperately to a 'merely rational' consciousness which is no longer able to deal adequately with the world.

Gebser developed his theory in the context of a European culture which was in grave danger of regressing to a deficient magical consciousness. He came to hold the more optimistic view that the destabilization of rational consciousness could be a sign of the emergence of a new structure. At the beginning of this millennium it seems that we are again being confronted with same danger and the same promise.

6

SELF-REALIZATION
AND THE ECOLOGICAL SELF

In *Living in the Borderland* (2005) Jerome Bernstein recounts his experience with a seriously depressed client, Hannah, who had a history of sexual abuse. The conventional analytic techniques had been helpful to some extent, but he always had the sense that he was missing something in their sessions. One day she arrived at his office very distressed. Driving home from the previous session she had found herself behind a truck carrying two cows. She sensed that they were being taken to be slaughtered and felt their distress. He suggested, as any good Jungian would, that she was projecting her own distress onto the cows. She went along with this for a while and then protested in frustration 'But it's the *cows!*'

Some weeks later, Hannah recounted how she had been followed by some stray dogs. As she described the experience the room was filled with pain. Again Bernstein talked about projection, until Hannah shouted out in anger 'You just don't get it. It's the *dogs!*'

Reflecting on his experience, Bernstein realized that he had heard the same message from Navajo elders, the message that 'Everything animate and inanimate has within it the spirit dimension and communicates in that dimension to those who can listen' (Bernstein, 2005: 8). He 'got it'.

Of course the 'it' does not fit well with modern Western notions of what sort of a world we live in. The deficient rational consciousness which enables scientific materialism, and which we have found so valuable in giving some of us more comfortable, healthier, more prosperous lives, has no way of acknowledging the existence of any other way of experiencing the world.

Bernstein's reflections on this led him to develop the notion of the 'borderland personality'. He uses this term to describe the person who 'straddles the split between the developed, rational mind and nature in the Western psyche' (Bernstein, 2005: 17).

He argues, as Jean Gebser does, that the split between the rational mind and nature, is at last being reconciled.

The Borderland is a recent evolutionary dynamic that appears to be rapidly gaining momentum and liminality in the Western ego. It is manifested through the collective unconscious – a natural evolutionary dynamic – that is moving the Western psyche to reconnect its present overspecialized ego to its natural roots. (Bernstein, 2005: 17)

He suggests that there is an evolutionary process that is moving us towards a new kind of collective consciousness that will be common to the many rather than the few, a kind of awareness that 'may become the predominant form of consciousness emergent in the 21st century' (Bernstein, 2005: 122). Jung, likewise, observed a shift in consciousness taking place, as the 'overvaluation of consciousness' characteristic of modernity met its inherent limitations.

The picture we have of the world gets broken down into countless particulars, and the original feeling of unity, which we integrally connected with the unity of the unconscious psyche, is lost. This feeling of unity … is now, after a long period of oblivion, looming up again on the scientific horizon, thanks to the discoveries made by the psychology of the unconscious and by parapsychology. (Jung, 1979, CW 11, para. 443)

However, for the time being, 'borderland' personalities in conventional Western culture have to be careful who they talk to about their connection to animals, trees and rocks, or they will be diagnosed, labelled and medicated as delusional 'borderline' personalities.

Bernstein argues that while 'borderland' phenomena are sometimes associated with pathology (e.g. post-traumatic stress disorder and depression) the experience of these phenomena is not itself pathological. People who are sensitive to experiences of which most of us are unaware, and see or hear or feel things which conventional wisdom tells them cannot possibly be real, naturally feel alienation and distress. However, we can argue that what they need if they are to live comfortably in a conventional community is not medication but a filter. We might argue, as the philosopher Henri Bergson did a century ago, that our senses function not so much to let information into us as to keep information out and without our filters we would be so overwhelmed by the flood of sensations that we would drown in them, as is the case in psychosis. In indigenous cultures shamans must undergo rigorous training to enable them to cope with the world beyond our senses.

INDIGENOUS WISDOM

Taking Hannah's exclamation 'It's the *cows!*' seriously led Bernstein into an exploration of Navajo cosmology, religion and healing. He found that for the Navajo, as for other 'first peoples' who have retained substantial elements of their pre-conquest culture, the kind of experience described by Hannah would be considered entirely normal, hardly worth a comment. He found a world in which everything is connected, where there is no split between mind and body, no boundary between self and other, a world where life is consciously lived within the 'big stories', and where 'men, animals, plants, Mother Earth, the sun, the moon, all physical bodies, have some of this great power or spirit within them which is indwelling intelligent life' (Gorman, in Bernstein, 2005: 128).

Jung had no doubt that a lot of the difficulties which we experience – personal, social and environmental – 'come from losing contact with [our] instincts, the age-old forgotten wisdom stored up in us' (Jung, 1977: 89). He was confirmed in this conviction when he visited the Pueblo Indians in New Mexico in 1925 and again when he travelled in Kenya and Uganda. He acknowledges that before these experiences he 'was still *caught up and imprisoned* in the cultural consciousness of the white man' (Jung, 1961: 248).

Jung regularly returns to the theme that, at depth, we retain the modes of experience characteristic of our remote ancestors. For Jung, we are all 'archaic' or 'primitive' at depth.

> *Every civilized human being, however high his conscious development, is still an archaic man at the deeper levels of the psyche. Just as the human body connects us with the mammals and displays numerous vestiges of early or evolutionary stages going back even to the reptilian age, so the human psyche is a product of evolution which, when followed back to its origins, shows countless archaic traits. (Jung, 1979, CW 10, para. 105)*

121

Jung has a disconcerting tendency to use the word 'primitive' for pre-conquest cultures where we would prefer other words such as 'primal' or 'pre-scientific'. He was aware that the term was problematic and pointed out that:

> *I use the term 'primitive' in the sense of 'primordial' and I do not imply any kind of value judgment. Also, when I speak of a 'message' of a primitive state, I do not necessarily mean that this state will sooner or later come to an end. On the contrary, I see no reason why it should not endure as long as humanity lasts. (Jung, 1979, CW 8, para. 218)*

Our problem, he says, is that in the civilizing process we have learned to 'control' ourselves, and in so doing 'we have increasingly divided off consciousness from the deeper instinctive strata of the human psyche, and even ultimately from the somatic basis of psychic phenomena' (Jung, 1964: 52). We only notice what we are receptive to noticing. Where the borderline personality lacks a filter, the problem for most of us most of the time, is that our filter is too effective. We are not even particularly sensitive to the non-verbal communications we receive from the human beings who surround us. We may be cut off completely from communications from the non-human world.

The notion that indigenous peoples might have retained knowledge of something that we have forgotten is regularly articulated in the deep ecology literature. The founder of the deep ecology movement, Arne Naess, makes this point explicitly (1995). George Sessions and Bill Devall, who introduced Naess' ecophilosophy to North America, expand on the argument in *Deep Ecology* (1985). Others who have looked to indigenous cultures for insights into our proper relationship to the planet include Theodore Roszak, David Suzuki, Andy Fisher and David Abram.

The capacity to 'hear' the language of animals and trees, even the language of place, is but one of the characteristics of people with a functioning and efficient magical consciousness. Anthropological studies, such as A.P. Elkin's (1946) study of Australian Aboriginal 'men of high degree' have shown that such powers, both 'efficient' magic (healing, rainmaking) and 'deficient' sorcery (evil eye, bone-pointing, voodoo) are often concentrated in particular members of a tribe or clan.

For Gebser, exploring the different structures of consciousness which have been dominant at different times and places in human history, it was clear enough that tribal cultures which are able to function within an efficient magical structure of consciousness have access to ways of knowing alien to modern Western rational culture, in which this structure is atrophied. When we come across phenomena such as 'precognition', 'distant sight', 'extrasensory perception' and 'mental telepathy', we try to bring them into the fold of rational science and perform experiments to determine their credibility. Scientific parapsychology is part of the Promethean project of sorting out cause and effect so that we can control and predict these 'anomalous' phenomena. People in cultures blessed with an efficient magical consciousness have no need for this. Such phenomena are regarded as not particularly worthy of mention. Magical consciousness, which in Gebser's words, is characterized by a 'point-related unity in which each and every thing intertwines and is interchangeable' (Gebser, 1949/1986: 48) may not, on its own, be able to deal with the full complexity of the universe, but neither can rational consciousness.

Aboriginal Australians have inhabited their continent for upwards of 50,000 years, living in harmony with a landscape which colonizing Europeans found threatening and which they have taken only 200 years to degrade, possibly terminally. This was not just a question of developing technologies such as 'firestick farming' which enabled them to live without exploiting or destroying the land they lived in. Rather, it was a function of their understanding of their organic connection with 'country'. Deborah Bird Rose suggests that if we want to understand the significance of 'country' in Aboriginal culture we must abandon the subject–object split for a poetics of interactive engagement.

> The inadequacy of subject–object, human–nature structures becomes fully evident in Aboriginal country. Country is not nature, and humans are not the only, or the necessarily privileged, participants. (Rose, 2009: 93)

She writes of 'opening up country to a poetic, ethical, aesthetic engagement' and sensing country:

> as a place of creation and continuity, of current action, of hopes and memories, of people long gone and people here today, and animals, some

gone, some expanding, and all doing their best to engage with life as it presents itself to them. We began to come alive in our understanding of country as a sentient and glimmeringly complex subjectivity. (Rose, 2009: 93)

If we want to understand the kind of relationship which primal cultures have had to the natural world we have to set aside our assumption that we are subjects dealing with objects. We are familiar enough with Martin Buber's distinction between I–It relationships and I–Thou relationships but we may not take him seriously when he suggests that the I–Thou encounter, which acknowledges the subjectivity of the other, extends to the whole of the natural world. Alfred North Whitehead put this notion at the centre of his philosophy, arguing that 'mentality' (interiority, subjectivity) is a fundamental feature of reality. He did not suggest that everything is 'aware' in any conscious way, but he did argue that something akin to 'experience' pervades the whole, alive universe.

Teilhard de Chardin likewise argued that:

It is a fact beyond question that deep within ourselves we can discern, as though through a rent, an 'interior' at the heart of things; and this glimpse is sufficient to force upon us the conviction that in one degree or another this 'interior' exists and has always existed. Since at one particular point in itself, the stuff of the universe has an inner face, we are forced to conclude that in its very structure – that is, in every region of space and time – it has this double aspect ... In all things there is a Within, coextensive with their Without. (De Chardin, 1965: 83)

It makes sense to abandon both the notion that only matter is real and the notion that only mind is real, and talk of 'embodied minds' and 'enminded brains', and even 'an ensouled universe'. Christian de Quincey suggests that the only adequate solution to the 'mind–body problem' is the assumption that matter and consciousness are coextensive and coeternal:

Where materialism, idealism, and dualism fall short as adequate ontologies for a science of consciousness, radical naturalism provides a coherent foundation. The central tenet of radical naturalism is that matter is intrinsically sentient – *it is both subjective and objective ... We*

exist as embodied subjects – as subjective objects *or* feeling matter. *We
know consciousness only as embodied beings, yet we know it not as body
or matter. It is simultaneously our most intimate reality and our deepest
mystery. (De Quincey, 2002: 48)*

De Quincey's *radical naturalism* only sounds radical because
mainstream science has been seduced by materialism. For most of
human history most people have taken it for granted that the universe
is alive. Even in the nineteenth century it was a commonly accepted
notion in science and philosophy. In the early twentieth century
Whitehead developed a comprehensive *theory of everything* which took
into account the findings of physics and proposed that the basic
ingredients of the world are 'moments of experience', that subjectivity
and something akin to experience are a quality of matter. After
Whitehead, the idea became unfashionable for most of the century,
though a significant minority of scientists continued to argue, like the
British geneticist C.H. Waddington (1961), that it is inconceivable
that consciousness could have originated from anything that did not
share something in common with it. The idea of an experiencing
universe is still mocked by die-hard materialists, However, in the past
couple of decades it is once again being taken seriously in both
science (Sheldrake,1990; Birch, 1993; Laszlo, 2004; Lanza, 2009;
Rosenblum & Kuttner, 2006) and philosophy (Mathews, 2003; Griffin,
1989; de Quincey, 2002).

It is no longer particularly controversial to suggest that our physical
selves are continuous with the material universe, that there is no clear
boundary between my body and its environment. It is much more
difficult to be taken seriously if we argue, as Jung did, that our minds
are continuous not only with the collective mind of the species but
with the soul (the *anima mundi*) of the universe.

We might ask why all of this matters when it comes to engaging in
our professional activities. In a sense it does not matter. People carry
on with their professional activities without meditating constantly on
the nature of the cosmos. However, what we do as counsellors and
how we perceive what we are doing depends very much on our notion
of what sort of beings humans are and what sort universe this is, even
if we rarely reflect on it.

Whiteheadians may argue about whether Whitehead's 'philosophy
of organism' is 'pan-psychist' or merely 'pan-experientialist', but the

distinction need not trouble non-philosophers. The essence of Whitehead's position is that if awareness exists anywhere in the universe, e.g. in that part of the universe represented by human beings, it must exist in some form or other 'all the way down to quarks or quanta or whatever may lie beyond' (de Quincey, 2005: 301). This doesn't necessarily mean that rocks know what is going on but, as de Quincey (2002) points out, it is just as unscientific to assume that rocks have no awareness as it is to assume that they can think and feel. Such a belief is based entirely on an assumption about what kind of world this is. Science currently has no way of proving it to be true.

John Collier in *On the Gleaming Way* (1949/1962) cites the Hopi belief that the universe 'is by nature a harmonious, integrated system operating rhythmically according to the principles of justice, and in it the key role is played by man' (p. 102). Not all ecophilosophers would agree that man has a central and indispensable place in the universe, but they are sympathetic to the conviction of the Hopi and many other indigenous peoples that they must participate in certain rituals to maintain the rhythms of the days and the seasons. Such ritual and ceremony is, to quote Dolores LaChapelle, an expression of the wisdom of such cultures that their relationship to the natural world required the whole of their being. The ceremonies of 'first peoples' are 'a sophisticated social and spiritual technology, refined through many thousands of years of experience' that maintained their relationship to the natural world much more successfully than we are able to do' (LaChapelle, 1995: 220).

Native peoples, who pray to the sun, see no essential difference between themselves and other animals, and talk to rocks and trees and ancestors, are not being stupid or ignorant. They are not even being unscientific. They are basing their beliefs on their experience, and behaving accordingly. If we can detach ourselves from the conventional materialistic assumptions about the world (also known as the 'mechanistic paradigm'), we may be prepared to believe something different about rocks and trees. At least we will not be contemptuous of those who do.

To be that self which one truly is

When Rogers took the above line from Kierkegaard and made it the title of a key chapter in *On Becoming a Person* (1961) he did not apparently find the notion of 'the self' problematic. He did not bother defining it. He was more interested in making some generalizations about 'the trends and tendencies which I see as I work with my clients' (Rogers, 1961: 167). He had observed that when clients found the opportunity and courage to authentically be 'themselves' within the safety of the therapeutic relationship they began to move in a specific direction: away from facades, away from 'oughts', away from meeting expectations, away from pleasing others, and toward self-direction, toward process, toward complexity, toward openness to experience, toward acceptance of others, toward trust of self. The client moves 'toward being, knowingly and accepting *me*, the process which he inwardly and actually is' (Rogers, 1961: 175).

Later in this book he writes of the 'actualizing tendency'. When discussing creativity he suggests that it derives from:

> the same tendency which we discover so deeply as a curative force in psychotherapy – man's tendency to actualize himself *[sic]*, to become his potentialities. *By this I mean the directional trend which is evident in all organic and human life – the urge to expand, extend, develop, mature – the tendency to express and activate all the capacities of the organism, or the self. (Rogers, 1961: 351)*

Here we have a clear indication of what Rogers means by the self. He is not confusing the self with the Freudian 'ego', the organizing, decision-making centre of awareness. Rather he is thinking of the human body – mind as an organism, responding 'organismically' to the world. He is suggesting that human beings are not essentially different in kind from other living beings. Along with plants and animals they move towards greater complexity, for there is, in all organic life, a directional tendency, a flow of movement towards fulfilment of life's possibilities.

In his writing about the actualizing tendency in the 1960s Rogers was thinking of the individual human organism being open to experience and fulfilling his or her potentialities. However, by the time he came to write *A Way of Being* (1980) he had thought through the consequences of putting life and creativity at the centre of his notion of what it is to be human. He argues that the actualizing tendency is not just a characteristic of human beings or, indeed, of all organic life, rather it is an attribute of the universe as a whole. There is, he asserts, 'a formative tendency at work in the universe, which can be observed at every level' (Rogers, 1980: 123).

So where is the self in this?

Defining the self appears to have little relevance for the pragmatics of counselling. Rogers was not particularly fussy about how he used the word. When he is being careful about definitions, as in his 1959 paper, he defines the self as a concept, rather than a thing. The self is 'the organized consistent perceptual gestalt consisting of perceptions of the characteristic of the 'I' or 'me'... together with the values attached to these perceptions' (Rogers, 1959: 200). Later, he came to emphasize the fluid nature of the self, understanding that human beings are, as Ivan Ellingham puts it, 'organized fields of evolving processes embedded in a similarly evolving overarching field' (Ellingham, 2009: 2). In describing the last of 'the successive stages by which the individual changes from fixity to flowingness' (Rogers, 1961: 132) Rogers provides a process definition of the self.

> *The self becomes increasingly simply the subjective and reflexive awareness of experiencing. The self is much less frequently a perceived object, and much more frequently something confidently felt in process. (Rogers, 1961: 153)*

In 1961 Rogers was arguing that 'Life, at its best, is a flowing, changing process in which nothing is fixed ... I find I am at my best when I let the flow of my experience carry me, in a direction which appears to be forward, towards goals of which I am but dimly aware' (Rogers, 1961: 27). Emerging individuals move 'from fixity to changingness, from rigid structure to flow, from stasis to process' (Rogers, 1961: 131). Following Rogers, we see ourselves moving from being something called a 'self' who thinks and feels in predictable ways (being determined by all our past moments of experience) to 'living subjectively in the experience, not feeling about it. ... The self, at this moment, is this feeling ... The self is, subjectively, in the existential moment. It is not something one perceives' (Rogers, 1961: 147).

Here he is identifying selfhood with the 'I' rather than the 'me'. The self is not something I 'have'. Rather, it is all that I am in this moment.

Whitehead's way of dealing with the subject–object duality (which includes the distinction between 'I' and 'me') was to suggest that the distinction is a product of time. Subjectivity is always in the present. Objectivity is always in the past. When I see you, or any other 'object', I am always looking into the past, as there is always a time gap between your present moment and my perception of you. When I reflect on who I am, I am also looking into the past, the recollection (accurate or not) of all my past experiences, which I put together and label as 'me'. At the human level I subjectively experience 'me', in each moment, as definite, concrete fact. This momentary experience immediately becomes part of the 'me' which I subjectively experience in the next instant. The subjective *becoming* immediately turns into objective *being*. In the next micro-second a new 'I' does it all again. The drop of experience which is 'I' is a microscopic element in the creative advance of the universe from subjective *becoming* to objective *being*.

With or without Whitehead's direct influence, Rogers came to the same conclusion, that through our actualizing tendency we are involved in something bigger than our individual selves.

> *Thus, when we provide a climate that permits persons to be – whether they are clients, students, workers or persons in a group – we are not involved in a chance event. We are tapping into a tendency which permeates all organic life – a tendency to become all the complexity of which the organism is capable. (Rogers, 1980: 134)*

We need to take seriously Rogers' notion of the formative tendency, and understand ourselves organically, not merely as individual organisms but as cells of a greater organism, the cosmos, so that our growing is not something we do as individuals, but a process through which we participate creatively in the universe's *becoming*. We can take him seriously when he asks us to think of self as process, not as content. To think of self as process means we cannot think ourselves apart from the world. There is one process and our becoming is part of it.

SELF-REALIZATION

When deep ecologists look for a philosophical framework within which to shape their ideas about the place of human beings in the universe, they are likely to find it in Buddhism, or in the Renaissance philosopher Baruch Spinoza. Spinoza rejected Rene Descartes' notion that there are two kinds of substance, matter and spirit, and argued that there is only one being, living nature, of which we are a part. His philosophy was inherited by many of the romantic poets and found its way into twentieth century philosophy through Henri Bergson and Whitehead.

Arne Naess first distinguished 'deep' ecology from 'shallow' ecology in the 1970s. The distinction he made at that time is now the basis for the division between ecopsychology and environmental psychology. Environmental psychology has been shaped by the dualistic, mechanistic, objectivist worldview of modern science which shapes most psychological thinking. Ecopsychologists, however, adopt a very different position, which owes much more to Spinoza than it does to Descartes and Isaac Newton. Where the shallow ecology movement (and environmental psychology) concern themselves with the fight against pollution and resource depletion, and focus on the health and affluence of people in developed countries, the deep ecology movement (and ecopsychology) reject the human-in-environment image completely. Humans do not live in an environment. They are as much part of the total relational field as anything else. Environmental psychologists are interested in the way we treat 'nature'. Ecopsychologists do not distinguish us from nature.

> *The total-field model dissolves not only the human-in-environment concept, but every compact thing-in-milieu concept – except when talking at a superficial or preliminary level of communication. (Naess, 1973: 101)*

In this model humans are not the centre of the universe, or even the most important inhabitants of Earth. This would come as no surprise to most people for most of human history. Taking the long view, the assumption that we are special appears to be a fairly recent one in both religious and philosophical discourse. Some ecophilosophers argue that humans have a special place in the universe because we represent a new phase in cosmic evolution – the universe's awareness of itself. Others are not persuaded.

Naess is clear about where he stands. When he talks about self-realization, he is not talking about individuals becoming all that they can individually become. That is too narrow a notion of self. He is talking about the self-realization of nature, and our limited part in it. For Naess, to identify self-realization with ego indicates a vast underestimation of the human self.

We underestimate ourselves. I emphasize 'self'. We tend to confuse it with the narrow ego.

Human nature is such that with sufficient all-sided maturity we cannot avoid 'identifying' our self with all living beings, beautiful or ugly, big or small, sentient or not. (Naess, 1995: 13)

Naess introduces the notion of the *ecological self*, a necessary broadening and deepening of the notion of self, for:

we may be said to be in, of and for Nature from our very beginning. Society and human relations are important, but our self is richer in its constitutive relations. These relations are not only relations we have to other humans and the human community ... Because of an inescapable process of identification with others, with growing maturity, the self is widened and deepened. We 'see ourselves in others'. Self-realization is hindered if the self-realization of others, with whom we identify, is hindered. (Naess, 1995: 14)

Jung was careful not to confuse the self with the narrow ego. It is conventional in Jungian writing to distinguish the ego (the decision-making centre of consciousness), the self (the whole person) and the Self (the personhood of the cosmos). Like Whitehead and Gebser, Jung was prepared to accept the possibility that the universe is not only alive but has a subjective existence as well as objective existence, that we dwell in mind, rather than contain mind within ourselves.

As I see it, the psyche is a world in which the ego is contained. Maybe there are fishes who believe that they contain the sea. We must rid ourselves of this habitual illusion of ours if we wish to consider metaphysical assertions from the standpoint of psychology. (Jung, 1979, CW 13, para. 75)

Reflecting on the sense of being that he experiences at his Bollingen tower, Jung gives voice to his ecological self.

> *At times I feel as if I am spread out over the landscape and inside things, in the splashing of the waves, in the clouds and the animals that come and go, in the procession of the seasons. There is nothing in the Tower that has not grown into its own form over the decades, nothing with which I am not linked. Here everything has its history, and mine; here is space for the spaceless kingdom of the world's and the psyche's hinterland. (Jung, 1961: 225–6)*

If our identity is connected with the identity of all other beings, then our experience and even our existence depend on theirs. One of the principles of environmental ethics from the deep ecology perspective is that we have no need for a notion of altruism. When we choose to act on behalf of other beings (people, animals, plants, places), rather than on behalf of ourselves, we are simply being who we naturally are, acting for ourselves, for our *self* is a manifestation of the greater self, as is theirs. Jung understood this well.

> *My self is not confined to my body. It extends into all the things I have and all the things around me. Without these things I would not be myself. (Jung, 1977: 202)*

Empathy for other beings is, as Gebser argues, simply an expression of who we are, at our basic, archaic level. The archaic structure of consciousness provides us with no way of distinguishing between self and environment, no way of distinguishing between interior and exterior experience. The magic structure gives us a numinous world in which everything is alive and everything is connected. It is only through the emergence of the mythical structure that we begin to get a sense of ourselves as individuals, and only through the mental structure that we separate ourselves from the world and act upon it. The emergence of the integral structure enables us once again to experience ourselves as one with the universe, to identify with the whole of creation, with the added capacity of being aware of this unity and able to reflect on it. Jung, who claimed to see the suffering of all humankind in each individual, reflected as he neared the end of his life:

This is old age, and a limitation. Yet there is so much that fills me: plants, animals, clouds, day and night, and the eternal in man. The more uncertain I have felt about myself, the more there has grown up in me a feeling of kinship with all things. (Jung, 1961: 359)

This brings us back to the question of the One and the Many. For Jungians, our tendency to see the universe as either unitary or fragmented is archetypal. We find the tension between our sense of unity and our sense of individuality played out in the Greek myths of Mother and Hero (Semele and Dionysos, Maia and Hermes, Themis and Prometheus, Leto and Apollo). Our experience of being isolated individuals doing our best to survive in a difficult world is a real one. So also, if we allow ourselves to acknowledge it, is our experience of being children of the Great Mother, who yearn to experience once again the bliss we once found in her womb.

Writing from the deep ecology perspective, Freya Mathews points out that while organisms are essentially interactive beings, incapable of existing independently of other beings, they do possess a genuine individuality. In the ordinary, atomistic way of thinking the whole consists of the sum of all the independent parts which determine the nature of the whole. However, in the holistic thinking which characterizes deep ecology, the individual parts are what they are – and only *exist* – through their interconnectedness with all the other parts.

Applying this principle of interconnectedness to the human case, it becomes apparent that the individual denoted by 'I' is not constituted merely by a body or a personal ego or consciousness ... But I am also constituted by my ecological relations with the elements of my environment ... I am a holistic element of my native ecosystem, and of any wider wholes under which that ecosystem is subsumed. (Mathews, 1995: 128)

To put it differently, we are all jewels in Indra's net.

For better or worse, counselling theory and practice have emerged from a culture which was embedded in the Hero narrative, and a psychological science which had not yet (unlike physics) challenged the nineteenth century assumption of an atomistic, mechanical universe. If we set aside that narrative and abandon that assumption, counselling theory and practice can take on a different aspect.

CONGRUENT BEINGS

Counselling as a profession is deeply rooted in the individualistic assumptions of twentieth century modernity. The humanistic-existential, psychoanalytical and cognitive behavioural approaches to psychological healing are all based on the assumption that human distress is a matter of individual consciousness. Of course, the most deeply suffering people on the planet do not get to see counsellors. Millions of diseased, starving, exploited, enslaved and abused people exist outside most discussions of the nature of counselling. Yet, even setting that aside and thinking only of that demographic which is the context for professional counselling, we have to challenge the assumption that psychological distress is essentially something that affects us, or even originates in us, as individuals.

The client in distress is not necessarily so because there is something wrong with him. The focus in therapy has conventionally been on the interaction between two individuals, one of whom has entered the relationship because they are experiencing distress through some dysfunction in their awareness or behaviour. People want to talk about relationships that are not working, a job that gives them no satisfaction, a boss who exploits or bullies them, a lack in their lives for which they do not have a name, their grief, pain, alienation or depression. Or they want to talk about experiences which they find painful and which the world around them believes delusional. They feel bad about it, even depressed about feeling depressed, and have a sense that there is something wrong with them. So we listen and help them explore, and trust that through the non-judgmental relationship we offer and the actualizing tendency of which they are barely aware, they will find a way to live more authentically.

The problem with this is that very often the dysfunction is not in them but in the world. People who seek counselling may not be distressed or depressed because they are doing something wrong. It is just as likely that they are distressed or depressed because the world is treating them badly. Not only is there something wrong with the specific social context which is the background to their distress, but there is something amiss in a culture in which such contexts are seen as 'normal'. The cultural world which is the occasion of their suffering is incongruent with the natural world. The individual's distress may be the manifestation of her frustrated sense of who she is, and the wrongness not only of the context in which she lives and works, but perhaps also of her relationship to the natural world. There may be an incongruity in her value system which fills her with unease without taking a form which she can put words to. As Terrance O'Connor points out, it is doubtful that helping people to adjust to a destructive society or a distorted vision of reality is in anybody's interest.

> *We sit in our offices helping parents raise children, divorcees get their bearings, couples find ways to deepen their relationships, while outside the air gets fouler and the ocean's ecosystems break down. In a year's time, if we are successful, the parents and children are doing well, the divorcee is enjoying her independence, the couple has developed a more satisfying relationship. Meanwhile hundreds, perhaps thousands of species, have vanished forever from the earth …*
>
> *We are facing an unparalleled global crisis, a disaster much greater than Hitler, Stalin, or the Khmer Rouge would ever create. What is the meaning of therapy, and what is the responsibility of the therapist in such a world? (O'Connor, 1995: 150)*

Rogers' label for the experience of being 'that self which one truly is' is congruence. When we talk about congruence in conventional person-centred terms we think of it in terms of individual experience – that our experience, awareness and communication are not in conflict with each other. However this perception comes from a kind of false consciousness in which Western culture has been embedded for some centuries. Congruence is more than the integration of experience, awareness and communication in an individual. Congruence goes beyond our individual encapsulated being; it involves our being at one with what we call 'the natural world'. From an ecopsychological perspective it is wrongheaded to talk about human beings and the natural world as though they are separate. What psychology ought to be about is the lived experience of our relationship with the natural world, non-human as well as human. If our relationship with the natural world, experienced in our organismic 'felt sense', is denied to our culturally informed awareness, we are in a state of unacknowledged pathological tension.

Psychological health used to be thought of in terms such as 'strong ego', 'autonomy' and 'internal locus of control'. This is no longer beyond argument. We are more inclined to argue now that maintaining our separateness from others is pathological. We can extend that argument to have 'others' include all organic being. If we stop thinking of 'self' as stopping at our skin, and realize that any boundary we put to our 'self' is an arbitrary one, our experience becomes the experience of 'the whole'. This may not be well represented in our awareness and communication, and we may have no idea why we are stressed, but we are stressed nonetheless. To quote R.D. Laing:

> *Only by the most outrageous violation of ourselves have we achieved our capacity to live in relative adjustment to a civilization driven to its own destruction. (Laing, 1967: 64)*

One of the key influences on Naess and the deep ecology movement was Mahatma Gandhi. Naess found in Gandhi's writing and action an appropriate expression of how we ought to think about the world and act in it. Gandhi's principle of non-violent interaction with others was based, like Naess', on a broad understanding of the self. Like Naess he proclaimed a belief in the essential oneness of all life. For Gandhi, self-realization is self-realization of the whole of the natural world. Violence against the planet, like violence against other people, is violence against ourselves. No wonder we are stressed.

LISTENING TO THE UNIVERSE

What is our experience of the whole? Our experience obviously depends on our perception. In spite of our acknowledgement that our senses sometimes deceive us, we are inclined to think that what we see, hear, touch and smell is exactly what is there – no more, no less. Whitehead suggests that this is too narrow a view. He argues that there are two quite different kinds of perception, which he calls 'presentational immediacy' and 'causal efficacy'. The first of these gives us data from our senses. We see colours and shapes, we feel textures. The second is the direct grasp of reality as we feel it 'in our gut'. This is a very primitive form of perception, and we may not even be aware of what we experience in our bodies. However, it is only when we connect what our conventional senses deliver as a particular set of shapes, colours, smells, sound and textures with what we simultaneously experience viscerally (an experience grounded in all our past experiences), that we can recognize that what we are looking at, listening to, smelling or touching is a human being, an octopus or a table.

Whitehead gave the label 'symbolic reference' to this more sophisticated form of perception, which integrates what our senses detect and what our whole organism connects with, and enables us to relate to a meaningful world. We experience the world in our body through causal efficacy all the time, but only occasionally does it reach our awareness. When psychics or indigenous people show the capacity to 'know' things that could not have been communicated through their senses, we imagine that they have a special talent called 'extrasensory perception'.

Jung was intensely interested in this kind of perception, and called it 'intuition'.

Bernstein's patient Hannah protested that she felt the pain of the cows. She was not saying that she had watched the cows carefully, listened to the sounds they were making, smelled something she interpreted as fear and then identified with them to the extent that she could feel their pain. She simply *knew*. She was claiming a direct felt connection with the cows, which did not have to detour through sight, hearing, smell and interpretation. Her awareness of their pain came through 'causal efficacy', felt immediately without the need for processing. 'Symbolic reference' connected this direct visceral sensation with what she was looking at and gave it meaning: 'It's the *cows*.' In Whitehead's language, Hannah's experience and the cows' experience are the same 'throb of experience' which includes the whole world. Hannah's ecological self includes the cows. It is worth noting that the best approximation of Whitehead's term 'prehension' is 'feeling', that Gebser points to emotion as the specific characteristic of subjectivity in the magic structure of consciousness, and that the phenomenon which we call telepathy is most likely to occur in moments of intense emotion.

Another philosopher with a special interest in perception was Maurice Merleau-Ponty. Taking the obvious point that what we perceive is largely determined by what we expect to perceive, he explored what our experience of the world is when we observe it without taking anything for granted.

In *The Phenomenology of Perception* (1962) Merleau-Ponty argues that if we set aside the assumptions of the mechanical paradigm and just explore our own experience without presuppositions, we find that perception is inherently interactive and participative, an interplay between the perceiver and the perceived. Unfortunately, we have learned to think of perception as an activity that we engage in, something in which we are active and nature is passive. It makes just as much sense (Merleau-Ponty would say *more* sense) to think of ourselves as passive and nature as active. Instead of saying 'I see, touch, hear the tree' we might just as well say 'This tree is communicating with me.' As is this room and this landscape and the stars.

Like Jung and Whitehead, Merleau-Ponty attacks our conventional distinctions between subject and object, between mind and body. We do not experience subjectivity apart from our physical body. We do not experience a disembodied 'I'. In our raw experience there is no evidence of a distinction between animate and inanimate phenomena, no self which is independent of the surrounding world, no split between subject and object, no way of separating our sensations from whatever it is we sense. For Merleau-Ponty, as for Whitehead and Jung, the Earth is alive and is saying something. There is always a non-verbal exchange going on between our flesh and what Merleau-Ponty (1968) calls 'the flesh of the world', a sentient world that we are not 'in' but 'of'.

Merleau-Ponty asserts that 'the flesh we are speaking of is not matter' (1968: 146). In reflecting on this, David Abram points out that our own senses are implicated in everything we sense. There is no 'objective', independent 'thing' that we sense, just as there is no sensing without something to sense. Both are included in 'the flesh'. Things do not exist because we see them, neither do we see them because they independently exist. Perception depends on both sides of the equation. Materialist–objectivist and idealist–subjectivist understandings of reality are both wrongheaded.

> *While both of these views are unstable, each bolsters the other; by bouncing from one to the other – from scientific determinism to spiritual idealism and back again – contemporary discourse easily avoids the possibility that both the perceiving being and the perceived being are* of the same stuff, *that the perceiver and the perceived are interdependent and in some sense even reversible aspects of a common animate element, that is* at once both sensible and sensitive. *(Abram, 1997: 67)*

EXPERIENCING

For Rogers the essence of incongruence is a disconnection between awareness and experience. The process of change, he says, involves a change in the manner of experiencing.

> *The continuum [of change] begins with a fixity in which the individual is very remote from [his] experiencing ... From this remoteness in relation to his experiencing, the individual moves towards the recognition of experiencing as a troubling process going on within him. Experiencing gradually becomes a more accepted inner referent to which he can turn for increasingly accurate meanings. Finally he becomes able to live freely and acceptantly in a fluid process of experiencing, using it comfortably as a major reference for his behavior. (Rogers, 1961: 157)*

In his essay on Ellen West, Rogers comments on the suffering which is a consequence of the tension between our attempts to live up to other people's expectations and our experience – our deep, and maybe inarticulate, sense of who we are, for:

> *the experiencing organism senses one meaning in experience, but the conscious self clings rigidly to another, since that is the way it has found love and acceptance from others. (Rogers, 1980: 165)*

Here Rogers was thinking of the individual trying vainly to live up to 'conditions of worth' imposed by family and social context, conditions which are antagonistic to the 'self' which is trying to actualize. If we take Rogers seriously in his theorizing of the formative tendency and his understanding of 'self' as process, we will realize that the meaning which the organism senses in experience is its identification with all living beings.

Eugene Gendlin writes of the 'life-forward direction': 'A client may feel something stirring inside, where before everything was long numb and dead. We want to notice such a stirring, if it is new and leads to more life' (Gendlin, 1996: 259). Gendlin's focus in this passage is on the stirrings which seem to be purely personal – blocked feelings, for instance, or unacknowledged perceptions. But for an ecopsychologist the 'life-forward direction' goes beyond the purely personal, or rather, the personal goes beyond the purely individual.

In *Radical Ecopsychology* (2002) Andy Fisher acknowledges that this central tenet of ecopsychology – that 'all meaning is grounded in the life process and that we feel in our bodies what is for and against this process' (2002: 63) – is not currently fashionable in conventional psychology. He remarks how:

> *many people are* surprised *to discover on learning to focus that their feelings are so intricate, that they mean something, that their bodies are ordered to spontaneously carry their lives forward ... Focusing is a deliberate way of 'dipping down' into the bodily felt place whence life-forwarding steps of change may come, where our organismic wisdom resides. (Fisher, 2002: 52)*

In Gendlin's philosophy there is a direct relationship between experience and the creation of meaning. When we use the focusing technique to check into the barely acknowledged sensations in our body and allow them to express themselves in images, we are checking into the life process and becoming aware of something that we already know somatically. Even bad feelings, if we acknowledge them, point us in the 'life-forward direction' for 'every bad feeling is potential energy toward a more right way of being if you give it space to move toward its rightness. The very existence of bad feelings within you is evidence that your body knows what is wrong and what is right' (Gendlin, 1981: 76). This 'rightness' or 'wrongness' is not sensed in a body which is a world to itself, independent of its environment. Rather it is a sense of congruence or incongruence with the whole organism of which it is a part.

Gendlin's focusing technique can be applied in the narrowest and broadest contexts. We can check the vague felt sense by which our organism responds to a particular person, issue or context. We can check the felt sense of a group of people which registers their collective organismic response to being together. A counsellor and client can individually or together check the felt sense of their mutual process in the present moment, or they can use felt sense to tune in to each other's process. Or we can ask our body: 'How is it for you down there?' and be aware of the very fuzzy, unclear, vague, felt sense, too faint and subtle to be labelled 'a feeling', of how we are in the world at this moment.

When Merleau-Ponty talks about our being recipients of communication from the natural world, or when Whitehead argues that 'causal efficacy' is prior to 'presentational immediacy', it is felt sense (or not-yet-felt sense) that they are describing. If I let myself be aware of it I can feel in my body the communication which I am receiving from a tree, a landscape or a building. People have relationships with non-human entities all the time. They talk to their animals, their plants, their cars, their computers. They can also 'listen' to them through their felt sense. If they can set aside their assumption that the proper position for human beings is that of mastery over the so-called 'objects' in their world and allow themselves to accept the world and be sensitive to its signals, they will be more in tune with the life process, which, as Gendlin says 'has its own direction' (Gendlin, 1981: 76).

Jung was very aware of the healing power of nature, arguing that natural life is 'the nourishing soil of the soul' (Jung, 1979, CW 8, para. 800). Nowadays we can find a persuasive literature arguing that simply reconnecting with nature is the magical path to wellness (Cohen, 1997; Louv, 2005). It is an idea supported by biologist E.O. Wilson's 'biophilia' argument. Wilson (1984) argues that we have a natural affinity with nature; after millions of years of evolution we are adapted to living in symbiotic relationship with the natural world, not with a constructed, industrial one. Paul Erlich similarly argues that:

> we are as likely to be programmed to a natural habitat of clean air and varied green habitat as any other mammal. To be relaxed and healthy usually means simply allowing our bodies to react in the way for which one hundred million years of evolution has equipped us. (Erlich, in Birch, 1993: 88)

However, we may argue that a more direct approach is required where the disconnection is toxic. Naess, in noting that compassion for others flows naturally if the self is widened through a deepened realism, so that protection of nature is felt and conceived of as protection of ourselves, argues that 'we must find and develop therapies which heal our relations with the widest community, that of all living beings' (Naess, 1995: 29). (He notes that 'If we can conceive of reality or the world we live in as alive in a wide, not easily defined sense, then there will be no non-living beings to care for!')

Many counsellors who bring a person-centred approach to their work will pause from time to time and ask their client to check their felt sense and hopefully discover what is going on beneath the words. Many follow Gendlin's advice and check their own felt sense for the same purpose. In focusing instructions it is conventional to remind clients to wait for a felt sense of 'the whole' of whatever it is they are attending to. It is only a small step to understanding, as Whitehead and Jung did, that the whole of the living planet, indeed the whole of the cosmos, presents itself both to us and through us, that the vague, fuzzy felt sense we tune into is our connection with all living beings and the creative process of the universe.

Jung pointed to dreams as the medium by which the universe speaks to us. Dreams, he says are not merely personal:

> *To concern ourselves with dreams is a way of reflecting on ourselves. It is not our ego-consciousness reflecting on itself; rather it turns its attention to the objective actuality of the dream as a message from the unconscious, unitary soul of humanity. (Jung, 1979, CW 10, para. 318)*

Accordingly, in Jungian dream work there is a step beyond exploring the dream images to grasp the message which is coming from the personal unconscious. The further step involves listening for the message coming from 'the unitary soul of humanity' which, we should note, is not distinct from the unitary soul of the earth.

The counsellor who attends to her clients' attempts to find words for whatever is going on within, will hear not only the clients' intensely personal experience, not only the collective voice of humanity, but the voice of the earth. When she listens to a client's dream or story she hears the client's unconscious self speaking: she also hears the voice of humanity and the voice of the planet, for:

> *Every tear ... can be said to express the sadness and suffering of the universe: the mute anguish of all the oceans, compressed into a single consuming droplet – just as it is equally less than any droplet, merely lachrymose and transitory like the rainfall or the oceans which too could pass away one day if the threatened visitation by fire becomes a reality. (Gebser, 1949/1986: 546)*

Erich Neumann, who was writing *Origins and History of Consciousness* (1954) at the same time and in much the same context as Gebser was writing *The Ever-Present Origin* (1949/1986) and Jung was writing

Modern Man in Search of a Soul (1955), shared with Gebser and Jung the conviction that the divisiveness generated by both tribal and individualistic consciousness was driving humanity to self-destruction. He argued, like Gebser, that we have an urgent need for a transformation of consciousness. He saw the necessary transformation to be in the development of a new sense of self, beyond identification with race, nation, tribe or group.

> *A future humanity will then realize the centre, which the individual experiences as his own self-centre, to be one with humanity's very self. (Neumann, 1954: 418)*

We can forgive Neumann for his species arrogance, since in 1954 it was still relatively possible to ignore the impact that human activity has on the planet of which we are a part. We have no such excuse. We must extend the notion of self-centre to the 'very self' of all living being.

7

ENTWINED AND ENTANGLED

When Carl Rogers came to describe what he had learned in his lifetime about communication, he emphasized the importance of 'realness', 'genuineness' or 'congruence' as a fundamental basis for good communication. In reflecting on this he went on to say:

> *What do I mean by being close to what is going on in me? Let me try to explain what I mean by describing what sometimes occurs in my work as a therapist. Sometimes a feeling 'rises up in me' which seems to have no particular relationship to what is going on. Yet I have learned to accept and trust this feeling in my awareness and to try to communicate it to my client. For example, a client is talking to me and I suddenly feel an image of him as a pleading little boy, folding his hands in supplication, saying, 'Please let me have this, please let me have this.' I have learnt that if I can be real in the relationship with him and express this feeling that has occurred in me, it is very likely to strike some deep note in him and advance our relationship. (Rogers, 1980: 15)*

This statement would come as no surprise to Jean Gebser, who saw such 'spaceless and timeless phenomena' as arising 'from the vegetative intertwining of all living things ... in the egoless magic sphere of every human being' (Gebser, 1949/1986: 49). He would have seen it as predictable that such an intuition should have emerged as feeling and image, because our magical connection with others of our species and tribe is pre-lingual. It would come as no surprise to Carl Jung, who argued that intuition is a 'function of the psyche' that is just as reliable as sensation. That Rogers could 'feel an image' would come as no surprise to Eugene Gendlin or to Maurice Merleau-Ponty, who argued that somatic experience is the basis of language, that our bodies experience what we want to say before ever we find the words or other symbols to express it. It would certainly come as no surprise to Alfred North Whitehead, who argued that it is only through 'the fallacy of simple location' that we would assume that communication between Rogers and his client has to pass through the space between them and then through their eyes and ears before it reaches their awareness.

They would not be surprised, either, by Rogers' claim that his intuitions are sometimes 'a step ahead' of his client's awareness:

> *What I wish is to be by her side, occasionally falling a step behind, occasionally a step ahead when I see more clearly the path we are on, and only taking a leap when guided by my intuition. (Rogers, 1980: 27)*

INTUITION

Rogers, at the end of his life, was convinced that the 'next great frontier of learning' is 'the area of the intuitive, the psychic, the vast inner space that looms before us ... the area that currently seems illogical and irrational' (Rogers, 1980: 312). He imagined intuition to be of the same nature as parapsychological or 'psi' phenomena, and to be most manifest when our whole organism is 'in tune with the pulse of the world' (Rogers, 1980: 313).

Rogers did not write a great deal about intuition. However, in his later writing he acknowledged its importance and professed that: 'We need ... to learn more about our intuitive abilities, our capacity for sensing with our whole organism' (Rogers, 1980: 313). This is as close as he came to providing a definition of intuition.

Defining intuition is not as simple as it might seem. However, after surveying the history of attempts since Aristotle to describe and theorize intuition, Noddings and Shore (1984) are able to come to the following conclusion:

> *Intuition is that function that contacts objects directly in phenomena. This direct contact yields something we might call 'knowledge' in that it guides our actions and is precipitated by our own quest for meaning. As we shall see, some things that are intuitive, for example, feelings in others, may be represented first and most directly to the dynamic faculty, thereby inducing an 'I must do something!' response. We might call this form of representation 'intuitive feeling'. When the intuitive representation is*

created primarily for cognition (but, of course, a report also goes to Will)
we may properly refer to that which guides us as 'intuitive knowledge'.
(Noddings & Shore, 1984: 57)

Tony Bastick (1982) discusses at length the development of the notion
of intuition in both philosophy and psychology, noting that intuition
tends to be defined in terms of empathy and vice versa, and that there
is a good deal of consensus (and research confirmation) around the
association of intuition with both empathy and creativity. He points in
particular to the kinesthetic dimension of intuition. He refers to the
process of simultaneously empathizing and projecting one's feeling
in a temporary identification as 'empathic projection', which, he
suggests, is 'a two-way channel of empathy and projection which allows
the person to use his [sic] body as an intuitive processor' (Bastick,
1982: 280). He extends the notion of empathy/intuition to include
identification not only with persons but with objects. He argues that
intuition transcends the subject/object split, citing the Buddhist
philosopher Suzuki's assertion that: 'The act of intuition is considered
complete when a state of identification takes place between the object
and the subject' (Bastick, 1982: 280).

Jung argued that intuition is a basic psychological function, in
contradistinction to sensation as an alternative mode of perception.
However, his discussion of intuition was largely ignored outside the
Jungian subculture until Isabel Myers found a way of quantifying it as
a dimension of psychological type. Jung's writing about intuition is
fairly tentative, and sometimes confusing. His interest is in describing
the pathology of patients who are dominated by their intuition, rather
than in imagining how a therapist may use intuition in assisting the
patient. He did not explore the implications of his thinking for what
goes on within the therapeutic interaction. Nevertheless he provides
us with some ideas which are worth exploring in this context. Intuition,
says Jung,

is that psychological function which translates perceptions in an
unconscious way. Everything, whether outer or inner objects or their
associations, can be the object of this perception. Intuition has this peculiar
quality: it is neither sensation, nor feeling, nor intellectual conclusion,
although it may appear in any of these forms. Through intuition, any
one content is presented as a complete whole without our being able to

explain or discover in what way this content has been arrived at. Intuition is a kind of instinctive apprehension, irrespective of the nature of its contents. (Jung, 1953: 568)

Jung distinguishes between *subjective* intuition (a perception of unconscious psychic facts whose origin is subjective) and *objective* intuition (a perception of facts which depend upon the 'subliminal perceptions of the object'). He distinguishes between *concrete* intuition, concerned with 'the actuality of things', and *abstract* intuition which focuses on ideas. He also distinguishes between *introverted* and *extraverted* intuition.

Intuition, for Jung, is 'a characteristic of infantile and primitive psychology' (Jung, 1953: 569). We should remember that Jung never uses these words in a pejorative sense. Rather, he is suggesting that it is the way 'archaic man' experienced the world, and is still a basic function in the way we experience the world, more basic than the conscious thinking and feeling which characterize the later development of both the individual and the species. Jung acknowledges that his thinking has been influenced by Baruch Spinoza and Henri Bergson, both of whom actually considered intuitive cognition to be the highest form of knowing.

The essence of Jung's understanding of intuition is, first, that it is one of our two ways of perceiving the world and, second, that it is an unconscious process, grounded in 'the inherited foundations of the unconscious mind' (Jung, 1953: 507). We can add to this that where sensation experiences the world's fragments, intuition experiences the world as an organic whole.

Conventional writing about intuition takes the view that intuition involves the unconscious processing of sensory information. We perceive things without knowing that we are perceiving them. These subliminal perceptions are processed unconsciously, and finally we arrive at a conclusion without knowing how we arrived at it. We 'just know'. This is Jung's *objective* intuition. However, Jung goes further. We also experience *subjective* intuitions, without sensory input. We access understandings held within the psyche but not previously available to our conscious awareness. And Jung is convinced that not everything in our unconscious gets there via the senses. In this regard, Guy Claxton (1998) points out that intuitions are not sitting in our unconscious waiting to be accessed but are rather created by our unconscious when we are receptive to their emergence.

One of the key features of intuition is its immediacy. The conventional way of talking about perception is to imagine that our senses collect data which is organized in our brains into a representation of the object that we perceive. We then become aware of that representation. That is not how Jung understands the kind of perception that he calls subjective intuition. For Jung it became increasingly clear that we sometimes experience mental and physical events which are meaningfully connected, independently of time and space. Conventional notions of causality do not seem to apply to them. In an attempt at explaining this phenomenon, Jung suggested that there is an 'acausal connecting principle' which he called synchronicity. Arguing that when two events (mental or physical) occur simultaneously without any possibility of communication, yet are meaningfully connected, there is clearly something at work other than a cause and effect relationship constrained by time and space. Jung associated his original reflections on this with his dinner conversations with Albert Einstein when the latter was living in Zurich (1909–1912).

> These were the very early days when Einstein was developing his theory of relativity. He tried to instil into us the elements of it, more or less successfully. As non-mathematicians we psychiatrists had difficulty in following his argument. Even so, I understood enough to form a powerful impression of him. It was above all the simplicity and directness of his genius as a thinker that impressed me mightily and exerted a lasting influence on my own intellectual work. It was Einstein who first started me off thinking about the possible relativity of time as well as space, and their psychic conditionality. More than 30 years later this stimulus led to my relation with the physicist Professor W. Pauli and to my thesis of psychic synchronicity. (Jung, 1976: 108)

For Jung, like Rogers, the experience of intuition seemed to be related to the experience of psi phenomena like telepathy and precognition. It is an idea taken up by Frances Vaughan, for whom these are sub-categories of the much wider category of intuitive experience.

> Intuitive experiences include, but are by no means limited to, mystical insights into the nature of reality. Experiences which are commonly called intuitive also include discovery and invention in science, inspiration in art, creative problem solving, assertion of patterns and possibilities,

extrasensory perception, clairvoyance, telepathy, precognition, retrocognition, feelings of attraction and rejection, picking up 'vibes', knowing or perceiving through the body rather than the rational mind, hunches, and premonitions. (Vaughan, 1979: 57)

PSI ANYONE?

In his later thinking about empathy Rogers includes the sense of direct, intuitive knowing, and a sense that he and his client are elements of a greater whole.

When I am at my best, as a group facilitator or as a therapist, I discover another characteristic. I find that when I am closest to my inner, intuitive self, when I am somehow in touch with the unknown in me, when perhaps I am in a state of slightly altered consciousness in the relationship, then whatever I do seems to be full of healing ... At those moments it seems that my inner spirit has reached out and touched the inner spirit of the other. Our relationship transcends itself and becomes a part of something larger. Profound growth and healing and energy are present. (Rogers, 1980: 129)

Rogers shows here his readiness to think beyond conventional notions of communication. Not all counsellors of a person-centred persuasion are prepared to go as far as he did in re-thinking the nature of the therapist–client connection. Rogers was adequately convinced that parapsychological science had demonstrated the existence of such phenomena as telepathy, precognition and remote viewing, and had provided evidence that 'most people can discover or develop such abilities in themselves' (Rogers, 1980: 344). This comment comes in the context of his observation that there was a gradual transformation of consciousness in the late twentieth century, as does his observation that 'there is an increased respect for and use of intuition as a powerful tool' (Rogers, 1980: 344).

Dean Radin in *The Conscious Universe* (1997) and *Entangled Minds* (2006) has presented ample experimental evidence for the reality of such 'psi' phenomena as telepathy, precognition, remote viewing, psychokinesis, extrasensory perception, healing at a distance and the feeling of being stared at. Side by side with the laboratory studies enumerated by Radin, we have a mountain of documented anecdotal evidence of such phenomena. Promethean science has been hard at work seeking to give credibility to phenomena which seem to resist mechanical measurement and theories of cause and effect. Promethean science has been much better at developing technologies which have enabled us to communicate efficiently and reliably at a distance. For much of our communication our intuitive capacities are now 'surplus to requirements'. Unfortunately, this has led us to neglect them, and they have atrophied for lack of use.

We know from contemporary neuroscience that even without conscious or unconscious neglect of our capacities we become aware of only a fraction of the information which reaches our organism. Studies of perception have shown that by the time we become aware of something, it has passed through a series of stages of selection and interpretation by which a great deal of the information is excluded. This is partly because our capacity to process information is limited and partly because we consciously or unconsciously exercise control over what we want to pay attention to. However, the information does reach our organism and even if it is 'selected out' part way through the processing, it still registers in our bodies (see Bowlby, 1988: 112*ff*). We may not let our brains process it into awareness, but our gut or our liver may have to deal with it.

Neuroscience also points to the role of the limbic system in intuitive or telepathic communication. Haule (2011) argues that the limbic system was designed by evolution for immediate life or death emotional connections, and

> *it often plays an essential role in spontaneous occurrences of telepathy. It is surely the reason that matters of life and death are so frequently the message delivered in such events. Limbic emotion is the main component in human–human (or, indeed, mammal–mammal) entanglement. (Haule, 2011, vol 2: 200)*

By the time Rogers became interested in psychic phenomena he had shifted his focus from investigating the one-to-one therapeutic interaction to describing a person-centred 'way of being' and developing a picture of the 'person of tomorrow'. Nevertheless, his acknowledgement of a broader role for such phenomena as intuition and telepathy in communication leads us to reflect on the relevance this has for counselling and, more broadly, for all human relationships. If we accept Rogers' proposition that 'full human functioning' involves 'getting back to basic sensory and visceral experience' (Rogers, 1961: 103) and being 'able to live freely and acceptantly in a fluid process of experiencing' (Rogers, 1961: 157), we have to accept the implication that, as Ervin Laszlo puts it:

> *Healthy and moral behaviour presupposes openness not only to the full range of information reaching the individual through the senses, but openness also to the subtle intuition of interpersonal, social, and ecological ties that in-form the subconscious or conscious mind, and the willingness to adopt the coherence-enhancing behaviours that are consistent with them. (Laszlo, 2003: 114)*

Rogers argues that visceral experience is grounded in 'subception', a phenomenon that is more usually termed 'subliminal perception'. Mentality and symbolization, for him as for Gendlin, begin in our 'gut experience'. Jung suggests that subliminal perception may be responsible for psi experiences, citing, for example, premonitions and the sense of a ghostly presence. However, Jung also suggests that occurrences of psi phenomena, like occurrences of intuition, represent the manifestation of an archetype, and, accordingly, are not constrained by time, space and individual personality.

> *Because of its ubiquity, the archetype can by its very nature manifest itself not only in the individual concerned but in another person or even in several people at once – for instance, in parallel dreams, the 'transmission' of which should be regarded more as a psi phenomenon than anything else. (Jung, 1976, vol 2: 542)*

The quotation marks around 'transmission' indicate that Jung does not want us to take the word literally. He is not suggesting that dreams pass from one person to another but rather that they occur in both people simultaneously. It was this kind of phenomenon that led him to develop his theory of synchronicity and pursue the metaphysical question: 'How does it come that even inanimate objects are capable of behaving as if they were acquainted with my thoughts?' (Jung, 1976, vol 2: 344). He suggested that there must be 'an interconnection or unity of causally unrelated events' and accordingly there must be 'a unitary aspect of being which can very well be described as the *unus mundus*' (Jung, 1954: 464). In a letter to J.B. Rhine, whose work in parapsychological research impressed him greatly, and whose empirical findings influenced his thinking about synchronicity, he writes:

> *Viewed from a psychological standpoint, extrasensory perception appears as a manifestation of the collective unconscious. This particular psyche behaves as if it were* one *and not as if it were split up into many individuals. It is* non-personal. *(I call it the 'objective psyche'). It is the same everywhere and at all times ... As it is not limited to the person, it is also not limited to the body. It manifests itself therefore not only in human beings but at the same time in animals and even in physical circumstances ... I call these latter phenomena the synchronicity of archetypal events. (Jung, 1976, vol 1: 394)*

Like Rogers, Jung saw the increasing acceptance of parapsychology as an indication of a shift in the consciousness of twentieth century, over-civilized humans. For Jung, however, as for Gebser, it is not a new development but a re-acknowledgement of capacities which had been lost through the overvaluation of rational consciousness in European civilization since the Enlightenment.

What we call 'psychic' capacities belong to what Jung calls the 'archaic man' within us. Similarly, in Gebser's understanding they are grounded in our basic nature, in which self and other are not differentiated, and emerge into awareness with the magic structure of consciousness. We may speculate on how and why we have lost the use of them, and whether, indeed, Rogers is correct in claiming that most of us can discover and develop them. Yet there is evidence enough that such capacities belonging to the magical structure of consciousness still find specific expression both in indigenous cultures that have retained an efficient magical structure and in specific individuals who, through either 'gift' or training, are sensitive to inner signals which, for most of us, are outside our awareness' (see Van de Castle, 1977; Haule, 2011). Moreover, there is evidence that some animals are better able to use these capacities than humans (Van de Castle, 1977; Haule 2011; Sheldrake, 2000, 2003). It is not surprising that it is notoriously difficult to repeat demonstrations of remote viewing and telepathy in the laboratory. They are most likely to occur when the 'sender' or 'receiver' is experiencing intense emotion. Unfortunately, the most likely emotion experienced in repeated laboratory trials is boredom.

To quote systems theorist Ervin Laszlo, we are not condemned to 'view the world through five slits in the tower' for:

> *by entering altered states of consciousness in which everyday rationality does not filter out what we can apprehend, we can open the roof to the sky. We access a broad range of information that links us to other people, to nature, and to the universe. (Laszlo, 2004: 116)*

Gendlin, whose theory of perception is strongly influenced by Maurice Merleau-Ponty, uses a similar image when he asserts that:

> *[our bodies] interact as bodies, not just through what comes with the five senses. Our bodies don't lurk behind the five peepholes of perception. (Gendlin, 1992: 344)*

There are numerous psychiatrists and psychotherapists who help patients or clients to gain access to these capacities by inducing in them in an altered state of consciousness, through trance, meditation, ritual, suggestion or breathing techniques, and there are countless healers in many cultures who have used drumming, chanting or chemical means to achieve the same end. Ralph Metzner, in *Green Psychology* (1999), notes how psychoactive plant medicines such as coca and psilocybin, which have had a sacramental, consciousness-expanding function in traditional cultures, have been adopted by their European colonizers as recreational drugs, commodified, abused and finally criminalized. Similarly, some synthetic consciousness-altering drugs such as LSD and ecstasy have shown some promise as aids to psychiatric healing, but have been commodified as recreational drugs, abused and subsequently prohibited.

It seems clear from research on 'anomalous' psychological phenomena that they do not depend on the ingestion of mind-altering substances. There are technologies such as Stanislaus Grof's 'holotropic breathing' which seem to facilitate 'non-ordinary' psychological experiences. Experimental research on psi phenomena has found them much more likely to occur when the dominant brainwaves of the 'receiver' are not the beta waves of our 'thinking' state, but the slower alpha, theta and delta waves characteristic of meditation, trance, dreaming and the 'hypnogogic' state between sleep and dreaming. They also occur more readily where the subject is in a state of sensory deprivation, as in 'ganzfeld' experiments (Radin, 1997, 2006). These findings parallel Rogers' observation that for him intuition is most in evidence when he is in a 'slightly altered' state of consciousness. It is an observation that has been reiterated in discussions of how to 'awaken' intuition. Both thinking and sensory stimulation appear to inhibit intuition. A meditative, calm, still, unfocused, open, receptive state of mind, even the dreaming state, seems to facilitate it (see Reik, 1948; Assagioli, 1970; Vaughan, 1979; Noddings & Shore, 1984; Charles, 2004; Orloff, 2010; Haule, 2011).

Wordsworth was reflecting on a similar insight about the circumstances in which our deep knowing becomes available to us when he wrote, in *Tintern Abbey*, of

> *that blessed mood,*
> *In which the burthen of the mystery,*
> *In which the heavy and the weary weight*
> *Of all this unintelligible world,*
> *Is lightened: – that serene and blessed mood,*
> *In which the affections gently lead us on, –*
> *Until, the breath of this corporeal frame*
> *And even the motion of our human blood*
> *Almost suspended, we are laid asleep*
> *In body, and become a living soul:*
> *While with an eye made quiet by the power*
> *Of harmony, and the deep power of joy,*
> *We see into the life of things.*

Telepathic dreams and shared dreams are not uncommon in therapy. Sometimes the client's dream reflects something which is going on in the therapist's life; sometimes the therapist's dream reflects the client's experience. Actually, shared dreams are common enough outside of therapy, especially among participants in an intensive group experience. Gordon Lawrence (2005) has done much to normalize this experience through his work on social dreaming. The phenomena of telepathic communication and remote viewing while in a dream state have been extensively researched (Ullman, 2003). In seeking an explanation for such phenomena, Montague Ullman calls on physicist

David Bohm's (1980) notion of the 'implicate order' – a seamless ground of interconnectedness out of which the experience we refer to as 'reality' (and which Bohm calls the 'explicate order') emerges moment by moment. Ullman suggests that the imagistic mode of the dream is closer to the implicate order than the discursive mode of waking consciousness. He argues, moreover, that:

> *the affective scanning that takes place while dreaming can, on occasion, bridge a spatial gap and provide us with information independent of any known communication channel. Emotional contiguity, under conditions we know very little about, appears capable of integrating transpersonal as well as personal content into the dream. Anecdotal accounts have for a long time pointed in this direction and the circumstances under which they occur strongly suggest that in matters of life and death the vigilant scanning of one's emotional environment reaches out across spatial boundaries in a manner that has yet to be explained. (Ullman, 2003: 41)*

When Freud and Jung were developing and publicizing their ideas at the beginning of the twentieth century, highly reputable psychologists and psychiatrists, such as William James, F.W.H. Myers and Pierre Janet were taking psi phenomena very seriously indeed and exploring their implications for mental health. Interest in these phenomena was particularly focused on their association with psychopathology. Freud himself seems to have had no doubt that unconscious telepathic communication was often a factor in psychoanalysis – for example in transference and counter-transference. However, his biographer, Ernest Jones, warned him not to say such things publicly as it might threaten his credibility (see Eshel, 2006). Jung, on the other hand, had no hesitation in recounting his own experiences of paranormal experiences. In the Swiss village in which he grew up, such experiences were taken for granted, and he had plenty of firsthand experience to confirm his impression that they were not delusional and to prompt his attempt to develop a theory (synchronicity) which could go some way to explaining them.

There is plenty of clinical evidence for the impact of psi phenomena in psychiatry and psychoanalysis (see Ullman, 1979, 1986; Eshel, 2006) which is variously theorized. Ullman cites Ehrenwald's (1955) theory that psi is an archaic or primitive faculty that is dominant in the early mother–child symbiotic relationship, is gradually submerged as the infant learns to adapt to external forces, and emerges only occasionally in later life in special circumstances (such as stress, trauma, danger or intense emotion). There are echoes here of Jung's view that intuition is 'a characteristic of infantile and primitive psychology', and Gebser's description of archaic and magical consciousness. In times of trauma, according to Ehrenwald, we may experience a failure of the mechanism which generally filters out 'heteropsychic influences' and enables us to retain our sense of intactness and identity.

Jung warns us that 'parapsychology plays a subtle part in psychology because it lurks everywhere behind the surface of things' (1976, vol 1: 378). We can argue like Ullman (1979) and Bernstein (2005) that psychotherapists need to be open and sensitive to the occurrence of such phenomena if they are to be of assistance to their clients, not only because these experiences have an impact on the relationship and the process of therapy – especially through transference and counter-transference phenomena (in which the unconscious of the client communicates directly with the unconscious of the therapist) – but because their clients may fear that what they have experienced as valid is of necessity pathological, and may be afraid to talk about it. We can argue further that therapists need to be sensitive to bodily sensations and images that arise in themselves when they are working with a client, because they may be 'transmissions' from their client, even in the client's absence. They need to acknowledge that their client is communicating with them in three ways: through words and images which are immediately present to their awareness; through non-verbal sensory information (facial expression, gesture, breathing patterns, bodily odour) which may or may not reach their awareness; and through direct, immediate, 'synchronistic' connection.

Until fairly recently, interest in psi phenomena and their implications for psychotherapy focused almost entirely on the experience (usually pathological) of the client and how the therapist might deal with it. In the *Diagnostic and Statistical Manual of Mental Disorders* (*IV-TR*) (American Psychiatric Association, 2000) 'clairvoyance' is listed as a symptom of psychosis. The notion that the therapist might be experiencing telepathic communication, intuitive impressions of the client's world, visual images or precognitive dreams has not entered much into the discussion. For instance, Ullman's

(2003) observations of dream telepathy in psychotherapy focus on the occurrence of such phenomena in people with mental illness of one kind or another, especially in patients who are 'teetering on the brink but not yet over on the psychotic side' (Ullman, 2003: 42). However, like Ehrenwald, he acknowledges that there are people who are able to accommodate with reasonable comfort to 'heteropsychic influences'. It is only because of an increasing interest in intuition that we are beginning to see psi phenomena being taken into consideration in observations of the therapeutic interaction. However, those therapists who discuss such experiences have been careful about their language, tending to use the word 'intuition' to cover diverse 'non-ordinary' experiences (Reik, 1948; Charles, 2004; Orloff, 2010).

In *A Way of Being* (1980), Rogers demonstrates that he does not experience any discomfort with 'heteropsychic influences' either in himself or others. He makes positive references to altered states of consciousness, telepathic communication, remote viewing, precognitive dreams and mystical experiences. He writes about the power of intuition, the 'almost telepathic knowledge' of each other's process that staff have experienced in workshops (Rogers, 1980: 188). He notes the emergence of a new level of consciousness, suggesting that 'there is alongside the obviously destructive forces on our planet, a growing current that will lead to a new level of human awareness' characterized by 'the recognition of undeveloped psychic powers within each individual; the mysterious, unspoken communication that is so evident in our groups' (Rogers, 1980: 204). He asks: 'Could it be that our Western culture has forgotten something [so-called primitive tribes] know?' (Rogers, 1980: 313). He is clearly impressed by Carlos Castenada's (1968, 1971) accounts of life with Don Juan and by the research of Lawrence LeShan (1974/2003). Of the latter he writes:

> *He shows the astonishingly close relationship of the person 'sensitive' to paranormal phenomena, the mystic of all periods, and surprisingly enough, the modern theoretical physicist. A reality in which time and space have vanished, a world in which we cannot live, but whose laws we can learn and perceive. A reality that is based not on our senses but on our inner perceptions, is common to all of these. (Rogers, 1980: 254)*

Those who do not want to take Rogers seriously when he reflects on such things may suggest that being impressed by the assertions of

Castenada and LeShan indicates a tendency to be seduced by sloppy, romantic, New Age ideas. However, when Rogers wants to establish the credibility of such ideas he goes to physicist Fritjof Capra and chemist Ilya Prigogine for confirmation:

> *Thus, from theoretical physics and chemistry comes some confirmation of the validity of experiences that are transcendent, indescribable, unexpected, transformational – the sort of phenomena that I and my colleagues have observed and felt as concomitants of the person-centred approach. (Rogers, 1980: 132)*

Rogers may have been remiss in overlooking the evidence that psi experiences, including so-called 'mystical' experiences, may sometimes be regressive or indicative of pathology, rather than signs of the emergence of a higher level of consciousness. By contrast, Gebser was careful to point out the difference between the different structures of consciousness through which we experience the world and the distinction between 'efficient' and 'deficient' structures. Our archaic mind gives us undifferentiated 'unity consciousness' – and leaves us under the control of our instinctive reactions to our environment. Our magic mind enables both intuition and delusion, both magic and sorcery. Our mythical mind embeds us either in a tribal narrative where such phenomena are normal or in a tribal narrative where such phenomena are impossible. Our mental mind can reflect on such experiences and decide whether they represent reality or illusion. The integral consciousness which emerges from these more primitive structures enables us to reflect not just on what we know but on our limited way of knowing it, to be receptive to the transparency of the cosmos in all its manifestations. The unity consciousness of the mystic is different from the 'participation mystique' of archaic humans who had not yet developed egoic (mental) consciousness. It also needs to be distinguished from the 'oceanic feeling' that Freud argued is a regression to our infantile consciousness – before we learned to separate ourselves from the external world. Integral mind incorporates archaic, mythical, magical and mental mind into a new kind of mind in which we experience both unity with 'all that is' and our own individuality within it.

Superficially, mystical experiences may be difficult to distinguish from narcissistic, grandiose, hallucinatory visions, whether spontaneous or drug induced. Ken Wilber (1983), in describing what he calls 'the pre/trans fallacy', points out how it is our worldview that leads us either to mistake transpersonal, ego-transcendent (integral) experiences for regressive, pre-egoic (archaic/magical) experiences or vice versa. Wilber argues that Freud made the first mistake. New Age and transpersonal therapists have a tendency to make the second.

BEING CONNECTED

In the Promethean vision of the universe which shapes most psychology and which, indeed, shaped Freud's and Jung's early understandings of psychology and pathology, the universe is composed of 'things' which act on each other in various ways, a universe in which human beings can ignore the gods and take charge for themselves. In such a universe it is difficult to get away from the notion that causes must come before effects. Even perception is understood as an action with consequences. We look, and therefore we see. We listen, and therefore we hear. We touch, and therefore we feel. Talking about an 'acausal' principle, as Jung does, is not a very satisfactory way of dealing with evidence from physics and elsewhere that something besides cause and effect is at work. Jung's own intuition gave him the insight that thinking of synchronicity in terms of individual, one-to-one, 'acausal' connections was wrong-headed. In the *unus mundus* there are ultimately no individuals, and 'everything that is stated or manifested by the psyche is an expression of the nature of things, whereof man is a part' (Jung, 1976, vol 2: 439). In commenting on Jung's theory of synchronicity, Gebser takes him to task for using the term 'acausal'. Synchronicitous events, he says, are not 'acausal' but 'pre-causal'. They belong to the 'natural relationality' of the magic structure.

> *Events not comprehensible causally belong to the magic realm and are pre-rational phenomena. Acausal events, by contrast, being free of causation, are arational by nature and as such cannot be experienced vitally ... They are perceived if at all only aperspectivally. Viewed in this light, Jung's concept of synchronicity has nothing in common with acausality and arationality, although it brings to our awareness the reality of pre-rational and pre-causal phenomena; and therein lies its merit. (Gebser, 1949/1986: 400)*

In the universe as Whitehead understood it, there is no need for an alternative principle to explain how events are mysteriously connected. Connection is an aspect of their being. We ourselves are events, and connection is an aspect of our being. There is no existence outside of relationship. Our experienced connection to another person (or to a tree or a rock or a galaxy, for that matter) is part of who we are and part of who they are. We participate directly in 'the other'.

The experience of 'the other' may or may not reach our awareness. For instance, Alison Talbot (1997), in her study of therapists' somatic experience in counselling, found that some therapists were happy to acknowledge that they regularly experience in their own bodies something that is integrally connected with the inner state of the client. They just do not talk about it much. Bastick (1982) refers to experiments which have measured physiological arousal during the intuitive process and concludes that it is a 'whole body' experience. The findings of research on psi phenomena are even more striking. The phenomenon (e.g. telepathic communication, remote staring and remote healing) may register in the body of the 'receiver' even when it does not reach the receiver's awareness (Sheldrake, 2003; Radin, 1997, 2006). Similarly, it is common enough for therapists to receive, as Rogers did, an image which turns out to be related to client issues which have not been verbalized, and of which the counsellor has been quite unaware (see Charles, 2004: 204).

ENTANGLEMENT

Ervin Laszlo, a key figure in the development of systems theory, has spent a great part of his life attempting to develop an understanding of how the world works. He found in Whitehead's process philosophy, in which everything both 'is' and 'becomes', a good starting point, but was not satisfied that Whitehead's philosophy adequately explained how the universe as a whole came to 'be' and 'become'. He turned to Ludwig von Bertalanffy's general systems theory, and collaborated with Bertalanffy in the development of what they jointly called 'systems philosophy'. He was still not satisfied, because he needed a way of explaining how systems change and evolve. This he found in Ilya Prigogine's theory of dissipative structures. The universe, he concluded, is 'an evolving thermodynamically open system' (Laszlo,

2004: 164). This conclusion would be purely academic for those of us outside the field of physics, chemistry and biology, were it not for the fact that Laszlo's theory purports to be a 'theory of everything', and has been applied to such issues as international relations and the evolution of human consciousness and values.

As Gebser did more than half a century ago, Laszlo has gone to the cutting-edge sciences for evidence of the 'crucial feature of the emerging worldview', which is:

> *the revolutionary discovery that at the roots of reality there is not just matter and energy, but also a more subtle but equally fundamental factor, one that we can best describe as active and effective in-formation. (Laszlo, 2004: 3)*

Erwin Schrodinger called this factor 'entanglement'. Einstein had stated that he was not prepared to believe in 'spooky actions at a distance' which seemed to be an aspect of the world described by quantum theory. Schrodinger's response was to assert that the phenomenon of 'entanglement' was central to the theory, stating that 'I would not call that *one* but rather *the* characteristic trait of quantum mechanics' (in Aczel, 2003: 70). Entanglement, for Schrodinger, is what happens when two independent systems are brought together and then separated again. They do not return to what they were before but remain 'entangled'. Such connections operate outside time and are independent of space. As Radin puts it, the connections that can be demonstrated in subatomic physics:

> *imply that at very deep levels the separations we see between ordinary isolated objects, are, in a sense, illusions created by our very limited perceptions. The bottom line is that physical reality is connected in ways we're just beginning to understand. (Radin, 2006: 16)*

Laszlo argues that it is 'in-formation' (a term, borrowed from physicist David Bohm, which implies the emergence of form) that links everything in the universe, atoms as well as galaxies, and bodies as well as minds. In *Science and the Akashic Field* (2004) and *The Connectivity Hypothesis* (2003) Laszlo explains how 'in-formation' connects everything to everything else and governs the evolution of the universe's basic elements into complex systems. The universe that contemporary science is exploring is not composed of fragments connected through cause–effect relationships, but is entirely coherent – a single indivisible unity. Laszlo's theorizing about what kind of universe we inhabit is shaped by the current findings of the physical sciences. Nevertheless his conclusions are a reiteration of what was intuitively known to many ancient cultures, stated by many philosophers, ancient, medieval and modern. Since the Enlightenment it has been a minority view, but this is rapidly changing. The world we know from quantum physics is one in which mind is totally entangled.

Gendlin and Lemke (Gendlin & Lemke, 1983) point to the direct connection between the philosophy which he articulates in *Experiencing and the Creation of Meaning* (1962) (and which is operationalized in experiential focusing) and a quantum theory which abandons notions of ultimate space and time. They take the Whiteheadean position that particles at the subatomic level are not fundamental notions. In a universe in which everything is in motion, and where one item can only be measured in relation to other items, there can be no ultimate space and time. Without ultimate space and time, nothing can exist at a precise point of space and time. Single points and single particles are an impossibility. It is interaction which generates particles rather than the other way around.

There is an evolving literature in consciousness studies which argues that the brain functions according to the laws of quantum physics (Penrose, 1991; Schwartz & Begley, 2002; Clarke, 2004; Rosenblum & Kuttner, 2006; Kauffman, 2008; Lanza & Berman, 2009). Specifically, numerous authors have called on quantum theory for an explanation of psi phenomena (Radin, 2006; Walker, 2000; Clarke, 2005). Others have looked to field theory (Sheldrake, 2003, 2005; Laszlo, 2004) or Bohm's holographic theory (Pribram, 1977; Grof & Bennett, 1993; Talbot, 1991).

For Whitehead, who had a career as a mathematician and physicist before he turned to philosophy, it was clear that we could not understand the universe unless we abandon what he called 'the fallacy of simple location'. Classical physics, and even Einstein's relativity theory, could not explain how the universe at the micro-level could be compatible with what we know of it at the macro-level and how we experience life at the human level. It was obvious to Whitehead that the world displayed to us by subatomic physics is the world 'all the way through'. So we should expect to find on the human level evidence that time and space are not constants, that events distantly removed can affect each other instantaneously, that we can have reliable intuitions of future events. Whether or not we are aware of it, we are, as Laszlo argues, 'literally in touch' with almost any part of the world, 'whether here on Earth or beyond in the cosmos' (Laszlo, 2004: 113). For physicist David Peat (1987) so-called 'synchronistic' phenomena are exactly what we should expect to find if 'reality' (both matter-events and mind-events) emerges out of a single unified field, as Bohm suggests it does.

We tend to accept without question the notion that sensation and perception are causally connected: it has seemed obvious to philosophers and brain scientists for centuries that perception is our mind's acknowledgement of the information that comes through our senses. However, Nicholas Humphrey in *Seeing Red* (2006) argues that sensation and perception are two very different, independent systems operating in our brains. Sensation does not provide the input for perception. The function of sensation is not to inform us but to select what matters to us. Perception is not dependent on our senses. We can have perception without sensation. Humphrey's evidence comes from a study of various pathological conditions such as anosognosia (where people cannot perceive their own disability), illusory conjunction (combining contrasting stimuli into a new perception), and Anton's syndrome (believing you can see when you are blind). The most striking evidence comes from the phenomenon of blindsight, in which a person or animal whose visual cortex has been destroyed is able to accurately point to or pick up objects which they clearly cannot see. Humphreys argues that there must be another way in which we receive information, without it having to pass through our senses. On the one hand, in a one-to-one encounter we may clearly be receiving information through our senses without being aware of it. Our hunch that someone is lying may come subconsciously via our below-awareness sense of smell or contact with their electromagnetic field, via a below-awareness sight of their aura, or some other sense we do not know we possess. On the other hand, there is plenty of evidence that some people, at least, can know what another is feeling, imagining or thinking when there is no possibility of sensate contact. There is plenty of anecdotal evidence that direct knowledge of another's inner state is most common when the 'sender' and 'receiver' are intimately connected as, for instance, twin-to-twin, mother-to-infant or lover-to-

163

lover. Experiments in parapsychology commonly isolate people in separate rooms, sometimes soundproofed and electromagnetically shielded, sometimes many kilometres apart (Radin, 2006). Sheldrake describes experiments on the 'sense of being stared at' in which people stared at the target subject's image on a television screen via CCTV, rather than directly at the subject. In either case there is strong evidence that the sense of being stared at is not an illusion: some people are more sensitive to being stared at than others, people become more sensitive with practice, and children are much more sensitive than adults (Sheldrake, 2003, 2005).

PRESENCE

Christian de Quincey in *Radical Knowing* (2005) suggests that being intensely engaged in relationship with another is the most vital manifestation of consciousness, and that we cannot have an adequate theory of consciousness without acknowledging that relationship is fundamental to it. Central to his argument is the notion of 'presence' which he takes from Islamic philosophy: 'This 'presence' – a nonsensory prehension of the being of the 'other' (whether Allah, human, or animal) – is the '*felt* unfolding of the other's being into a unity that transcends the dichotomy of separate subject and object' (de Quincey, 2005: 175).

When Gebser set out to document the integral structure of consciousness which he found himself observing, one of the key features that he noted was the dissolution of dichotomies. The mental structure which had been dominant during the preceding centuries appeared to be disintegrating, and with it the dualistic assumptions which had enabled materialistic science and the Promethean project of making a better world. In the emerging consciousness, as he saw it, there was no clear-cut distinction between mind and matter, between self and other, between subject and object, between I and thou, between you and me.

Conventionally, theorists of the person-centred approach have focused on the power of Rogers' six conditions of therapeutic growth as the principal agents of change. In recent years, however, there has been a challenge to this rather instrumental view. Within the person-centred framework Peter Schmid, Dave Mearns and Godfrey Barrett-

Lennard, among others, have argued that it is relationship itself which is healing. Our congruence is not congruence as individuals but as relational beings. We are only congruent in relationship. Indeed, we only exist in relationship.

In Rogers' later writing on empathy, he abandons his earlier notion that it is an 'as if' experience, in which the therapist enters the client's world only through imagination, and describes moving beyond a sense of separateness and really entering the client's world: 'It means temporarily living in the other's life' (Rogers, 1980: 142). To achieve this level of empathy he advises the counsellor to 'lay aside your self and experience becoming the client' (Rogers, 1980: 143). He points to this transcendence of self, even of the subject/object dichotomy, in *On Becoming a Person* (1961).

> *When there is complete unity, singleness, fullness of experiencing in the relationship, then it acquires the 'out-of-this-world' quality which therapists have remarked upon, a sort of trance-like feeling in the relationship from which both the client and I emerge at the end of the hour, as if from a deep well or tunnel. In these moments there is, to borrow Buber's phrase, a real 'I-Thou' relationship, a timeless living in the experience which is between the client and me. It is at the opposite pole from seeing the client, or myself, as an object. It is the height of personal subjectivity. (Rogers, 1961: 202)*

Rogers is persuaded that it is the existential encounter which is important. The relationship is the central factor in the healing. He argues that this goes both ways. In the moments when each of the people in the interaction experiences the realness of the other, growth occurs in both of them.

> *In those rare moments when a deep realness in one meets a deep realness in the other, a memorable I-Thou relationship, as Martin Buber would call it, occurs. Such a deep and mutual encounter does not happen often, but I am convinced that unless it happens occasionally we are not living as human beings. (Rogers, 1980: 9)*

Some writers on 'deep empathy' talk about this experience of connection as a kind of 'fusion' or 'melding' (Mahrer, 1993; Hoffman, 2001). Others think of it as 'sympathetic resonance' (Sprinkle, 1985; Larson, 1987;

Rowan, 1986). Tobin Hart (2000) reminds us of the need to distinguish 'trans-egoic fusion' of counsellor and client from the 'mindless pre-egoic fusion' of narcissistic projection. Confusing the two is a further instance of Wilber's 'pre/trans fallacy', in which archaic or magical experience is mistaken for integral experience. In a process conception of relationship, however, it is not necessary to think of two separate existences being 'fused' or resonating with each other. The fundamental connectedness, the 'interbeing', is prior to the sense of separatedness. This connectedness is not limited to whatever is in range of our senses. Hart takes up this notion in discussing deep empathy:

> As the gap between subject and object (or, self and other) is crossed and we become more available to the world at large, we may discover that our empathic meeting is not limited to the person sitting in front of us. For example, we may experience empathy for another at a distance, experience others not seemingly available to our senses, and experience openness to the world in general ... Finally we discover that the world – from a plant, to our pet, to the planet – may be available to direct knowing. (Hart, 2000: 262)

Rachel Charles (2004) associates deep empathy with the phenomena of 'emotional contagion' and 'interactional synchrony'. Our identification with others is not necessarily a positive experience. In psychoanalytic theory it is accepted as axiomatic that the unconscious connection between therapist and client has to be acknowledged and attended to, lest it impede the therapeutic process. For Freud as for Jung, it was clear that the unconscious processes of therapist and client were entangled. As Theodore Reik argued:

> We can attain to psychological comprehension of another's unconscious only if it is seized on by our own, at least for a moment, as if it were part of ourselves; it is a part of ourselves. (1948: 464)

Recent research in neuroscience has confirmed the existence of 'mirror neurons' which are alleged to be the basis of the human capacity for empathy and the evolution of what we call 'culture'. It appears that if we watch someone doing something or having an experience (e.g. of pain) the neurons that our brain would use to do or experience the same thing become active – just as if we were having that experience ourselves. We are biologically in tune with those around us, with an unconscious urge to copy what they do (Ramachandran, 2011, pp. 117*ff*; Hannaford, 2010, *passim*). It has been commonly observed that the bodily rhythms of people confined together become synchronized. There is evidence also that people in conversation unconsciously mirror each other, and that this extends to such things as heart rate and galvanic skin response. The anthropologist E.T. Hall (1981) discusses the phenomenon of 'syncing' where whole groups of people unconsciously synchronize their movements. Such entanglement is our default position, one that we share with termite nests and flocks of birds. We can avoid it only by deliberately reflecting on our behaviour and controlling it. Conversely, we can turn it into a technique for 'tuning into' and influencing another person by subtly mirroring them, as in neurolinguistic programming (Grinder & Bandler, 1976). The synchrony we experience in the world of our experience appears to be paralleled by analogous phenomena in the worlds of physics and biology, variously labelled 'coherence', 'correspondance', 'resonance ' and 'entrainment'.

In his discussion of synchronicity, Jung calls on Taoist and medieval philosophy for a similar understanding of how the world works. He refers to the classical idea of '*the sympathy of all things*', citing the Greek philosopher Hippocrates:

> *There is one common flow, one common breathing, all things are in sympathy. The whole organism and each of its parts are working in conjunction for the same purpose … the great principle extends to the extremest part, and from the extremest part returns to the great principle, to the one nature, being and non-being. (Jung, 1979, CW 8, para. 924)*

Jung comments that the interconnectedness of all being was once taken for granted. However, with the dominance of Western science the 'great principle' – that the smallest part of creation contains the whole, and that consequently meaning should not be seen to be exclusively the province of humans – was 'banished to such a remote and benighted region that the intellect lost track of it altogether' (Jung, 1979, CW 8, para. 928).

Barrett-Lennard (2007) noted in his recent writing that 'person-centred thought is transcending the philosophy of individualism in which it is rooted, while preserving its belief in the worth and dignity of each person (p. 135). In the broad context of the development of person-centred theory since Rogers' original formulation, he comments:

> *Almost imperceptibly, an image of the person as a sovereign and potentially autonomous being has been receding in favour of an understanding that lives are inherently interwoven and interdependent and that relationship is at the core of life. (Barrett-Lennard, 2009: 91)*

He writes of 'we-consciousness' in a relationship as 'something that goes beyond between-person dialogue to a process that has its own nature and individual dynamism emergent from the interplay of the participants' (Barrett-Lennard, 2009: 84).

Rogers left us the notion that empathic understanding is a necessary and sufficient condition for the particular kind of transformation that can take place through the interaction between counsellor and client. Whitehead's process philosophy takes it further, proposing that there is actually no space between us, that we are not encapsulated in our individuality, exchanging messages with each other. We are all aspects of each other. The interpersonal implications of Whitehead's philosophy are explored by de Quincey (2005), who argues that intersubjectivity precedes subjectivity. This is a radical departure from the conventional understanding of intersubjectivity, which involves individual subjects communicating with each other through language, interpreting each other's meaning and reaching agreement. De Quincey notes that there is a stronger kind of intersubjectivity, in which the subjective experience of each of the participating subjects is 'influenced and conditioned' by their mutual interaction, so that they share each other's presence. This comes close to what Rogers seems to mean by empathy in most of his writing. However, when he writes in *On Becoming a Person* (1961) of 'complete unity, singleness, fullness of experiencing in the relationship', and 'a timeless living in the experience which is *between* the client and me' (p. 202) he is going further than this, coming close to de Quincey's own radical definition of intersubjectivity as the 'mutual co-arising-and-engagement of interdependent subjects ... that *creates* their respective experience' (p. 281). Intersubjectivity, de Quincey argues, is a process of co-creativity, where *relationship* is ontologically primary.

All individuated subjects co-emerge, or co-arise, as a result of a holistic 'field' of relationships. The being of any one subject is thoroughly dependent on the being of all other subjects with which it is in relationship. (De Quincey, 2005: 281)

For Rogers, it is the acknowledgement and enhancement of the relationship between counsellor and client which enables the actualizing tendency, and it is the actualizing tendency – 'the directional trend which is evident in all organic and human life' – which enables creativity. Within the therapeutic relationship as Rogers imagines it, client and counsellor are co-creating themselves, participating in each other's becoming.

This focus on the intersubjectivity of the relationship, rather than the experiences of two interacting individuals, has been taken up by Schmid and other person-centred theorists in their discussions of 'relational depth'. Central to this discussion is the notion of dialogue. Schmid (2006) argues that 'dialogue is the authentic realization and acknowledgement of the underlying We' (p. 244). Dialogue is understood to be a primary and irreducible aspect of being human. It is not 'transmission of information; it is participation in the being of the other' (Schmid, 2006: 246). Citing Emmanuel Levinas, he states that dialogue is 'a place where transcendence happens'.

Levinas' position is that we only exist through our relationship with others, that being a person essentially means being-for-the-other. Being in the world inevitably means being in dialogue, and the true dialogue which is basic to our nature is dialogue which is in the service of the other.

Rogers would agree that dialogue is essential to our nature, that unless we can occasionally engage in real dialogue, where our realness meets the realness of another, 'we are not living as human beings' (Rogers, 1980: 9). When he aligns himself with Martin Buber, and proclaims that 'living in the experience which is between the client and me' is 'the height of personal subjectivity' (Rogers, 1961: 202), we can see him challenging the dichotomous thinking which frames conventional notions of counselling and healing. No longer does the therapist as subject do something *to* or *for* the client; they are intertwined subjects sharing a single experience.

Merleau-Ponty used the image of the hand to argue that we need to abandon our subject–object way of thinking. If you shake my hand, it is clear that your hand both touches and is touched. The two experiences cannot be separated. Merleau-Ponty argues that if you touch anything, even something you consider to be inanimate, this is equally true. It is true of all our interaction with 'the other'. We are totally intertwined with the world. Merleau-Ponty pointed out that there really is no boundary between self and other. When we imagine ourselves to be living *on* the earth we are failing to see that we are really living *inside* the earth, the series of concentric spheres which make up the biosphere. We now know that we are an intrinsic part of a complex, living system, no longer able to separate ourselves, as individual subjects, from the rest of the earth, human and non-human, as object. We are part of what he calls 'the flesh of the world', which is not mere insensate matter, but a living being which both senses and is sensed.

> One can say that we perceive the things themselves, that we are the world that thinks itself – or that the world is at the heart of our flesh. In any case, once a body–world relationship is recognized, there is a ramification of my body and a ramification of the world and a correspondence between its inside and my outside and between my inside and its outside. (Merleau-Ponty, 1968: 136)

Since Merleau-Ponty wrote these words we have been presented with Lovelock's 'Gaia hypothesis' and increasing evidence to support it. Merleau-Ponty's insight is now backed up by science and we know that the biosphere, the sensible world that surrounds us, is 'a coherent living entity regulating its temperature and internal composition much as one's own body metabolically maintains its own internal temperature and balances the chemical composition of its bloodstream' (Abram, 1988: 111). In such a world there is no sharp division between subject and object, or between humans and other organisms. Subjectivity (interiority, spirit), for Merleau-Ponty as for Whitehead, goes 'all the way through'. As Jung argued again and again, 'Nature is not matter only, she is also spirit ... There is nothing without spirit, for spirit seems to be the inside of things ... Everything that is stated or manifested by the psyche is an expression of the nature of things, of which man is a part' (Jung, 1979, CW, passim).

In the context of such ideas we can understand that at the centre of the person-centred counselling interaction is what de Quincey calls 'engaged presence'. 'This', says Rogers (1961: 202), 'is the height of personal subjectivity'. What Rogers did not articulate, but which is implicit in his worldview as soon as he starts to talk about the formative tendency, is the notion that 'engaged presence' is the proper expression of our relationship, not only to the particular person sitting across from us, but to the whole of human and non-human creation.

AFTERWORD

Carl Jung bewailed the loss of magic consciousness:

> *Through scientific understanding, our world has become dehumanized. Man feels himself isolated in the cosmos. He is no longer involved in nature and has lost his emotional participation in natural events, which hitherto had a symbolic meaning for him. Thunder is no longer the voice of a god, nor is lightening his avenging missile. No river contains a spirit, no tree means a man's life, no snake is the embodiment of wisdom, and no mountain still harbours a great demon. Neither do things speak to him nor can he speak to things, like stones, springs, plants, and animals. He no longer has the bush-soul identifying him with a wild animal. His immediate communication with nature is gone forever, and the emotional energy it generated has sunk into the unconscious. (Jung, 1979, CW 18, para. 585)*

We should not think that Jung is suggesting that we abandon rationality and return to a magical world, only that our denial of the magical world has serious consequences for our mental well-being. Jung was well aware of the dangers of a regression into magical consciousness. Like Jean Gebser, Jung witnessed Nazism and Fascism up close and lamented 'the over-stimulation of the magic components in present-day man' (Gebser, 1949/1986: 60). After witnessing the mass behaviour associated with Nazism, Jung remained suspicious of groups for the rest of his life. Gebser was equally suspicious of the relapse into magic culture, which he witnessed in wartime Europe. He argued that it represented 'the flight backwards into the vitality and unity of the magical' and that:

this disposition to regress is brought about by the absence nowadays of
these aspects in our rationalized world, as well as by anxiety in the face
of the emerging mutation. All of these negative phenomena ... are rooted
in the reactivated predisposition to magic in contemporary man. (Gebser,
1949/1986: 60)

The aspects whose absence is precipitating the 'disposition to regress'
are the 'vitality and unity of the magical'. Gebser argued that the
European overvaluation of rationality in the past few centuries had
weakened the magical structure, so that it was no longer providing
the vitality needed. Meanwhile, the breakdown of rational
consciousness was bringing anxiety. The consequence was that instead
of a robust magical and mental consciousness co-operating in the
experience of life, rationality was abandoned, and Europe saw a relapse
into a pre-rational magic culture, unsupported by a critical intelligence.

The 'contemporary man' that Gebser was referring to was living
in middle of the twentieth century. I doubt that he would have much
reason to express it differently if he was writing today. One of his key
ideas was the need to distinguish between efficient and deficient
manifestations of the various structures of consciousness. Both Gebser
and Jung had seen only too clearly how magical consciousness was
manifested in the incantations, rituals, emotional contagion and
tribalism of National Socialism. This prevented them from having a
romantic view of psychological and cultural regression. However, it
did not prevent them from appreciating 'the vegetative intertwining
of all living things' and our deep need for 'the vitality and unity of the
magical'. Gebser argued against the notion that human consciousness
has evolved from a primitive, archaic structure to an advanced rational
structure which represents the 'highest and best' form of consciousness.
For him, 'primitive' meant the least complex and the first to emerge
in our species. There is no 'best' and 'worst', no 'lowest' and 'highest'.
There is only 'different'. The 'all that is' is always present. It is simply
manifest through different modes of consciousness at different times.

The instinct and emotion of magical consciousness was a perfectly
valid way of relating to the world in the Stone Age. It is not on its own
a valid way of relating to the world today. Without the backing of our
mental, critical consciousness and the reflective and purposive ego
that comes with it, magical consciousness is manifested not only in
outbursts of tribal violence, in apparently sophisticated cultures, but

in credulity, superstition and a vulnerability to manipulation by politicians, the media and the advertising industry. Yet mental consciousness, especially not the deficient form of mental consciousness represented by materialist science, is unable to save us.

Gebser warned us that only a new kind of consciousness will save us from catastrophe. He coupled that warning with the observation that a new kind of consciousness appeared to be emerging in the twentieth century, a consciousness which integrates the unity consciousness of proto-humans and the magical consciousness of the Stone Age with the other more complex structures of consciousness which have emerged in the last 20,000 years. When Gebser sets out to describe this new structure, he uses words like arational (as opposed to both rational and irrational), aperspectival (as opposed to both perspectival and non-perspectival), space-free (as opposed to both spatial and spaceless), ego-free (as opposed to both egocentric and egoless), and transparency (as opposed to both duality and unity).

If we do our thinking within the frame of the archetype of the One and give all our worship to Gaia, we may live our personal and professional lives as though human beings do not count for anything in the greater scheme of things: we may assume that the fate of the Earth is out of our hands; we may trust in the Earth Mother to save us; or we may abandon hope and await the revenge of Gaia. If our perspective comes from the archetype of the Many, if we give all our worship to Prometheus, we will assume that we are masters of our fate and can use our brains to ward off disaster. Gaia tells us to enjoy our unity consciousness, locked in the comfort of her womb. Prometheus tells us not to submit to the whims of the gods, but to take responsibility for making a better world for ourselves. Hermes, tells us to listen to the voices of all the gods – in our heads and in our gut – and respect them all.

If we look critically at the evidence and decide that the universe is entirely mechanical, that humans are essentially isolated and alienated from each other and the natural world, that nothing exists but dead matter, we are exercising our mental consciousness and justified in coming to such a conclusion. If we look at the evidence and conclude that only the existence of a transcendent creator can account for the kind of world we find ourselves in, we are likewise making a rational decision. If we look at the evidence and decide that we live in the kind of organic, living universe described in this book, we are being no less rational. However, this is not usually what happens. We are more likely to accept one worldview or another simply because 'that's just the way it is'. We give up on the evidence, make some assumptions and accept a myth, whether a religious myth or a scientific one, because we find that it provides a container within which life is possible and even meaningful for us. Even an inadequate myth is better than no myth at all, for without a myth our lives make no sense.

Myth is a narrative we take for granted. We may be born into it, may simply absorb it from our subculture, or may adopt it as ours because we need a narrative to frame our lives and there is no other available that satisfies us. Science, on the other hand, purports to involve rational reflection on the current myths and the data that supports them. We seek objective truth and may even claim to have found it. Our egoic, mental consciousness is perspectival. We look at reality from a particular point in time and space and report on what we see. We may then be inclined to make dogmatic statements about it. However, when it becomes a taken-for-granted, this-is-just-the-way-it-is, culturally endorsed statement of the truth about things, we have moved from science to myth. The myth of modern science – that if we observe carefully enough and think hard enough we will find the truth – pretends to be the only story worth listening to. This myth, the myth of Apollo, has no more absolute a right to our commitment than any other myth. Nevertheless, history tells us that a myth is generally a good deal more powerful in human affairs than the facts.

Charles Birch cites Theodore Roszak's image of Jack in the Box to express the challenge of our times. 'Jack is in the box. Jack does not know he is in the box. Jack must get out of the box.' We are imprisoned in the myth of modernity, and must somehow find the will to break out of this prison and abandon the dominant modern worldview.

The modern worldview is derived from the Scientific Revolution, the Enlightenment and the Industrial Revolution. The postmodern worldview is more concerned with the subjective, feelings, values, consciousness and internal relations. It is an organic or holistic view contrasted with the mechanical or 'substance' view of things ... The beginning of wisdom is the awareness that what Jack knows in his box is not the world, but only a small box within the world, a very small box indeed. (Birch, 1993: 199)

Postmodern consciousness does not accept any statement of the truth as ultimate. Many of us are not true believers any more. We prefer to line up apparently incompatible 'truths' as 'both/and' rather than 'either/or'. We may be able to balance multiple perspectives. We may even be able to handle the paradoxes that light is both particle and wave, that the universe is both being and becoming, both object and subject, or that our behaviour is somehow both determined and free, and that we are both separate, decision-making individuals and totally intertwined in nature. Rogers suggests that in the emerging world:

Men and women, individually and collectively, are inwardly and organismically rejecting the view of a single, culture-approved reality. I believe they are moving inevitably towards the acceptance of millions of separate, exciting, informative, individual perceptions of reality. (Rogers, 1980: 106)

Here Rogers is not taking the radically relativistic position that 'anything goes'. Rather, he is taking what Gebser calls an aperspectival view of reality, suggesting that the truth about reality is in the whole, not in any single perspective. As long as the perceptions of the men and women he is talking about are 'exciting' and 'informative' they may well be contributing to the creation of the universe. After all, as Whitehead remarks: 'It is more important that a proposition be interesting than that it be true (Whitehead, 1953: 14). (He remarks also that an interesting proposition is more apt to be true than a false one.)

I have written elsewhere (Neville, 1992, 2008) of Hermes as the god of what Lyotard called 'the postmodern condition'. He could also be called the god of what Gebser calls the emerging integral structure of consciousness. Whether we are aware of it or not, many of us live our lives embedded in the narrative of Hermes. Many of us are prepared to accept his advice and worship a host of squabbling gods, without being too much disturbed by the contradictions and paradoxes this involves. We can understand that we are but cells in the body of Gaia, and at the same time appreciate our significance as individuals – free, able and willing to craft our future. We may be sympathetic with Alfred North Whitehead's comment on the prevalence of 'the fallacy of dogmatic finality':

The Universe is vast. Nothing is more curious than the self-satisfied dogmatism with which mankind at each period of its history cherishes the delusion of the finality of its existing modes of knowledge. Sceptics and believers are all alike. At this moment scientists and sceptics are the leading dogmatists. Advance in detail is admitted; fundamental novelty is barred. This dogmatic common sense is the death of philosophic adventure. The Universe is vast. (Whitehead, 1953: 5)

The most charming and friendly of the gods, the god of information, process, complexity and magic, Hermes gives us a perspective which – paradoxically – is aperspectival. We can see the world from a particular perspective while being fully aware that it is one perspective among many. We are able to see our dangerous situation from more than one direction at once. We can seek solutions through both our rationality and our intuition. We can avoid being constrained by holding on to absolute truths and values, yet not suppose that there is no truth or value to be had. We can cease to be egocentric without abandoning our sense of self. We can live in the enchanted world of magical consciousness while retaining our ability to monitor our own gullibility and our tendency to delude ourselves.

The peculiar consciousness of the postmodern era has enabled us to let go of the certainties of the Promethean age from which we are emerging and give Hermes' mother, the Earth Mother, the honour he promises her. However, while the god of flexibility and motility makes transformation possible, he does not guarantee it. Nothing is determined. Hermes, for all his charm, is a slippery god, not totally trustworthy, who may lead us to the underworld and leave us there.

Carl Rogers has been accused of having too romantic a view of human nature and the direction in which we are moving. So have Jung and Whitehead. Gebser's insights have been misread by those who want to imagine humanity evolving inexorably towards a higher consciousness. Yet they were all well aware that organisms not only grow; they also decay. In fact, they can only grow because they also decay.

Whitehead asserted that 'the teleology of the Universe is directed towards the production of Beauty' (Whitehead, 1929/1978: 341). Rogers concluded that 'there is in every organism, at whatever level, an underlying flow of movement towards constructive fulfilment of its inherent possibilities' (Rogers, 1980: 117). Jung was able to say that

177

'Nature, psyche, and life appear to me like divinity unfolded – what more could I ask for?' (Jung, cited in Sabini, 2002: 221). Gebser looked through human history and saw the emergence of 'the ever-present origin' into human awareness. They all saw the process of the universe, and our part in it, as directional. The direction appears to be positive but the movement is towards a possibility, not towards a predetermined end.

After a lifetime of reflection, Rogers decided that ultimate truth is beyond our reach, and suggested that those of us who are keen to find the truth should make the assumption that there are as many realities as there are persons. At the end of his massive opus, Gebser claims to have merely 'attempted to point towards clarification of a complex situation'. Jung, at the end of his life, decided that the best he could do was to develop hypotheses. Whitehead proposed that there are no whole truths, only half-truths, and that we get it seriously wrong when we mistake half-truths for truths.

The particular myth, the particular story about the universe which has shaped this book, has a long history, not only in European science and philosophy, but in the science and philosophy of the Middle East, India and China. In the European context it has had to stand against more dominant myths for a few centuries, but it seems to be currently gathering adherents in both popular culture and serious science, among those who find that it makes more sense to them than the alternative stories. Not only does it make more sense metaphysically, but it has clear implications for their personal and professional lives.

It may be a myth, but that does not mean that it is not true. On the other hand, the attractiveness of the Gaian myth should not blind us to the counter-truth of the Promethean myth. James Lovelock, who brought scientific credibility to Gaian thinking four decades ago, argues in *The Vanishing Face of Gaia* (2010) that it is already too late to prevent catastrophic climate change. That we do not have time to wait for consciousness transformation and we have to find technical solutions to buy time while we learn to adapt to the inevitable catastrophe.

Gaia worshippers are inclined to have an optimistic view of our capacity to experience the transformation of consciousness which will enable us to live in harmony with the planet. They may look with some disdain at the Promethean fantasy which drives the efforts of scientists and engineers to develop the technical fixes that they hope will save us from destruction. This is as narrow a view as that which ignores our condition as cells in an organic, self-regulating system.

It has not been my purpose in this book to argue about whether we are doomed or not, or even to argue that counselling within the Promethean fantasy of the heroic individual is necessarily inappropriate or ineffective. Rather, I have wanted to say that life is more complex than the view of it we get from this single perspective. Conventional theory and practice in counselling is shaped by a particular image of humanity, and we find that image is increasingly unable to represent life as we experience it in this universe. The alternative image offered in this book seems to me to have more to offer to counselling in the planetary emergency which frames our thinking. However, it is not so simple. Whitehead had a maxim: 'Seek simplicity and mistrust it.' We are not talking here about competing images or competing truths and arguing that we should adopt the one and abandon the other. I like the way Luce Irigaray puts it:

> *Instead of being light opposed to darkness, or knowledge opposed to ignorance, truth is light which does not give up mystery ... never total, never authoritarian or dogmatic, but light always shared between two subjects irreducible to one another. (Irigaray, 2001: 110)*

The Australian biologist and process philosopher, Charles Birch (2008), whose ideas have helped to shape the way I have talked about counselling in these pages, ends his account of his lifetime's mission of reconciling science and soul with a quotation from Whitehead:

> *Philosophy begins in wonder. And at the end, when philosophic thought has done its best, the wonder remains. There have been added, however, some grasp of the immensity of things, some purification of the emotion by understanding. (Whitehead, 1938: 168)*

I cannot vouch for the purification, but I do relate to the wonder and the immensity.

REFERENCES

Abram, D (1988) Merleau-Ponty and the voice of the earth. *Environmental Ethics, 10,* 101–20.

Abram, D (1997) *The Spell of the Sensuous.* New York: Vintage.

Aczel, A (2003) *Entanglement.* New York: Plume.

Aizenstadt, S (1995) Jungian psychology and the world unconscious. In T Roszak, ME Gomes & AD Kanner (Eds) *Ecopsychology: Restoring the earth; healing the mind* (pp. 92–100). San Francisco: Sierra Club Books.

American Psychiatric Association (2000) *Diagnostic and Statistical Manual of Mental Disorders* (4th ed, rev). Washington, DC: American Psychiatric Association.

Angyal, A (1941) *Foundations for a Science of Personality.* New York: Commonwealth Fund.

Assagioli, R (1970) *Psychosynthesis.* London: Penguin.

Barrett-Lennard, G (1998) *Carl Rogers' Helping System: Journey and substance.* London: Sage.

Barrett-Lennard, G (2003) Human relationship: Linkage or life form? *Person-Centered & Experiential Psychotherapies, 6*(3), 183–95.

Barrett-Lennard, G (2005) *Relationship at the Centre: Healing in a troubled world.* London: Whurr.

Barrett-Lennard, G (2007) The relational foundations of person-centred practice. In M Cooper, M O'Hara, PF Schmid & G Wyatt (Eds) *The Handbook of Person-Centred Psychotherapy and Counselling* (pp. 127–9). Houndmills: Palgrave Macmillan.

Barrett-Lennard, G (2009) From personality to relationship: Path of thought and practice. *Person-Centered & Experiential Psychotherapies, 8*(2), 79–93.

Bastick, T (1982) *Intuition: How we think we act.* New York: Wiley.

Bateson, G (1980) *Mind and Nature.* New York: Bantam.

Bernstein, J (2005) *Living in the Borderland: The evolution of consciousness and the challenge of healing trauma.* London: Routledge.

Birch, C (1993) *Regaining Compassion for Humanity and Nature.* Kensington: New South Wales University Press.

Birch, C (2008) *Science and Soul.* West Conshohocken, PA: Templeton.

Boer, C (Trans) (1970) *The Homeric Hymns* (pp. 18–58). Dallas, TX: Spring Publications.

Bohm, D (1980) *Wholeness and the Implicate Order.* London: Routledge & Kegan Paul.

Bookchin, M (1980) *Toward an Ecological Society.* Montreal: Black Rose Books.

Bowlby, J (1988) *A Secure Base: Parent–child attachment and healthy human development.* London: Routledge.

Brizee, R (2000) Process relational psychotherapy: Creatively transforming relationships. *Process Studies, 29*(1), 151–67.

Burnet, J (1930) *Early Greek Philosophy.* London: Black.

Campbell, J (1968) *The Masks of God.* New York: Viking.

Capra, F (1975) *The Tao of Physics.* Boulder, CO: Shambala.

Capra, F (1982) *The Turning Point: Science, society and the rising culture.* London: Wildwood House.

Capra, F (1997) *The Web of Life: A synthesis of mind and matter.* London: Flamingo.

Carkhuff, R (1969) *Helping and Human Relations: A primer for lay and professional helpers.* New York: Holt, Rhinehart & Winston.

Castenada, C (1968) *The Teachings of Don Juan: A Yaqui way of knowledge.* Berkeley, CA: University of California Press.

Castenada, C (1971) *A Separate Reality.* New York: Washington Square Press.

Charles, R (2004) *Intuition in Psychotherapy and Counselling.* London: Whurr.

Clarke, C (2004) Quantum mechanics, consciousness and the self. In D Lorimer (Ed) *Science, Consciousness and Ultimate Reality* (pp. 65–92). Exeter: Imprint Academic.

Clarke, C (2005) The sense of being stared at: Its relevance to the physics of consciousness. *Journal of Consciousness Studies, 2*(6), 78–81.

Claxton, G (1998) *Hare Brain, Tortoise Mind: Why intelligence increases when you think less.* London: Fourth Estate.

Cohen, MJ (1997) *Reconnecting with Nature: Finding your wellness through restoring your bond with the earth.* Corvallis, OR: Ecopress.

Collier, J (1962) *On the Gleaming Way; Navajos, Eastern Pueblos, Zunis, Hopis, Apaches, and their land; and their meanings to the world.* Denver, CO: Sage. (Original work published 1949)

Damasio, A (2010) *Self Comes to Mind: Constructing the conscious brain.* New York: Pantheon.

Davies, P (1992) *The Mind of God.* London: Penguin.

De Chardin, T (1965) *Hymn of the Universe.* London: Collins.

De Quincey, C (2002) *Radical Nature: The soul of matter.* Rochester, VT: Park Street Press.

De Quincey, C (2005) *Radical Knowing: Understanding consciousness through relationship*. Rochester, VT: Park Street Press.

Dell, W (2005) *Notes for a New Mind: Brain lateralization, deconstruction, and the new myth*. Boca Raton, FL: Universal Publishers.

Devall, B & Sessions, G (1985) *Deep Ecology: Living as if nature mattered*. Salt Lake City, UT: Peregrine Smith Books.

Donald, M (1991) *Origins of the Modern Mind*. Cambridge, MA: Harvard University Press.

Donald, M (2001) *A Mind so Rare*. New York: Norton.

Egan, K (1997) *The Educated Mind*. Chicago: University of Chicago Press.

Ehrenwald, J (1955) *New Dimensions of Deep Analysis*. New York: Grune & Stratton.

Eliade, M (1971) *The Myth of the Eternal Return: Cosmos and history*. Princeton, NJ: Princeton University Press.

Elkin, AP (1946) *Aboriginal Men of High Degree*. Sydney: Australasian Publishing Company.

Ellingham, IH (1997) On the quest for a person-centred paradigm. *Counselling, 8*(1), 52–5.

Ellingham, IH (2001) Carl Rogers' 'congruence' as an organismic not a Freudian concept. In G Wyatt (Ed) *Rogers' Therapeutic Conditions: Evolution, theory and practice. Vol 1: Congruence* (pp. 96–115). Ross-on-Wye: PCCS Books.

Ellingham, IH (2009) Person-centred therapy and the mindful, I–Thou, mystical/spiritual dimension: The multi-level nature of relational depth and mental distress. *Person-Centred Quarterly*, November, pp. 2–4.

Eshel, O (2006) Where are you, my beloved? On absence, loss, and the enigma of telepathic dreams. *International Journal of Psychoanalysis, 87*, 1603–27.

Fisher, A (2002) *Radical Ecopsychology: Psychology in the service of life*. Albany, NY: SUNY Press.

Fox, W (1990) *Toward a Transpersonal Ecology: Developing new foundations for environmentalism*. Boston: Shambhala.

Freud, S (1961) *Civilization and its Discontents*. New York: Norton.

Gare, A (2006) *Reviving the Radical Enlightenment: Process philosophy and the struggle for democracy*. Paper presented at the 6th International Whitehead Conference, Salzburg, 3–6 July.

Gebser, J (1986) *The Ever-Present Origin*. (N Barstad & A Mickunas, Trans) Athens, OH: Ohio University Press. (Original work published 1949)

Gendlin, E (1962) *Experiencing and the Creation of Meaning: A philosophical and psychological approach to the subjective*. New York: Free Press of Glencoe.

Gendlin, E (1981) *Focusing*. New York: Bantam.

Gendlin, E (1984) The client's client: The edge of awareness. In R Levant & JM Shlein (Eds) *Client-Centered Therapy and the Person-Centered Approach* (pp. 76–108). New York: Praeger.

Gendlin, E (1992) The primacy of the body, not the primacy of perception. *Man and the World, 25*(3–4), 341–53.

Gendlin, E (1996) *Focusing-Oriented Psychotherapy: A manual of the experiential method.* New York: Guilford Press.

Gendlin, E & Lemke, J (1983) A critique of relativity and localization. *Mathematical Modelling, 4,* 61–72.

Goerner, S (1999) *After the Clockwork Universe: The emerging science and the culture of integral society.* Edinburgh: Floris Books.

Goleman, D (1995) *Emotional Intelligence.* New York: Bantam.

Gribbin, J & Gribbin, M (2009) *He Knew He Was Right: The irrepressible life of James Lovelock and Gaia.* London: Allen Lane.

Griffin, DR (1989) *God and Religion in the Postmodern World.* Albany, NY: SUNY Press.

Grinder, J & Bandler, R (1976) *The Structure of Magic.* Palo Alto, CA: Science & Behavior Books.

Grof, S & Bennett, HZ (1993) *The Holotropic Mind: The three levels of human consciousness and how they shape our lives.* Los Angeles: Harperone.

Haisch, B (2006) *The God Theory: Universes, zero-point fields and what's behind it all.* San Francisco: Weiser Books.

Hall, ET (1981) *Beyond Culture.* New York: Random House.

Hannaford, C (2010) *Playing in the Unified Field.* Salt Lake City, UT: Great River Books.

Hart, T (2000) Deep empathy. In T Hart, P Nelson & K Puhakka (Eds) *Transpersonal Knowing: Exploring the horizon of consciousness* (pp. 253–70). Albany, NY: SUNY Press.

Haule, J (2011) *Jung in the 21st Century* (2 vols). London: Routledge.

Hillman, J (1975) *Revisioning Psychology.* New York: Harper & Row.

Hillman, J (1982) Anima Mundi: The return of the soul to the world. *Spring,* 71–93.

Hiltner, S (1949) *Pastoral Counseling.* New York: Abingdon Press.

Hoffman, M (2001) *Empathy and Moral Development: Implications for caring and justice.* Cambridge: Cambridge University Press.

Humphrey, N (2006) *Seeing Red: A study in consciousness.* Cambridge, MA: Harvard University Press.

Irigaray, L (2001) *To Be Two.* New York: Routledge.

Israel, J (2009) *A Revolution of the Mind: Radical enlightenment and the intellectual origins of modern democracy.* Princeton, NJ: Princeton University Press.

Jacob, M (2006) *The Radical Enlightenment: Pantheists, Freemasons and Republicans.* New Orleans: Cornerstone Books.

Jantsch, E (1980) *The Self-Organising Universe.* Oxford: Pergamon.

Jaynes, J (1976) *The Origin of Consciousness in the Breakdown of the Bicameral Mind.* New York: Houghton Mifflin.

Jung, CG (1953) *Psychological Types*. New York: Pantheon. (Original work published 1923)

Jung, CG (1955) *Modern Man in Search of a Soul*. New York: Harcourt Harvest.

Jung, CG (1961) *Memories, Dreams, Reflections*. New York: Random House.

Jung, CG (1964) *Man and His Symbols*. New York: Doubleday.

Jung, CG (1969) *The Structure and Dynamics of the Psyche*. London: Routledge & Kegan Paul. (Original work published 1954)

Jung, CG (1976) *Letters* (2 vols) (G Adler, Ed). London: Routledge & Kegan Paul.

Jung, CG (1977) *Jung Speaking: Interviews and encounters* (W McGuire & RFC Hull, Eds). Princeton, NJ: Princeton University Press.

Jung, CG (1979) *Collected Works* (H Read, M Fordham & G Adler, Eds). London: Routledge & Kegan Paul.

Kauffman, S (1995) *At Home in the Universe: The search for the laws of self-organization and complexity*. Oxford: Oxford University Press.

Kauffman, S (2008) *Reinventing the Sacred: A new view of science, reason and religion*. New York: Basic Books.

Kegan, R (1983) *The Evolving Self: Problem and process in human development*. Cambridge, MA: Harvard University Press.

Kegan, R (1998) *In Over Our Heads: The mental demands of modern life*. Cambridge, MA: Harvard University Press.

Knox, J (2003) *Archetype, Attachment, Analysis: Jungian psychology and the emergent mind*. New York: Brunner-Routledge.

LaChapelle, D (1995) Ritual is essential. In A Drengson & Y Inoue (Eds) *The Deep Ecology Movement: An introductory anthology* (pp. 219–25). Berkeley, CA: North Atlantic Books.

Laing, RD (1967) *The Politics of Experience and the Bird of Paradise*. New York: Ballantine.

Lanza, R & Berman, B (2009) *Biocentrism: How life and consciousness are the keys to understanding the true nature of the universe*. Dallas, TX: Benbella Books.

Larson, VA (1987) An exploration of psychotherapeutic resonance. *Psychotherapy, 24*(3), 321–4.

Laszlo, E (2003) *The Connectivity Hypothesis*. Albany, NY: SUNY Press.

Laszlo, E (2004) *Science and the Akashic Field: An integral theory of everything*. Rochester, VT: Inner Traditions.

Lawrence, GW (2005) *Introduction to Social Dreaming: Transforming thinking*. London: Karnac Books.

LeShan, L (2003) *The Medium, the Mystic, and the Physicist: Toward a general theory of the paranormal*. New York: Allworth Books. (Original work published 1974)

Lloyd, G (1996) *Spinoza and the Ethics*. New York: Routledge.

Lorimer, D (Ed) (2004) *Science, Consciousness and Ultimate Reality*. Exeter: Imprint Academic.

Louv, R (2005) *Last Child in the Woods: Saving our children from nature-deficit disorder*. Chapel Hill, SC: Algonquin Books.

Lovelock, J (1979) *Gaia: A new look at life on earth*. Oxford: Oxford University Press.

Lovelock, J (2006) *The Revenge of Gaia*. London: Allen Lane.

Lovelock, J (2010) *The Vanishing Face of Gaia*. London: Penguin.

Lyotard, J (1983) *The Postmodern Condition*. Manchester: Manchester University Press.

Maclean, P (1990) *The Triune Brain in Evolution*. New York: Springer.

MacLean, P, Campbell, D & Boag, T (Eds) (1973) *A Triune Concept of the Brain and Behaviour*. Toronto: University of Toronto Press.

Mahrer, A (1978) *Experiencing: A humanistic theory of psychology and psychiatry*. New York: Brunner/Mazel.

Mahrer, A (1986) *Therapeutic Experiencing*. New York: Norton.

Mahrer, A (1993) Transformational psychotherapy sessions. *Journal of Humanistic Psychology, 33*(2), 30–7.

Marlan, S (Ed) (2008) *Archetypal Psychology: Reflections in honor of James Hillman*. New Orleans: Spring Journal Books.

Mathews, F (1995) Conservation and self-realization: A deep ecology perspective. In A Drengson & Y Inoue (Eds) *The Deep Ecology Movement: An introductory anthology* (pp. 219–25). Berkeley, CA: North Atlantic Books.

Maturana, H & Varela, F (1980) *Autopoiesis and Cognition: The realization of the living*. London: Reidl.

McKinnon, P (2012) *Living Calm in a Busy World: Stillness meditation in the Meares tradition*. Melbourne: David Lovell Publishing.

Meares, A (1967) *Relief without Drugs: The self-management of tension, anxiety and pain*. New York: Doubleday.

Mearns, D & Cooper, M (2005) *Working at Relational Depth in Counselling and Psychotherapy*. London: Sage.

Merleau-Ponty, M (1962) *The Phenomenology of Perception*. London: Routledge & Kegan Paul.

Merleau-Ponty, M (1968) *The Visible and the Invisible*. Evanston, IL: Northwestern University Press.

Metzner, R (1999) *Green Psychology: Transforming our relationship to the earth*. New York: Park Street Press.

Miller, A (2009) *Deciphering the Cosmic Number: The strange friendship of Wolfgang Pauli and Carl Jung*. New York: WW Norton.

Naess, A (1973) The shallow and the deep, long-range ecology movement: A summary. *Inquiry, 16*, 95–100.

Naess, A (1995) Self-realization: An ecological approach to being in the world. In A Drengson & Y Inoue (Eds) *The Deep Ecology Movement: An introductory anthology* (pp. 13–30). Berkeley, CA: North Atlantic Books.

Neumann, E (1954) *The Origin and History of Consciousness.* Princeton, NJ: Princeton University Press.

Neville, B (1992) The charm of Hermes: Hillman, Lyotard and the postmodern condition. *Journal of Analytical Psychology, 37*(3), 337–53.

Neville, B & Dalmau, T (2008) *Olympus Inc.: Intervening for cultural change in organizations.* Greensborough, Australia: Flat Chat Press.

Noddings, N & Shore, P (1984) *Awakening the Inner Eye: Intuition in education.* New York: Teachers College Press.

O'Connor, T (1995) Therapy for a dying planet. In T Roszak, M Gomes & A Kanner (Eds) *Ecopsychology: Restoring the earth; healing the mind* (pp. 149–55). San Francisco: Sierra Club Books.

O'Riordan, T (1999) *Environmental Science for Environmental Management.* London: Longman.

Orloff, J (2010) *Second Sight: An intuitive psychiatrist tells her extraordinary story and shows you how to tap your own inner wisdom.* New York: Crown Publishing Group.

Ornstein, R (1997) *The Right Mind: Making sense of the hemispheres.* New York: Harcourt.

Peat, D (1987) *Synchronicity: The bridge between matter and mind.* New York: Bantam Books.

Penrose, R (1991) *The Emperor's New Mind.* London: Penguin.

Popper, K (1982) *The Open Universe: An argument for indeterminism.* Cambridge: Routledge.

Pribram, K (1977) *Languages of the Brain: Experimental paradoxes and principles in neuropsychology* (2nd ed). Monterey, CA: Brooks/Cole.

Prigogine, I (1997) *The End of Certainty: Time, chaos and the new laws of nature.* New York: The Free Press.

Prigogine, I & Stengers, I (1984) *Order Out of Chaos: Man's new dialogue with nature.* New York: Bantam.

Proctor, G, Cooper, M, Sanders, P & Malcolm, B (2006) *Politicizing the Person-Centred Approach.* Ross-on-Wye: PCCS Books.

Radin, D (1997) *The Conscious Universe: The scientific truth of psychic phenomena.* New York: HarperOne.

Radin, D (2006) *Entangled Minds: Extrasensory experiences in quantum reality.* New York: Pocket Books.

Ramachandran, VS (2011) *The Tell-Tale Brain: A neuroscientist's quest for what makes us human.* New York: Norton.

Reanney, D (1994) *Music of the Mind: An adventure into consciousness.* Melbourne: Hill of Content.

Reik, T (1948) *Listening with the Third Ear: The inner experience of a psychoanalyst.* New York: Grove Press.

Riffert, F (2005) Whitehead's cyclic theory of learning and empirical research. In F Riffert (Ed) *Alfred North Whitehead on Learning and Education* (pp. 89–120). Cambridge: Cambridge University Press.

Rogers, CR (1951) *Client-Centered Therapy: Its current practice, implications and theory.* Boston: Houghton Mifflin.

Rogers, CR (1958) The characteristics of a helping relationship. *Personnel and Guidance Journal, 37*(1), 6–16.

Rogers, CR (1959) A theory of therapy, personality and interpersonal relationships developed in the client-centred framework. In S Koch (Ed) *Psychology: A study of a science. Vol 3: Formulations of the person and the social context* (pp. 184–256). New York: McGraw-Hill.

Rogers, CR (1961) *On Becoming a Person.* Boston: Houghton Mifflin.

Rogers, CR (1980). *A Way of Being.* Boston: Houghton Mifflin.

Rogers, CR (1986) A client-centered/person-centered approach to therapy. In IL Kutash & A Wolf (Eds) *Psychotherapist's Casebook: Theory and technique in practice* (pp. 197–208). San Francisco: Jossey-Bass.

Rogers, CR (1990) A client-centered/person-centered approach to therapy. In H Kirschenbaum & VL Henderson (Eds) *The Carl Rogers Reader* (pp. 135–52). London: Constable.

Rose, DB (2009) Journey to sacred ground: Ethics and aesthetics of country. In M Paranjape (Ed) *Sacred Australia: Post-secular considerations* (pp. 85–95). Melbourne: Clouds of Magellan.

Rosenblum, B & Kuttner, F (2006) *Quantum Enigma: Physics encounters consciousness.* Oxford: Oxford University Press.

Roszak, T (1995) Where psyche meets Gaia. In T Roszak, ME Gomes & AD Kanner (Eds) *Ecopsychology: Restoring the earth; healing the mind* (pp. 3–23). San Francisco: Sierra Club Books.

Rowan, J (1986) Holistic listening. *Journal of Humanistic Psychology, 26*(1), 83–102.

Sabini, M (2002) *The Earth Has a Soul.* Berkeley, CA: North Atlantic Books.

Samuels, A (1989) *The Plural Psyche.* London: Routledge.

Schmid, PF (2002) Knowledge and acknowledgement: Psychotherapy as 'the art of not-knowing'. *Person-Centered & Experiential Psychotherapies, 1*(1&2) 56–70.

Schmid, PF (2006) The challenge of the other: Towards dialogical person-centered psychotherapy and counseling. *Person-Centered & Experiential Psychotherapies, 5*(4), 240–54.

Schwartz, J & Begley, S (2002) *The Mind and the Brain: Neuroplasticity and the power of mental force.* New York: Harper.

Sheldrake, R (1981) *A New Science of Life: The hypothesis of formative causation.*

London: Blond & Briggs.

Sheldrake, R (1990) *The Rebirth of Nature: New science and the revival of animism.* London: Rider.

Sheldrake, R (2000) *Dogs that Know when their Owners Are Coming Home: And other unexplained powers of animals.* London: Arrow.

Sheldrake, R (2003) *The Sense of Being Stared At: And other aspects of the extended mind.* London: Hutchinson.

Sheldrake, R (2005) The sense of being stared at. Part 2. *Journal of Consciousness Studies, 12*(6), 32–49.

Shostrom, E (1986) *Three Approaches to Psychotherapy* [VHS]. Corona Del Mar, CA: Psychological & Educational Films.

Snygg, D & Combs, A (1959) *Individual Behavior.* New York: Harper & Row.

Sprinkle, L (1985) Psychological resonance: A holographic model of counseling. *Journal of Counseling and Development, 64,* 206–8.

Stevens, A (1999) *Ariadne's Clue: A guide to the symbols of humankind.* Princeton, NJ: Princeton University Press.

Szent-Gyoergyi, A (1966) The drive in living matter to perfect itself. *Journal of Individual Psychology, 22*(2), 153–62.

Talbot, A (1997) *The Body of Knowledge.* Unpublished PhD thesis. La Trobe University, Melbourne.

Talbot, M (1991) *The Holographic Universe.* London: HarperCollins.

Tudor, K (2010) Person-centered relational therapy: An organismic perspective. *Person-Centered & Experiential Psychotherapies, 9*(1), 53–68.

Tudor, K & Worrall, M (2006) *Person-Centered Therapy: A clinical perspective.* New York: Routledge.

Ullman, M (1979) Psi and psychiatry. In J White (Ed) *Edgar D. Mitchell: Psychic exploration – A challenge for science* (pp. 247–68). New York: Putnam's Sons.

Ullman, M (1986) Psychopathology and psi phenomena. In B Wolman (Ed) *Handbook of Parapsychology* (pp. 557–76). New York: Van Nostrand Reinhold.

Ullman, M (2003) Dream telepathy: Experimental and clinical findings. In N Totton (Ed) *Lands of Darkness: Psychoanalysis and the paranormal* (pp. 15–46). London: Karnac Books.

Van Belle, HA (1990) Rogers' later move towards mysticism: Implications for client-centered therapy. In G Lietaer, J Rombauts & R Van Balen (Eds) *Client-Centered and Experiential Psychotherapy in the Nineties* (pp. 47–58). Leuven: Leuven University Press.

Van de Castle, R (1977) Parapsychology and anthropology. In B Wolman (Ed) *Handbook of Parapsychology* (pp. 667–86). New York: Van Nostrand Reinhold.

Vaughan, F (1979) *Awakening Intuition.* New York: Anchor Books.

Waddington, CH (1961) *The Nature of Life.* London: Unwin.

Walker, EH (2000) *The Physics of Consciousness.* Cambridge, MA: Perseus Books.

Whitehead, AN (1927) *Science and the Modern World.* Cambridge: Cambridge University Press.

Whitehead, AN (1933) *Adventures of Ideas.* Cambridge: Cambridge University Press.

Whitehead, AN (1938) *Modes of Thought.* Cambridge: Cambridge University Press.

Whitehead, AN (1953) *Dialogues of Alfred North Whitehead* (L Price, Ed). Boston: Nonpareil.

Whitehead, AN (1978) *Process and reality: An essay in cosmology* (Corrected ed, DR Griffin & DW Sherburne, Eds). New York: Free Press. (Original work published 1929)

Whitehead AN (1982) *An Introduction to Mathematics.* Oxford: Oxford University Press. (Original work published 1911)

Wilber, K (1983) *Eye to Eye.* New York: Anchor.

Wilber, K (1996) *A Brief History of Everything.* Melbourne: Hill of Content.

Wilson, EO (1984) *Biophilia: The human bond with other species.* Cambridge, MA: Harvard University Press.

Witoszek N & Brennan, A (Eds) (1999) *Philosophical Dialogues: Arne Naess and the progress of ecophilosophy.* Lanham, MD: Rowman & Littlefield.

INDEX

A

Aboriginal culture 122, 123
Abram, D 122, 138, 170
acceptance vi, 50, 54
activism
    reframing political and environ-
        mental 55–6
actualization vi, 21, 46, 47, 60, 78, 107
actualizing tendency 20, 34, 47, 62, 63,
        66, 77, 83, 97, 107, 127, 128,
        129, 134, 169
    is creative 84
    and the universe 63, 128 (*see also*
        formative tendency)
Aczel, A 161
advertising industry 174
Aizenstadt, S 33
altruism 132
Angyal, A 44, 64
anima mundi 33, 125
animals, five-minded 88–91
anthropocentrism iii, iv, 33, 69
anxiety
    about the state of the Earth 45, 46,
        55, 93
    separation from mother and cosmos
        56
    vulnerbility to 55, 56
Aphrodite 6, 7, 15, 18, 25
apocalyptic nihilism 39
Apollo 6, 10, 14, 19, 22, 133
Apollonine
    myth of an absolute reality 14, 175
    rationality 22
archaic man/mind 121, 147, 152
archetypal
    analysis 22

    image 3, 6, 38, 42, 133
    patterns 2, 3, 4, 25, 26
    perspective 4, 8, 133
    psychology v, 1, 2, 3, 15, 16, 25
archetype/s 1, 3, 8, 65
    definitions of 39
    of Hermes 21
    of the Many and the One 133, 174
    as Sheldrake's 'habits' 65
    theory 70
    variations on the notion of 2
Ares 7, 18, 38
Aristotle 63, 145
Artemis 6, 19, 25
Assagioli, R 154
    psychosynthesis 102
Atavistic Theory of Mental Homeostasis
    93
Athena 6, 9, 17, 25
    therapy 17

B

Bandler, R 167
Barrett-Lennard, G i, 57, 58, 164, 167,
    168
Bastick, T 146, 160
Bateson, G 45, 71
Begley, S 162
behaviour 15, 19, 75, 76, 94, 101, 105,
    108, 151
    archetypal patterns in 2, 3, 4, 25, 26
    change 6, 10
    collective 1
        pathological 46, 172
    egoic control of 38
    magical 98
    unconscious, robotic 92

behaviourism 8, 94
being and becoming 72
Bennett, HZ 162
Bergson, H 63, 71, 120, 130, 147
Berman, B 71, 162
Bernstein, J 119, 120, 137, 156
Bertalanffy, L von 160
biofeedback 8
biophilia hypothesis 42, 68, 141
Birch, C 71, 125, 141, 175, 179
body 64, 82, 94, 127
    holotropic breathing 153
    intuition 141, 146, 149, 160, 170
    language 91
    /mind duality 82, 102, 112, 121,
        124, 138
    rhythms 79, 167
    therapies 1
    wisdom 136, 150
Boer, C 22
Bohm, D 67, 68, 71, 72, 155, 161, 163
    holographic theory 162
Bohr, N 56
Bookchin, M iv, 50, 69
boundaries of the self 44–6
Bowlby, J 150
brain (see also mind)
    bicameral 115
    left 22, 102, 104, 110, 115, 116
    hard-wired 26, 27
    MacLean's model of the 115
    neo-cortex 115
    neo-mammalian 115
    paleo-mammalian 115
    pre-frontal cortex 116
    reptilian 115
    right 22, 102, 104, 115
        therapies of the 102
    scientists 163
    second 82
    triune 114–15
    waves 79, 153
brainstem 115, 116
Brennan, A 69
Brizee, R 78
Bruno, G 71
Buber, M vi, 20, 57, 112, 124, 165, 169
    I–Thou relationship 112, 124, 164, 165
    –Rogers dialogue 20

Buddha 73
Buddhism v, 130
    Hua-yen 74
Buddhist
    natural link to ecopsychology v
    philosopher DT Suzuki 146
Burnet, J 73

C
Campbell, J 28
capitalism 21, 35
Capra, F 63, 65, 71, 158
Carkhuff, R 10, 17, 30, 31, 94
    Hero literature 10, 30
Cartesian–Newtonian fantasy 51
Castenada, C 157, 158
catastrophe 40, 178
causal efficacy 76, 136, 137, 141
ceremonies, traditional healing 99, 126
Ceres 27 (see also Demeter)
change 107
    model of 55
Charles, R 154, 157, 160, 166
Christian orthodoxy 70
civilizing process 122
Clarke, C 162
Claxton, G 147
client passim
    in distress due to disfunction in
        world 45, 46, 134–5
    experience and behaviour,
        influences on iv
    and therapist inside a process bigger
        than themselves 34
client-centred
    ecopsychologist 3ff
    therapists 44, 45, 55, 117
client-centred therapy v, vii, 9, 13, 14,
        16, 18, 20, 31, 39, 43, 46, 110
        (see also person-centred
        counselling/therapy)
    and belief in supremacy of humans v
    and link to individualism 58, 59
    a polytheistic therapy 15–22
    political implications of 57
    and Rogers' political convictions 17
climate change 41, 178
cognitive behavioural therapy 1, 21,
        29, 134

Cohen, MJ 141
Coleridge, Samuel Taylor 71
Collier, J 126
Combs, A 9
communication 144*ff*, 150
    psychic 149–59
communitarian movements 55
compassion 47, 141
    for whole creation vi
'conatus' 46
conditions of worth 29, 51, 54, 55, 107,
    139
Conforti, M 2
congruence vi, 11, 62, 95, 100, 135,
    139, 140, 144, 165
    ecocentric 53–6
congruent beings 134–6
connecting 56–8, 159–60
    with client 76–7
consciousness 69, 87, 89, 116, 125,
    150, 158, 174
    of adolescence 101
    altered state of 153, 154, 157
    archaic 91–5
    of childhood 100
    complex ironic 111
    continuous improvement of 87
    cosmic 48
    creates the world 77
    deficient magical 118
    deficient rational 119
    distributed throughout the body
        82
    is dynamic system iii
    and the Enlightenment 87
    evolving towards a higher 177
    expansion of 153
    false 135
    fifth order 110, 111
    of five-minded animals 88, 90, 114
    fourth order 104, 107, 110
    in Greek culture 104
    in the gut (second brain) 82
    higher 173
    individual, impact of culture on 89
    Kegan's five orders of 90, 114*ff*
    magical 109, 172–3
        and mythical roots of 87
    mental 104, 174, 175

–rational 109, 114, 117
mimetic 91
models of 116
new 174
postmodern 8, 42, 176
of primate ancestors 90
rational 97, 113, 118
    breakdown of 173
    overvaluation of 152
second order 100
structure/s 3, 87–8, 90, 123
    archaic 91–5, 109, 114, 132, 158
    efficient and deficient 158, 174
    integral 3, 108*ff*, 114, 117, 132,
        176
    magical 3, 95*ff*, 99, 102, 114,
        123, 132, 137, 152, 158, 172,
        173
    mental 89, 114, 132
        –rational 104*ff*
    mythical 91, 100*ff*, 114, 132, 158
        and images 102
studies 162
theory of 164
third order 101, 104
transformation of 56, 149, 178
    in 20th C 149
unity 142, 174
    of the mystic 158
universal 34, 48
Cooper, M 57
cosmic
    'creative advance' 75, 79
    balance 56
    order 33, 56
    paradox 58
cosmology, Navajo 121
cosmos (*see also* universe)
    as living organism v, 64, 65
    personhood of the 131
counselling
    essence of is listening 14
    shaped by image of humanity 179
    as a profession 29, 134
    psychology 29
    theory and practice 133
        systems approaches in 57
counsellor (*see also* therapist)
    and client, connection between 77

–client relationship (*see* relationship, counsellor and client)
manipulating the client 94
postmodern 38
counter-transference 96, 103, 155, 156
'creative advance' 77, 79, 81, 129
creativity 9, 37, 58, 84, 127, 128, 169
and the actualizing tendency 84, 127, 128
cultural
collective 55, 56
philosophers 36
psychology v
culture/s 54, 90, 133, 166
beliefs and values of 54
causing distress in clients 134
classical 59
client's 15, 46
conditions of worth imposed by 55
and congruence with planet 54
destructive aspects 55
effect on individual consciousness 89
indigenous 54, 121, 152
individualistic–competitive global 55
and the Hero narrative 133
pre-scientific 86, 96
primal 124
of scientific-industrial era 28
traditional 104, 153
tribal
community 98
narratives 3
Western 135, 157
-dominated global 54
rational 87, 123

D

Damasio, A 115
Darwin's theory of evolution 2, 66
Davies, P 71
de Chardin, T 124
deep ecology (*see* ecology, deep)
deep ecologists (see ecologists, deep)
Dell, W 115
Demeter, 6, 9, 19, 25, 27, 35
depression as a natural response to current conditions 33

de Quincey, C 71, 124, 125, 126, 164, 168, 170
radical naturalism 125
Descartes, R 63, 130
mind–body distinction 82 (*see also* dualism)
Devall, B v, 122
dialogue 9, 11, 14, 38, 57, 169
Dionysos 7, 9, 14, 15, 16, 17, 133
disconnection is toxic 139, 141
disease, planetary 23, 55
Donald, M 90, 91
dream/s 142, 151, 154
shared 154
telepathy 157
work, Jungian 142
dreaming 154
Dreamtime 25
dualism v, 82, 124, 129, 138, 164 (*see also* body/mind duality)

E

Earth (*see also* Gaia; planet)
living system 41, 138
Mother 24, 174
nurtures and devours 35
eclecticism 38
ecocentric
congruence 53–6
empathy 51–3
valuing 50–1
ecological self, self-realization and the 119*ff*, 131, 132, 137
ecologists
deep 45, 49, 70, 130
psychologically oriented 44
ecology
deep iv, 122, 132, 133
homocentric iv
science of 41
shallow iv, 130
social iv, 69
systemic 35
ecophilosophy 122
ecopsychologist, client-centred 43*ff*
ecopsychology iv, v, 33, 51, 58, 130, 135, 140
literature of 59
radical 59

Egan, K 10, 31, 89, 91, 109, 116
   criticism of 10
   five minds 90
ego iii, 24, 29, 31, 38, 42, 109, 127,
      131, 133, 135
   foundation of 113
   -free 174
   individual 24
   -pathology 31
Ehrenwald, J 155, 156, 157
Einstein, A 71, 148, 161
   relativity theory 162
electro-convulsive therapy 21
Eliade, M 25
Eliot, TS 109
Elkin, AP 122
Ellingham, I 62, 128
empathy vi, 10, 11, 13, 15, 34, 51, 55,
      76, 77, 93, 95, 98, 105, 106, 146,
      149, 165, 166, 168
   with animals 34
   boundary-crossing experience of
      52
   deep 165, 166
   ecocentric 51–3
   intuition and creativity 146
   mythical 100
   for other beings 132
   with the planet 34
   with rocks and stones and trees 35
Enlightenment, the vii, 66, 87, 89, 162,
      175
   mechanistic worldview of vii,
   moderate, finding truth via
      propositional logic 70
   radical, valuing imagination and
      intuition 70
   supremacy of humans v
entanglement 160–4
entropy 66
environmental
   degradation iii, 23
   ethics 51, 132
   psychology 130
environmentalism iv
Erlich, P 141
Eros 7, 9, 16, 17
   therapy 17
Erysichthon 27

Eshel, O 155
evolution 69, 74
   biological 115
   as mechanical vs organic process 66
   and move towards greater complexity
      69
   as selection and self-organisiation 69
evolutionary
   adaptation 2, 26
   biology 115
   flow 74–6
   psychology 92
existence, brought about by relationship
      76–7
existential therapy 21
experiencing 36, 139–43
experiential psychotherapy 18, 52 (see
      also psychotherapy; therapy)

F
facilitation 9, 12, 13
fallacy of dogmatic finality viii, 37, 176
fantasy 24
   of control 36, 43
   of the Many and the One 24
fascism 172
felt sense 81, 82, 102, 135, 140, 142
female gods of the pantheon 6
feminism 55
field theory 62, 162
Fisher, A 59, 122, 140
'flesh of the world' 138, 170
flow, evolutionary 74–6
focusing-oriented therapy 79, 81, 140
Fordham, M 96
formative tendency i, 17, 21, 34, 55,
      60, 81, 128, 129, 139, 171
   self-realization and the 46–50
   universal 48
Fox, W v, 45, 49, 59
frame of reference 75
Freud, S 29, 30, 62, 82, 96, 127, 155,
      158, 159, 166

G
Gaia 5, 20, 25, 32–5, 36, 39, 40, 41, 51,
      56, 67, 170, 176 (see also earth;
      planet)
   fantasy 33, 34, 38, 41, 51

hypothesis 170
images of birthing and growth 55
revenge of 174
story 33
worshippers 41, 68, 178
Gaian
    language of biology 43
    myth 178
    perspective 42
Gandhi, M vi, 136
ganzfeld experiments 154
Gare, A 70
Gebser, J v, vii, 3, 86, 87, 88, 91, 92, 93,
    94, 95, 96, 97, 108, 113, 114,
    116, 117, 120, 123, 131, 132,
    137, 142, 143, 144, 152, 158,
    159, 161, 164, 172, 173, 174,
    177, 178
    focus on culture 87, 90
    structures of consciousness 87–8,
      90 (see also consciousness,
      structures)
Gendlin, E 50, 72, 79, 80, 81, 82, 102,
    139, 141, 142, 144, 151, 153, 162
    contribution to ecopsychology 59
    focusing technique 140
    philosophy 140
global
    crisis 135
    culture, stuck in Hermes myth 42
    financial crisis 40
    warming iii
Gloria 106, 107
god/s 41, 70
    female gods 6
    Greco-Roman 3, 4
    many, many therapies 5–8
    many, many truths 41–2
    Olympian 28
    pre-Olympian 5
Goerner, S 66
Goethe, J von 71
Golding, W 32
Goleman, D 116
Gorman, C 121
Greek mythology 3, 4, 26, 133
Green
    movement 41
    technologies, limited impact of 41

Gribbin, J 41
Gribbin, M 41
Griffin, DR 36, 37, 125
Grinder, J 167
Grof, S 153, 162
growth (see formative tendency)
gut, as second brain 82, 150

H

Haisch, B 71
Hall, ET 167
Hannaford, C 167
Hart, T 166
Hartshorne, W 72
Haule, J 2, 116, 150, 152, 154
healing, magical 112
Heidegger, M v
Hephaistos 7, 17
Hera 5, 6, 15, 20, 22
Herakles 18
Heraklitus 73
Hermes 8, 9, 11, 12, 13, 14, 16, 17, 22,
    25, 35, 36–40, 41, 133, 174, 176,
    178
    Age of 36
    archetype of 21
    charm of 11–15
    consciousness 22, 39, 41
    myth 14, 39, 42
    pathology 12, 21, 39
Hermetic perspective 42
Hero 1, 25, 41, 45, 47, 58, 133
    and the Mother 26–8
    myth 29
    perspective 54
Hestia 8, 18, 21, 25
Hillman, J v, 3, 4, 31, 34, 46, 102, 103
Hiltner, S 72
Hippocrates 167
Hitler, Adolf 86, 135
Hoffman, M 165
holotropic breathing 153
human/s
    activity, impact of 143
    behaviour, zombie dimensions of
      94
    beings, unimportance of 24
    breaking their connection to the
      Earth 26

as cells of a greater organism v
connected to all things 35, 130
early 91
evolution 81
as new phase in cosmic evolution
130
and progress, fantasy of 36
and the universe 24, 130
humanity
Rogers' image of 47
unitary soul of 142, 174
Humphrey, N 163

I
ideas in process 84–5
imagining
therapy 1*ff*
the universe 62–4
incongruence 54
is disconnection 134, 139
indigenous
cultures 54, 121, 152
Hopi belief in the universe 126
Navajo cosmology 121
first peoples, ceremonies of 126
peoples 122, 126
wisdom 121–6
individual/s 56
congruence of 55
ego 24
and freedom vs determinism 61
insignificance in cosmic order
56
isolated 133
vs planet 44
primacy of the 58
psychology 87, 89
subjectivity 57
survival 54
individualism 167
individualistic assumptions of 20th C
55, 134
individuality, fantasy of 28
Indra's net 74, 133
Industrial Revolution 175
'in-formation' 151, 161
interconnectedness 76, 133, 151, 155,
167
internal locus of control 135

intuition 137, 144, 145–9, 163
with both empathy and creativity
146
for Jung 147
kinesthetic 82
and the limbic system 150
(*see also* body, intuition)
Irigaray, L 179
Islamic philosophy 164
Israel, J 70
I–Thou relationship 112, 124, 164, 165

J
Jacob, M 70
James, W 70, 85, 155
James, William 155
Janet, P 155
Jantsch, E 71
Jaynes, J 104, 115
Jones, E 155
Juan, Don 157
Jung, CG v, vii, 1, 2, 3, 20, 24, 31, 32,
43, 44, 59, 70, 89, 96, 103, 107,
114, 117, 120, 121, 122, 125,
131, 132, 137, 138, 141, 142,
143, 144, 148, 151, 155, 156,
167, 172
collective psyche 103
intuition and 146, 147
and dream work 142

K
Kauffman, S 69, 162
Kegan, R 90, 91, 100, 101, 104, 106,
109
Kierkegaard, S 127
Klein, M 96
knowledge 51, 91, 177
commodification of 11, 36
organismically felt 82
intuitive 79, 122, 145, 146, 157, 163
Knox, J 26
Koestler, A 44
Kuttner, F 71, 125, 162

L
LaChapelle, D 126
Laing, RD 136
Lanza, R 71, 125, 162

Larson, VA 165
Laszlo, E 69, 71, 72, 125, 151, 153,
    160, 161, 162, 163
Lawrence, GW 154
Leibniz, G 64, 71
Lemke, J 162
LeShan, L 157, 158
Leto 133
Levinas, E 57, 169
life 64, 69
    not accidental 63
    essential quality of the universe 65
    -forward direction 139, 140
    rhythmical 79–83
limbic system 115, 116
    and intuition 150
lizards 116
Lloyd, G 70
Louv, R 141
Lovelock, J 32, 34, 40, 41, 67, 71, 170,
    178
Lyotard, J 11, 14, 36, 176

M
MacLean, P 114, 115
    three-brain model 114–15
magic 98, 99, 144, 172, 173, 177
    consciousness 2
    Hermes, god of 38
magic mind (see mind, magical;
    consciousness, structure, magic)
Mahrer, A 52, 105, 165
Maia 25, 35, 38, 40, 133
mammals 116
Many, fantasy of the 23, 25
Marlan, S 103
Maslow, A 59
Mathews, F 125, 133
Maturana, H 71
McKinnon, P 93
meaning 140
    creation of 140
    of wholeness 68
Meares, A 93
Mearns, D 57, 164
mechanistic worldview vii, 36, 66
media, the 174
meditation 92, 153, 154
    impact on health 92–3

Merleau-Ponty, M 137, 138, 140, 144,
    153, 169, 170
Metzner, R 153
mind/ed
    archaic 91–5
    five-, animal 88–91, 114–18
    integral 108–13
    magical 95–100
    mental–rational 104–8
    mythical 100–4
mind-in-matter 71
mirror neurons 166
mirroring 167
Mother 35, 38, 54, 59, 133 (see also
    Earth Mother; Gaia)
    anxiety of separation 56
    –child symbiotic relationship 156
    Great 5, 6, 19, 25, 33, 35, 133
    and the Hero 26–8
    stories of religious traditions 41
mundus imaginalis 103
Murayama, M 63
Myers, I 146, 155
mystical universalism 48
myths 24, 30, 38, 41, 175, 178 (see also
    stories)
    of classical cultures 59
    four functions of 28
    of Gaia 178
        and Prometheus 36
    more important than facts 175
    as narrative 175
    of modernity 175
    Promethean (see also Prometheus)
mythical mind (see consciousness
    structure, mythic)

N
Naess, A iv, v, vi, vii, 46, 47, 69, 122,
    130, 131, 136, 141
narrative/s 14, 100, 101
naturalism, radical 124
nature
    is alive 65
    damaged relationship to 33
    fantasy of the control of 38
    healing power of 141
Navajo
    cosmology 121

elders 119
Nazism 172
Neumann, E 142, 143
neuroscience 116, 150
　mirror neurons 166
　research 166
Neville, B 176
New Age 36, 41, 97, 159
　consciousness 113
　thinking 68, 158
'new science' 65–71
Newton, Isaac 60, 63, 130
Newtonian
　physics 73
　–Cartesian worldview 71
Noddings, N 145, 146, 154
non-human world
　valuing and preservation of v
nuclear devastation iii, 23

O
O'Connor, T 135
O'Riordan, T iv
Odysseus 14
One, fantasy of the 24, 25
organism/s
　cycles of 79
　enhancement of the 60
　philosophy of 125
organismic psychology
Orloff, J 154, 157
Ornstein, R 115
Ovid 27

P
pan-experientialism 35, 71, 125
Paracelsus 71
parapsychology 96, 120, 123, 145,
　149ff, 152, 156, 164 (see also psi
　phenomena; telepathy)
　clairvoyance as a symptom of
　　psychosis 156
　experiments in 164
　extrasensory perception 123, 137,
　　149
　healing at a distance 149
　research into 152
pathology iii, 31
　not an aberration iii

as frustration of the life process 50
and healing the planet iii
personal iii
of the planet 35
Pauli, W 70, 148
Peat, D 163
Penia 27
Penrose, R 162
perception 138, 163
　primitive form of 136
　sophisticated 137
　studies of 150
　subliminal 151
Persephone 14
personal transformation 84
personality
　'borderland' 119, 120
　borderline 122
　theory of 43, 47
person-centred approach iv, 15, 16, 17,
　45, 72, 107, 141, 164
　attacked for nacissism 20
　link to understanding the universe 60
　and organicist vs mechanistic
　　concepts of 62
　paradoxes and contradictions 1
　politics of the 46
　and postmodern consciousness 11
　radical ordinariness of vi
　Whitehead's influence on 72
person-centred counselling/therapy iv,
　12, 56 (see also client-centred
　therapy)
　anthropocentric assumptions iv
　as dialogue 57
person-centred
　counsellor/therapist 12, 21, 31, 60,
　　94, 99, 102
　pluralism 8–11
　psychology 48
　　organism is 'root metaphor' of
　　　48, 64
　theory iv, vi, 57, 48, 62, 64, 98, 168
personal contruct therapy 1
Piaget, J 89, 91
　heirarcical stages of development 89
Picasso, Pablo 86
planet 23
　anthropocentric image of the 69

awareness of itself 54
healing the 23*ff*
as object, iii, 23
as a patient 23
primacy of the 58
planetary crisis iii, 23
Platonic forms 25
political life, corruption of 23
politicians, manipulation by 174
polytheistic therapy 15–22
Popper, K 61
positivist science 3
post-industrial society 36
postmodern
condition 11, 14, 36, 176
consciousness 8, 11, 42, 176, 177
counsellor 38
worldview 36, 37, 175
presence 164–71
precognition 123, 148, 149
prehension 75, 76, 77, 83, 137
Pribram, K 162
Prigogine, I vi, 61, 62, 63, 71, 72, 85,
158, 160
dissipative structures 61, 160
primal unity 56
process 72, 78
philosophy v, 37, 49
psychology 78–9
Proctor, G 57
Progoff, I 108
progress 87
projective identification 96
Promethean
conquest 107
fantasy 8, 28, 30, 41, 50, 178, 179
image of control 45
image of emancipation 55
language 43
mindset 50, 51
myth 30, 32, 178
Western culture enmeshed 30
project of control 29, 40, 42, 123,
159, 164
science 38, 150
values 31
vision of the universe 159
Prometheus 8, 10, 17, 28–32, 35, 37,
38, 39, 107, 108, 123, 133, 174

Age of 36
psi phenomena 149–59, 160, 162 (*see
also* parapsychology, telepathy)
research into 153, 160
psychiatry, biomedical 8
psychoactive plant medicines 153
psychoanalysis 1, 6, 8, 21, 75, 155
psychological
development 89, 90
distress 134
environment 24
function of myth 28
health 33, 135
maladjustment 81
psychology 3, 33, 135, 159
behaviourist 43, 93
developmental 26, 29, 92
environmental (*see* ecopsychology)
evolutionary 92
individualist 87, 89
organismic 47, 64
person-centred 48, 64 (*see also*
person-centred counselling;
client-centred therapy)
process 78–9
psychological
connection 76–7
processes, eco-compatible insights
into 59
psychosis 121, 156
psychotherapy/ies (*see also* therapy)
all influenced by culture 4
experiential 52
focusing technique 79, 162

Q
quantum physics 52, 56, 162
reflects brain function 162
theory 70, 73, 77, 161

R
radical enlightenment 70, 85
Radin, D 149, 150, 154, 160, 161, 162,
164
Ramachandran, VS 167
Rank, O 56
relationship therapy 43
rational thinking 3, 66, 91, 103, 104, 114
rationality 86, 87, 103 (*see also*

consciousness, mental–rational)
  collapse of 86
  masculine 28
reality 89
  multi-perspectivist understanding of
    3
  transcendent, relationship between
    the physical world, consciousness
    and 71, 117
  two ways of approaching 22
recreational drugs 153
Reichian therapy 1
Reik, T 82, 154, 157, 166
relationship/s vi, vii, 9, 56, 58, 76, 100,
    160, 164, 168, 169
  between client and counsellor iv, 45,
    56–7, 76, 93
  between individual and universe 37, 57
  congruence in 134, 165
  Eros, god of 7, 9
  I–Thou 53, 112, 124, 165
  with the natural world 45, 55, 66,
    68, 126, 135, 141
  to the planet 42, 55
  therapeutic 21, 29, 77, 98, 111, 169
  therapy 43
religious traditions, mother stories of 41
Rhine, B 152
Riffert, F 80
Rilke, RM 109
ritual 98, 99, 153
  ceremony 126
Rogers, CR v, vii, 1, 8, 9, 11, 13, 14, 15,
    16, 19, 21, 30, 31, 34, 39, 45, 46,
    47, 49, 50, 53, 54, 55, 56, 58, 59,
    60, 64, 66, 67, 74, 81, 96, 113,
    127, 128, 144 passim
  –Buber dialogue 20
  and creativity 84
  definition of intuition 145
  interest in psychic phenomena 150
  and personality as process 49
  political convictions 17
  psychology and therapy 43
  therapeutic conditions vi, 10, 30,
    50, 164 (see also empathy,
    unconditional positive regard)
Rose, DB 123
Rosenblum, B 125, 162

Roszak, T 33, 59, 122, 175
Rouge, K 135
Rowan, J 166

S
Sabini, M 108, 178
Samuels. A 96, 103
Schmid, PF 57, 164, 169
Schrodinger, E 161
Schwartz, J 162
science 37, 175
  coming to our rescue 31, 40
  ecological 41
  of the Enlightenment 66
  European 178
  mainstream 60, 125
  materialist 126, 174
  and meaning-making 68
  and mechanistic worldview vii, 36,
    37, 60ff, 130
  myth of modern 175
  the new 65–71
  positivist 38
  postmodern 3, 38, 68
  Promethean shaping of 30, 36, 37,
    150
  revolution in modern physics 71
  and scientific thinking from the
    distant past 70
  and technology 29
  and truth 37
scientific
  materialism 119
  pre- 122
  Revolution 175
  worldview 117
self, the 47, 78, 113, 127, 128, 135,
    139, 143
  -actualization vi, 47, 78, 107
  autobiographical 115
  boundaries of the 44–6
  -consciousness, is mental 104
  core 115
  defining the 128
  differentiation of from
    environment 30, 141
  direction 127–9
  ecological 131, 132, 137
  and ego 131

identified with 'all that is' 45, 47
images of 78
notion of a substantial, enduring 39
-organizing planet 69
and the physical organism 44–5
pre-egoic 116
proto 115
-realization iv, 130–3
    and the ecological self 119*ff*
    and the formative tendency 46–
        50
    key concept of deep ecology
        46–7
    sense of 47
    Spinoza's idea of 47
    as stopping at our skin 136
Semele 133
Senex 5, 12, 20
sensation 163
Sessions, G v, 122
Sheldrake, R 65, 69, 71, 72, 125, 152,
    160, 162, 164
Shore, P 145, 146, 154
Shostrom, E 106
Smuts, J 63
Snygg, D 9
somatic
    experience 81, 111
        is basis of language 144
    understanding 109
Spinoza, B v, 46, 47, 64, 70, 130, 147
Sprinkle, L 165
Stengers, I 66, 71, 72
Stevens, A 2, 26
Stone Age 173, 174
    ancestors 98
stories 24, 25, 32, 42, 100
    as grand narratives 3, 25, 102, 121
    hard-wired within 24
    Hero 41, 42
Suzuki, D 122
Suzuki, DT (Buddhist philosopher) 146
'symbolic reference' 137
synchronicity 148, 152, 155, 159, 163,
    166
syntropy 66
systems
    approaches in counselling theory
        6, 57

closed 66
cyberneticians 45
    philosophy 160
    theory 62, 68, 153, 160, 161
Szent-Gyoergyi, A 63, 66

T
Talbot, A 52, 160, 162
Taoism 167
technocentric environmentalism iv
technology/ies
    Green, limited impact of 41
    progress of 41
    salvation through 29
    solutions to problems 178
    sustainable 40
telepathy 96, 123, 137, 148, 149, 150,
    156, 157
Themis 35, 38, 133
therapist/s (*see also* counsellor)
    as agents of cultural change 55
    –client relationship and the 'we' 75–
        6, 149
    responsibility of the 135
    role 15
    somatic experience in counselling
        160
therapeutic
    conditions 10, 17, 94
        apply to species and planet vi
    interaction between counsellor and
        client 76–7
therapy (*see also* psychotherapy)
    aim of 106
    commercialization of 11
    existential 21
    focusing 80, 140, 162
    imagining 1*ff*
    modernist understandings of 45
    monotheistic 16, 21
    narrative 1
    neurolinguistic programming 8,
        21, 167
    no need for 55
    non-directive 20, 134
    personal construct 1
    polytheistic 15–22
    primal 21
    psychoanalytic 98

rational-emotive 21
relational depth 57
relationship 43
transpersonal 48, 159
time-freedom 108, 109
trance 92, 153, 154
transcendent reality 71, 117
transference 155, 156
and projection 7, 98
Truax, C 10, 30
truth, deconstruction of 37
Tudor, K 47, 48, 64

U
Ullman, M 154, 155, 156
unconditional positive regard 11, 15, 50,
55
unconscious, the 13, 75, 147, 150
and intuition 147
understanding, ironic 109
unity-in-process 52
universe 24, 60, 72–4, 136, 161, 162,
177 (see also cosmos)
as connection between events 57
as emerging process 63, 73
formative tendency in the 60
is fractal 83
as seen by Heraklitus 73
and Hopi beliefs 126
humans and the 23–4
imagining the 62–4
listening to the 136–8
living vs mechanistic 63–4, 65, 125,
131
at the micro-level 162
pan-experientialist understanding of
71
is self-organizing 67
self-realization of 69
soul of the 125
no substance, only process 72–3
unfolding of the 56
unus mundus 152, 159

V
valuing, ecocentric 50–1
Van Belle, HA 48
Van de Castle, R 152
Varela, F 71

Vaughan, F 148, 154
vegetative entwinement 3, 95, 96–7,
144, 173

W
Waddington, CH 71, 125
Walker, EH 162
West, Ellen 139
Western
culture 135, 157
in the Promethean myth 30
-dominated global culture 54
psyche 119
rational culture 123
Whitehead, AN v, vii, viii, 1, 25, 37, 49,
57, 63, 70, 71, 72ff, 74, 76, 77,
78, 79, 81, 84, 95, 124, 125, 126,
129, 130, 131, 136, 137, 138,
140, 142, 145, 160, 162, 176, 177
creative advance of the universe 79,
81
process philosophy 72, 160, 168
universe is fractal 83
Whyte, L 63
Wilber, K 44, 59, 159
Wilson, EO 42, 68, 141
biophilia 141
wisdom, indigenous 121–6
Witoszek, N 69
Wordsworth, William vii, 154
worldview/s
constructive postmodern 37
deconstructive 37
mechanistic 36–7, 130, 133, 137
modernist 37, 175
Newtonian–Cartesian 71
postmodern 36–7, 175
of positivist science 68
transformation of 71
Worrall, M 64

Z
Zeus 5, 6, 15, 20, 22, 28, 38, 39

Wild Therapy:
Undomesticating inner and outer worlds

Nick Totton

ISBN 978 1 906254 36 0
£16.99 RRP, pp. 249

In our 'civilised' society, wild has come to mean dangerous, savage, crazy or being out of control. This highly original book restores the balance to the meaning of wild, suggesting that wildness – both of the human psyche and of the land – is vital for our sanity. Drawing together insights from psychotherapy, geography, ecology and anthropology, Nick Totton suggests that wild mind, like wild nature, has an order of its own. Furthermore, that wild therapy can support the restoration of this balance inherent in our psyche.

> Nick Totton's *Wild Therapy* is a call from nature to rediscover the earth and relationship to the universe. Totton's 'wildness' is a breath of fresh air, freeing therapies and cultures to live closer to the Tao. Read, dream, and be moved by his book!
> Arnold Mindell, author of *Processmind*

Nick Totton is a therapist and trainer with over 25 years' experience. Originally a Reichian body therapist, his approach has become broad based and open to the spontaneous and unexpected. He has an MA in Psychoanalytic Studies, and has worked with Process Oriented Psychology and trained as a craniosacral therapist. He has written or edited twelve books, including *Body Psychotherapy: An Introduction*; *Psychotherapy and Politics*; *Press When Illuminated: New and Selected Poems*; and *Wild Therapy*. He lives in Calderdale with his partner and grows vegetables.

Available from PCCS Books www.pccs-books.co.uk